CRUSHING
CAPITALISM

NORBERT J. MICHEL

CRUSHING CAPITALISM

HOW POPULIST POLICIES ARE THREATENING THE AMERICAN DREAM

CATO INSTITUTE

WASHINGTON, D.C.

Print ISBN: 978-1-964524-48-1
eBook ISBN: 978-1-964524-49-8
Cover: Keith Negley

Library of Congress Cataloging Number: 2025931956

Printed in the United States of America.

CATO
INSTITUTE

1000 Massachusetts Ave. NW
Washington, DC 20001

www.cato.org

CONTENTS

In this book, I present empirical evidence showing that, contrary to recent narratives of stagnation and decline, Americans have been doing better, materially and income-wise, for many decades and continue to do so. Not just rich Americans, but *most* Americans, have been sharing in the nation's increased prosperity for the full post–World War II period. None of this evidence suggests, however, that things couldn't be even better. And none of this evidence suggests that it's easy for anybody to consistently earn more money or make it to the top of the income distribution. In fact, I wish that more folks my age would tell younger people the simple truth—it takes an enormous amount of work, and some luck, even if you go to college!

I grew up the son of a mechanic. And my dad taught me many things; yet he constantly steered me away from a career where I would have to "pull wrenches." I owe him a great deal, not just the fact that I don't come home every day smelling of diesel fuel, parts cleaner, and sweat. But although I make more money than he ever did, I work even longer hours than he did. And job security is no more reliable in the white-collar workforce than in the blue-collar one—everyone can be replaced, no matter what. As it turns out, even if you work in an office building, nobody is willing to pay you hundreds of thousands of dollars to sit around and do nothing. As you're reading this book, please keep that in mind.

Separately, I want to flag that most of the economic data discussed in this book do not go past 2019. So the book presents, for example, income growth and trade data through 2019, as opposed to 2022 or 2023. That's not an accident or omission. It's on purpose because the

COVID-19 pandemic and the resulting government shutdowns temporarily reversed all kinds of trends, from employment to prices. They also resulted in an abnormally large burst of government spending starting in 2020. In short, things got out of whack for a few years starting in 2020, and many economic trends are just now getting back to pre-pandemic levels.

As a result, this book focuses mainly on the long-term economic trends before the COVID-19 pandemic. Given that the book counters political rhetoric that began several years before the pandemic, this choice of an end date does not weaken the book's main arguments. In fact, many of the arguments the book addresses deal with economic events that allegedly occurred before (sometimes long before) the 2008 financial crisis. All that said, I sincerely hope that you enjoy this book, and that it helps inform better policies that can help more people become even more prosperous going forward.

1

INTRODUCTION

The popular reality television show *Naked and Afraid* demonstrates how people live when they can't alter their environment with modern conveniences. The contestants typically build a crude shelter and then spend most of their time and energy trying to obtain food, water, and firewood. Many contestants give up within three weeks.

In the developed world, human beings do not live this way. They live so differently that it's easy to take food, water, and shelter for granted. It's all too easy to forget, but our modern lives are a historical anomaly. Most of the humans who have inhabited planet Earth lived in conditions like those on *Naked and Afraid*.

It's also too easy to forget that human flourishing didn't just happen.[1] And it is especially easy for Americans to take for granted—or simply ignore—the hard work and cooperative processes that help create their modern lifestyle.

Americans have been growing richer since the end of the 19th century and now enjoy levels of abundance and opportunity far greater than 50 years ago, and utterly unimaginable 150 years ago. The typical

American can buy any fruit or vegetable in the dead of winter for a relatively small share of his or her wages, can own a wireless communications device with access to virtually unlimited information, and can enjoy more transportation options, a cleaner environment, more years of education, more leisure choices, and better long-term health than at any point in history. But all these benefits did not simply materialize, and they will not remain in such abundance if we fail to nurture the combination of knowledge, effort, and cooperation that enables their production.

Nurturing these institutions that make modern life so attractive is especially important for those Americans who need more opportunities to prosper.

Unfortunately, during the past few years, countless politicians, commentators, and economists have fueled a bleak economic narrative, claiming that "the American economy is failing its citizens" and that "the status quo isn't working, unless you're already affluent."[2] To remedy the situation, these critics call for the United States to implement industrial policy, a broad-based federal program to develop select industries based on national economic goals, such as the Chinese government's "Made in China 2025" initiative.[3] They're misreading both the current level of prosperity in America and how it was created.

At a 2019 US Senate hearing titled "Economic Mobility: Is the American Dream in Crisis?," most of the witnesses—including conservatives Ramesh Ponnuru and Yuval Levin—testified that the American dream is, in fact, in peril.[4] Ponnuru referred to the "widespread sense" that the kind of economic progress that enables the "bulk of our population" to raise their living standards is "a thing of the past," while Levin bemoaned the lack of opportunities for "Americans at the bottom of the income scale . . . to move up," as well as the "many in the middle" who "feel stuck."[5]

Only one witness—Oren Cass, the domestic policy director for Mitt Romney's 2012 presidential campaign—painted a less gloomy picture, though he still presented income statistics that he believes "should worry us deeply."[6] Yet Cass's 2018 book, *The Once and Future Worker,* decisively answers yes to the question posed by the title of the Senate hearing:

> American public policy has lost its way. Since the middle of the last century, it has chased national economic growth, expecting that the benefits would be widely shared. Yet while gross domestic product (GDP) tripled from 1975 to 2015, the median worker's wages have barely budged. Half of Americans born in 1980 were earning less at age thirty than their parents made at that age.[7]

According to Cass, "Most Americans expect that the next generation will be worse off than themselves."[8]

Oddly enough, Cass's Senate testimony suggests that most Americans do *not* think things are so bad. "The American people," he says, "appear to have a much richer and more nuanced view of the determinants of their quality of life than do many of their leaders."[9] Cass then cites a Pew Research Center survey that reports that 36 percent of adults say their family has achieved the American dream, and another 46 percent say they are "on their way" to achieving it.[10] Combined, 82 percent believe they have or will be able to achieve the American dream. Both blacks and Hispanics are more likely than whites to say that they are on their way to achieving the American dream. Among the 17 percent who considered the dream out of reach, whites, blacks, and Hispanics were essentially equally represented.[11]

Still, in 2016, politicians campaigned on themes entirely inconsistent with these survey results. Donald Trump's campaign, for example, promoted the idea that many Americans had grown poorer because of both low-priced imports and low-cost labor.[12] His supporters argued that the Trump presidency was a unique opportunity to bolster the middle class, and that the core of Trump's new populism was that free trade and unchecked immigration were the main drivers behind increasing income inequality.[13]

Yet Trump's brand of populism was far from new. The 20th century was rife with politicians who relied on many of these same themes, most recently in the early 1990s.[14] Bill Clinton, for instance, announced that he was running for the presidency because he refused "to stand by and let our children become part of the first generation to do worse than their parents."[15] Pat Buchanan, who unsuccessfully sought the Republican nomination for president in 1992 and in 1996, argued that US manufacturing jobs were disappearing because domestic companies could not compete with low-cost foreign labor.[16] Although his message resonated with some Americans, his anti-immigration/anti-free-trade message was controversial, particularly among conservatives.[17]

Still, income statistics suggest that the Pew survey respondents were more in tune with reality than many politicians. The truth is that Americans of all backgrounds have done well over the past few decades. Their wages have not been stagnant, and income disparities have not widened. The middle class has shrunk only in the sense that former middle-income earners have moved *up* the income ladder.

Though it rarely makes headlines, the difference between economic reality and political rhetoric has not gone entirely unnoticed. In 2018, for instance, *Washington Post* economics columnist Robert Samuelson observed:

> We in the media have a problem. Actually, it's a big problem for all Americans. We have become addicted to the notion that, except for the top 1 percent or the top 10 percent, the incomes of most Americans have stagnated for decades. The problem is that, at best, this is an exaggeration and, at worst, an untruth.[18]

Indeed, virtually all the evidence points toward broad prosperity in the United States over the past few decades, with strong gains in income growth, and upward mobility at least as strong as in previous decades, even for lower-income groups.[19]

Over the past 40 years, 70 percent of working-age Americans spent at least one year among the top 20 percent of income earners. Over the same period, 80 percent never spent more than two consecutive years in the bottom 10 percent. The share of US households earning more than $100,000 (adjusted for inflation) essentially tripled over the past five decades, and the share earning less than $35,000 fell by 25 percent. During much of this period, workers in the lowest 10 percent of the income distribution realized stronger income growth than workers with higher incomes, typically earning enough to move out of the bottom

10 percent. Essentially, the conventional narrative could not be more wrong.

Despite these growth figures, critics of the American economy attribute supposed income stagnation to policymakers' misguided reliance on free markets and economic growth. They call for industrial policy—whereby government officials would "direct" economic activity—to remedy the situation. Brookings scholar Isabel Sawhill, for instance, rejects "the primacy of markets" in favor of a system that relies on public–private partnerships "to rebuild infrastructure, train workers," and "redirect rather than supplant the market."[20] Both Sen. Elizabeth Warren (D-MA) and Oren Cass call for, among other policies, subsidizing research and development and job training, as well as restricting trade and boosting manufacturing.

These ideas are misguided because it is impossible to redirect the market without supplanting it. Industrial policy advocates view the market as a policy device that government officials can manipulate, but in fact, the market is a group of people cooperating to get what they need while offering each other something in exchange. And in the United States, the market is a *very* large group of people. Even to "redirect" this market would require persuading—or forcing—hundreds of millions of people to do something they would otherwise not do. It's a core reason that so many experiments with government-directed economies have failed.

Misguided as they may be, such central planning ideas are also far from new. In the 1980s, countless academics and government officials blamed US economic problems on an overly zealous faith in markets. These critics saw Japan, with its supposedly successful industrial policy, as a major economic threat to America. They proposed, just as these more recent critics recommend, an industrial policy that restricts trade, subsidizes favored industries, and expands partnerships between select businesses and the federal government.

History was not on the critics' side in the 1980s and it is even less so today. These kinds of industrial policies have been promoted and tried repeatedly, in multiple countries, and rejected in favor of more open, less intrusive policies that bolster markets by expanding economic freedom.[21]

Is there any truth at all, then, to the more recent critics' claims of income stagnation? Is it true that increased international trade, immigration, and automation have imperiled the American dream? And, true or not, what would be the consequences of policies being recommended to address these alleged problems? This book addresses these, and related, questions. It argues that rejecting increased government direction in favor of policies that expand economic freedom is the best way to help all Americans create more economic opportunity and improve their living standards.

2

ECONOMIC FREEDOM—NOT INDUSTRIAL POLICY— CREATES THE MOST OPPORTUNITY

Proponents of bringing formal industrial policy to the United States insist that America carelessly opened its economy to foreign competition during the past few decades. They insist that America did so at the expense of its own workers. They blame these open policies for everything from income stagnation and worsening inequality to lower labor force participation and higher suicide rates.[1] They also credit Donald Trump with winning the presidency in 2016 because he, better than others, understood and exploited Americans' frustrations over these harmful economic policies. Adam Posen, president of the Peterson Institute for International Economics, describes this view as follows:

> The protectionist instinct rests on a syllogism: the populist an-
> ger that elected President Donald Trump was largely the product
> of economic displacement, economic displacement is largely the
> product of a laissez-faire approach to global competition, and
> therefore the best way to capture the support of populist voters
> is to firmly stand up against unfettered global competition. This
> syllogism is embraced by many Democrats, who are determined

to recapture an industrial working-class base, and many Republicans, who use it as evidence that the government has sold out American workers in the heartland.[2]

Posen also makes the case that "every step of this syllogism is wrong," and notes that America "has not been pursuing openness and integration over the last two decades."[3] Although America has not had an industrial policy, a federal program aimed at developing select industries for achieving national economic goals, the US economy is far from a laissez-faire paradise.[4] In fact, during the past five decades, there has been no shortage of growth in government through invasive economic, regulatory, and social policy—all of which restrict Americans' freedom and weaken the foundations of free enterprise.

More than 250 federal agencies now impose regulations related to everything from basic business activity to family leave, wages, privacy, and disability.[5] The number of pages in the *Federal Register*—the official journal of the federal government that contains agency rules, proposed rules, and public notices—has been steadily increasing each decade since the 1950s and has already exceeded 800,000 pages in the 2020s.[6] Similarly, the *Code of Federal Regulations* now contains more than 100 million words, approximately three times the count in 1970.[7] The raw volume and complexity of these regulations make estimating their cost exceedingly difficult, but a study conducted for the National Association of Manufacturers reports that the annual cost of federal regulation is nearly $3.1 trillion as of 2022, a figure that represents 12 percent of US gross domestic product (GDP).[8]

The critics are also wrong about income stagnation. Although income growth could have been higher, and likely would have been without such a high regulatory burden, Americans have experienced robust income growth during the past several decades. It has been nothing like what supporters of the stagnation story would have people believe.

For instance, the share of US households earning more than $100,000 (adjusted for inflation) *tripled* over the past five decades, and the share earning less than $35,000 fell by 25 percent. Over much of this period, workers in the lowest 10 percent of the income distribution realized the

FIGURE 2.1

Total nonfarm and manufacturing employment over time, 1939–2023

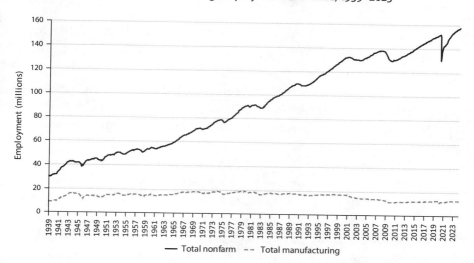

Source: US Bureau of Labor Statistics, "All Employees, Total Nonfarm and All Employees, Manufacturing," March 27, 2024; US Bureau of Labor Statistics, "All Employees, Manufacturing [MANEMP]."

strongest growth of all workers, typically earning enough to move into a higher income quintile. The data for the past five decades also show that 80 percent of working-age Americans never remained in the lowest 10 percent of the income distribution for more than two consecutive years, and more than 60 percent never stayed in the bottom 20 percent for more than two straight years. (Chapter 7 goes into greater detail on income growth.)

What makes this record even more impressive is that it occurred while the US population increased from about 203 million in 1970 to 328 million in 2019. The long-term trends in the labor market show a similar story. In January 1939 (the beginning of the data series), the total number of nonfarm jobs was 29.2 million, with 9 million of those in manufacturing. By January 2019, the total number of jobs in the US economy was 150.1 million, with 12.8 million of those in manufacturing (see figure 2.1).[9] Many critics of US economic policy like to focus on the decline in manufacturing jobs that occurred after 2000 (from 17.1 million down to 12.8 in 2019); however, the total number of manufacturing jobs never exceeded 20 million between 1939 and 2019 even though the total number of jobs increased by more than fivefold.

Rather than ask what can be done to continue such large overall job growth, critics have chosen to focus on "fixing" the decline—an incredibly small decline compared with the overall increase—of jobs in just one sector of the economy. Their favorite proposal for boosting manufacturing jobs is to institute industrial policy in the United States. Yet the massive increase in American jobs and prosperity during the past several decades occurred without industrial policy.

Few of these critics see increased government interference in markets as the main hindrance to broader prosperity. Instead, most blame the free-enterprise system. Brookings Institution scholar Isabel Sawhill, for example, argues: "My critique of market fundamentalism is not a narrative about evil people or simple greed. It's a story about the alleged miracle of markets turned into an ideology that has permeated policy making for almost half a century. . . . Markets, they are told, grow the pie and eventually everyone will get a piece of it."[10] Similarly, Oren Cass insists that US policy "lost its way" because it was overly focused on GDP growth and consumption, wrongly assuming that the benefits from growth would be widely shared.[11]

In 2016, Peter Navarro and Wilbur Ross, both of whom later served in the Trump administration, complained, "From 1947 to 2001, the nominal US gross domestic product (GDP) grew at an annual rate of 3.5% a year," but from 2002 to 2016 "that average has fallen to 1.9%."[12] They did acknowledge that high regulation and taxes contributed to slower growth, but they argued that "four decades of one-sided globalization and chronic trade deficits" were the main culprit.[13]

Navarro, Ross, Cass, and Sawhill are hardly alone. Sen. Elizabeth Warren's (D-MA) *Plan for Economic Patriotism*, for example, decries "a generation of stagnant wages, growing inequality, and sluggish economic growth."[14] A recent speech by Federal Reserve governor Lael Brainard warns that income inequality "could pose challenges to the health and resilience of our economy."[15] To improve outcomes, these critics call for expanding the government's role in the economy through industrial policy.

Sawhill, for instance, favors a new approach that rejects "the primacy of markets" in favor of one that "would rely on public–private partnerships to rebuild infrastructure, train workers," and "redirect rather than supplant the market."[16] Similarly, Cass calls for "efforts at sensible industrial policy."[17] He promotes proposals to

- Subsidize private-sector research and development (R&D),
- Provide tax benefits to those who generate profits "from the productive use of labor,"[18]
- Implement retaliatory tariffs against "mercantilist countries that undermine market competition,"[19]
- Impose local content requirements "in key supply chains,"[20] and
- Create federally funded apprenticeships with grants to employers of "roughly $10,000 per year" that attach to the trainee.[21]

Sounding much like Pat Buchanan, Senator Warren describes her plan as "an agenda of economic patriotism, using new and existing tools to defend and create quality American jobs and promote American industry."[22] Her proposal calls for expanding federal subsidies for exports, R&D, and apprenticeships, as well as a host of policies aimed at boosting US manufacturing. It also calls for creating a federal Department of Economic Development to implement industrial policy because "our international competitors like China, Germany, and Japan develop concrete plans for promoting domestic industry and then make serious investments to achieve their goals."[23] Sen. Marco Rubio (R-FL) wants to support "critical industries" with $2 billion per year and to provide export incentives.[24] Cass, too, calls for industrial policy to bolster manufacturing, a process that he sees as critical to "the ability of individuals, their families, and their communities to participate as productive contributors to society."[25] He argues:

> Our popular obsession with manufacturing isn't some nostalgic anachronism. (Here I use "manufacturing" to encapsulate the sector of our economy that makes physical things—traditional manufacturing, resource extraction, energy production,

agriculture, some construction, and so forth.) Manufacturing provides particularly well-paying, stable employment—especially for men with less formal education. Manufacturing also tends to deliver faster productivity growth because its processes are susceptible to technological advances that complement labor and increase output.[26]

Setting aside Cass's overly expansive definition of manufacturing, his critique ignores that total employment in the United States has increased roughly fivefold since the 1930s, whereas manufacturing jobs, as a share of the total, decreased, and income consistently increased for most Americans.[27] The same pattern holds, though less dramatically, from 2000, when manufacturing jobs sharply declined. Between January 2000 and January 2019, when manufacturing jobs declined by 4.5 million, total jobs in the US economy increased by 19 million. And while manufacturing wages are not particularly high (see chapter 7), outside of the 2008 recession, income consistently increased for most Americans over those two decades.

Senator Warren and her fellow critics also ignore several theoretical and practical problems with their proposals. First, it is impossible to redirect the market without supplanting it. The market is not some device that people can manipulate with various levers depending on what a single person—or a government committee—views as important. The market is a group of people cooperating to satisfy their needs. In the United States, the market is a *very* large group of people. Thus, to "redirect" the market in America requires persuading—or forcing—millions of people to do something they would otherwise not do (to a much larger degree than the existing regulatory framework does already).[28] The critics also have a problem because history is not on their side—their preferred proposals have been promoted and tried repeatedly, in multiple countries, and rejected in favor of more open, less intrusive policies that expand economic freedom.

Few, if any, of the American Founders would have used the term "industrial policy" in the same manner as recent critics; they started the nation largely by rejecting such policies.[29] Still, calls to implement these types of policies in the American market date to the 1700s. Alexander

Hamilton's 1791 *Report on Manufactures*, for instance, called for supporting domestic manufacturers with subsidies and tariffs. Although Congress did not adopt Hamilton's subsidy recommendations, it did enact most of Hamilton's tariff recommendations by 1792. However, most of those tariffs were relatively small, and even Hamilton feared discouraging imports with high tariffs.[30] Jumping ahead to the 1980s, countless policymakers proposed industrial policy measures that would have restricted trade, subsidized key industries, and increased the federal government's involvement in the economy.[31]

In 1982, for instance, Robert Reich, who later joined the Clinton administration, wrote, "Perhaps it is fairer to say that the nation itself has lost its economic innocence—the genial assurance that American industry would, without government intervention, provide an unfailing engine for bettering the American standard of living."[32] Reich noted: "In Japan, West Germany, and France policy has focused on reducing costs for promising industries. Indeed, through subsidies, loans, and special tax advantages, these governments vigorously promote industries with the greatest promise of international competitiveness."[33]

In the 1990s, high-ranking Clinton administration officials, such as Laura D'Andrea Tyson and Robert Reich, argued that it was necessary for the government to promote specific industries or firms whose health was vital to the economy. They argued that America's "ideological attachment to laissez-faire economics had blinded us to the fact that the rules of the game in international trade had changed."[34] Other prominent economists, such as Lester Thurow, former dean of the MIT Sloan School of Management, and University of California, Berkeley, economists Stephen S. Cohen and John Zysman, regularly promoted the idea that investing public funds in a stronger manufacturing base—particularly in high-tech manufacturing, much like the Japanese were doing at the time—was the key to America's economic future.[35]

Supposedly, large spillover effects from high-tech manufacturing would lead to more and more manufacturing opportunities.[36] One common example was Japan's strength in TV production, which supposedly provided the base for Japanese firms to expand into the production of other products, such as semiconductors.[37] Cohen and

Zysman also argued that Japanese high-tech manufacturers were so strong because isolationist trade and industrial policies kept many imported products out of the country.[38] Incidentally, even though the United States did not follow the Japanese approach, as of February 2024, 7 US companies were among the 10 largest semiconductor makers; none are Japanese.[39]

Regardless of the Japanese semiconductor experience, the notion that US economic policy should be based on public–private partnerships, tariffs, isolationism, and subsidized domestic manufacturing to save jobs has been continuously recycled for decades. In 1983, Clemson economics professor Richard McKenzie pointed out: "The trouble with this new talk about industrial policy is that it is not new. It is at least as old as the 18th century's mercantilism and as familiar as this century's disastrous experiments with central planning, the corporate state, and five-year plans."[40] McKenzie also cited Brookings scholar Robert W. Crandall's quip, "German and French readers of Reich's book will be amazed to read of their government's success in industrial policy."[41] Industrial production in both France and West Germany, it turns out, grew more slowly than in the United States. Writing in 1983, Crandall pointed out: "Reich's contrary conclusions are drawn from a period ending in 1979. Were he to extend his calculations to 1981, he would find that the United States has outperformed every major industrial country in the world except Japan since 1975."[42]

Despite the insistence that industrial policy will improve the status quo in the United States because, as Cass argues, China and "other market democracies like Germany and Japan have pursued the approach successfully,"[43] these countries' policies have not had great success. For the remainder of this chapter, most of the discussion regarding other countries' experiences with industrial policy focuses on Germany and Japan because critics regularly use those countries as examples of success stories. However, these two countries are not the only ones with poor track records on industrial policy. For instance, the so-called Asian Tiger economies of Hong Kong, Singapore, South Korea, and Taiwan went through sustained high growth periods after World War II because they did not engage in (or, in some cases, stopped engaging in) targeted industrial policies and restrictive trade policies.[44] Starting in the 1950s, India also went through periods of growth thanks to more liberalized economic policies, interspersed with periods of retraction owing to restrictive trade and targeted industrial policies.[45]

Germany, Japan, and the United States Experience Similar Manufacturing Trends

Despite their extensive use of industrial policy, Japan and Germany have been unable to insulate their manufacturing sectors from the same forces that have affected manufacturing in the United States and other developed nations. From 1990 to 2016, manufacturing employment in the United States fell by 25 percent, whereas it decreased by 31 percent in Japan, and by 24 percent in Germany.[46] Out of 11 developed countries, only Taiwan (12 percent) and South Korea (2 percent) realized an increase in manufacturing employment from 1990 to 2016; the smallest decrease reported was Canada's 22 percent decline.[47]

In the wake of the Great Recession, virtually all advanced economies experienced declines in manufacturing employment, but the United States experienced one of the mildest decreases. From 2008 through 2016, employment in the manufacturing sector fell by 4 percent in the United States, a smaller decrease than experienced in Sweden (−16 percent), Italy (−15 percent), France (−14 percent), Canada (−11 percent), Japan (−10 percent), the Netherlands (−9 percent), and the United Kingdom (−8 percent).[48] German manufacturing employment increased by 1 percent from 2008 to 2016, but the diminished importance of employment in the manufacturing sector is clearly a broader trend among developed nations and not simply an American phenomenon.

Furthermore, part-time employment has been on the rise in both Germany and Japan, and the share of such nonregular employment in both nations is now more than one-third, roughly double the share in the United States.[49] In spite of their respective industrial policy regimes, Germany and Japan exhibit a smaller share than the US labor market of the type of stable 40-hour-per-week jobs that critics insist industrial policy will bring to the United States.

Just as in other developed countries, though, the increase in part-time employment in both Germany and Japan is due to companies' becoming more flexible and to an increased share of service-based industries.[50] In both countries, the increase in atypical employment is clearly a long-term trend. In Japan, part-time workers increased from 15 percent of the labor force in 1982 to 38 percent by 2014.[51] According to Harvard history professor Andrew Gordon, this "steady rise in 'non-regular employment' has been underway in Japan for over three decades," and the raw number of people holding part-time jobs roughly tripled from 6.7 million to more than 20 million.[52]

As economic conditions have changed in recent decades, the German and Japanese governments have introduced market-oriented reforms into their labor markets and social welfare systems.[53] Beginning in the 1990s, Germany underwent major institutional reforms—namely, the restructuring of collective bargaining over wages, working time, and job stability—that dramatically transformed its manufacturing sector.[54] In particular, these reforms led to increased flexibility regarding employers' ability to adjust pay and working time. German manufacturers came to rely more on outsourcing and offshoring, largely redefining Germany's core labor force along narrower lines.[55] Overall, since the mid-1990s, the only substantial gains in "standard" German employment contracts occurred in the private service industries that employed high-skilled workers, offsetting the employment declines in manufacturing.[56]

It is true that the German labor market is still characterized by stable employment and respectable wages, especially in the high-skilled service and manufacturing sectors that remain covered by collective-bargaining agreements and social protections.[57] Germany does, indeed, have government programs that provide job tenure and wage guarantees for some workers. However, the coverage is much lower in the more dynamic service sector, which has been growing for decades.[58] As of 2014, the service sector was responsible for about 75 percent of total employment in Germany.[59]

According to economic researchers at the IZA Institute of Labor Economics, although overall employment in Germany grew by approximately 7 percent between 2000 and 2012, "a mixed picture emerges of the German labour market" when one takes into account "persistent issues such as long-term unemployment, a predominantly part-time-based employment pattern of mostly women, and issues with respect to labour market integration of low-skilled people."[60] According to IZA's research, the lower-paid segment of Germany's labor market grew substantially during this time, posing a particular problem for women, as well as workers in lower-skilled occupations.[61] This last finding is particularly damning for recent critics of the US economy who insist that German-style industrial policy should be used to bolster living standards for lower-skilled American workers.

Moreover, the German labor market has not been sufficiently robust to prevent a massive population flight as people seek more economic opportunities elsewhere.[62] As of 2011, Germany had the fifth-largest emigrant population among member countries of the Organisation for Economic Co-operation and Development (OECD), with 3.4 million Germans living in another OECD country, numbers only slightly behind those of China and India.[63] The OECD also notes that Germany's annual outflows—more than 140,000 per year—have been high in recent years and that the "education level of German emigrants is high and keeps rising."[64]

Of all the OECD countries, Germany has the most students studying abroad, and those emigrants leaving the country are more likely to have previously been employed than have former emigrants returning to the country.[65] Again, this finding is problematic for proponents of bringing German-style industrial policy to the United States.

The German and Japanese economies have clearly shifted more toward higher-skilled employment and service-sector jobs, much like what has occurred in the United States and most other developed nations.[66] Still, many critics of US policy remain fixated on the idea that boosting manufacturing is the best way to help workers.

Manufacturing Has Changed, but It Hasn't Disappeared

The American manufacturing sector looks very different than it did in the 1950s, but it has not been decimated.[67] Countless critics have blamed US job market problems on the supposed fact that "we do not produce

FIGURE 2.2
Manufacturing real output, 1919–2023

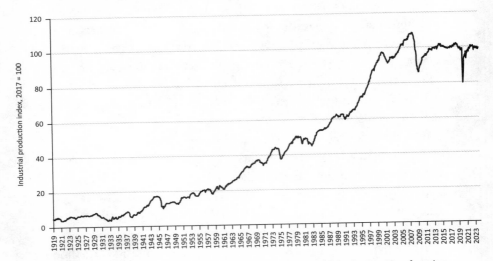

Source: Board of Governors of the Federal Reserve System, "Industrial Production: Manufacturing (SIC) [IPMANSICS]."

anything anymore."[68] In reality, outside of recessions, the inflation-adjusted value of US manufacturing output has been increasing for decades (see figure 2.2).[69] In the wake of the Great Recession, critics such as Oren Cass and Robert Reich insisted that the alleged demise of US manufacturing was the problem. Reich, for instance, argued that manufacturing's decline led to the disappearance of jobs "once relied on for steady work with good pay and generous benefits," particularly for those with lower levels of education.[70] According to Reich, these higher-paying jobs have been "replaced by lower-paying service jobs in places like retail stores, restaurants, hotels, and hospitals."[71]

It is true that service-sector jobs, many of which pay below median wages, have grown as a share of the US labor force since 1980; however, these critiques are misguided for several reasons. First, the focus on the post-1970s demise of manufacturing is wholly inappropriate. As a share of total employment, manufacturing employment has steadily declined since 1945 (see figure 2.3).[72] Additionally, the relative importance of the service sector has *always* been a key feature of the US economy.

FIGURE 2.3

Manufacturing share of total employment, 1939–2023

Source: US Bureau of Labor Statistics, "All Employees, Total Nonfarm [PAYEMS]"; US Bureau of Labor Statistics, "All Employees, Manufacturing [MANEMP]."

In fact, and contrary to widely held belief, the service sector has been a major contributor to American prosperity. It has accounted for a larger share of the US labor force than heavy industry since 1840 and agriculture since the early 20th century.[73] Additionally, the service sector's share of total output has exceeded the share for heavy industry during most of US history, with the only exception being a brief period around 1890.[74] Contrary to what many critics suggest, this long-term trend toward an increasingly service-based economy is exactly what should be expected as people become wealthier.[75]

Separately, it is difficult to support the claim that manufacturing jobs in general are higher paying than jobs in the rest of the economy.[76] For example, nonsupervisory workers in manufacturing earned 5.1 percent more in hourly wages than nonsupervisory workers in the service sector in 2000, but they earned almost 2.5 percent *less* in 2017. Separately, in 2018, nonsupervisory workers in manufacturing earned an average hourly wage of $21.54, less than the $27.74 for nonsupervisory construction workers and less than the $36.77 for nonsupervisory electric utility workers.[77] As of September 2019, average hourly earnings for

FIGURE 2.4
Share of sector workers under age 20, 2023

Source: US Bureau of Labor Statistics, "Labor Force Statistics from the Current Population Survey," table 18b.

nonsupervisory workers in manufacturing were lower than average earnings in 7 out of 10 service-sector categories, and they were less than $1 higher than average hourly earnings in the other services category.[78]

Manufacturing wages are also inflated relative to those in many other sectors—especially in service industries—because the manufacturing sector's workforce is older. A large share of the workers in major service-sector categories is under age 20 (15 percent in leisure and hospitality, 7 percent in retail), but only 1 percent of manufacturing workers are under age 20 (see figure 2.4).[79] Given the typical age-earnings profile of a career, this larger share of young workers clearly places downward pressure on average income for service jobs at the industry level.

Perhaps more importantly, the nature of manufacturing has been changing for decades. The image of hundreds of less-educated workers on an assembly line in a cavernous factory may warm the hearts of industrial policy enthusiasts, but it simply has not described the American manufacturing sector for many years. The number of very large

US factories—defined as those that employ more than 1,000 workers—is now well below levels reached even in the 1990s. Collectively, these large production establishments employ fewer than two million workers around the country, representing only about 1 percent of the US labor force and 16 percent of the manufacturing labor force.[80] Manufacturers have shifted to more specialized production, relying on automation, smaller plants, and smaller workforces.

Although fewer people are needed to manufacture, for example, air-conditioning units, more people are needed to make items such as orthopedic implants, surgical tools, and pharmaceuticals.[81] Naturally, manufacturers' educational requirements have changed as these shifts have occurred. For example, in 1970, nearly 36 percent of men in the United States without a college degree who worked full time were employed in manufacturing, but this figure fell to approximately 17 percent by 2015.[82] This change took place because manufacturers needed more highly educated workers, not because they stopped producing things. Using data from the Current Population Survey, the Congressional Research Service reports:

> In 2000, 53 percent of all workers in manufacturing had no education beyond high school. Between 2000 and 2018, that share dropped by 11 percentage points, even as the proportion with bachelor's or graduate degrees rose by 9 percentage points, to 31 percent. Despite the significant loss of manufacturing jobs between 2000 and 2018, the number of manufacturing workers with graduate degrees *increased* by approximately 357,000, or 36 percent.[83]

Because of these increased specialization and higher education requirements, it is true that some manufacturing workers earn relatively higher wages than workers in other industries. However, there is too much variation in the types of industries and jobs within the overall manufacturing sector to say that manufacturing in general provides particularly well-paying jobs. For instance, as of May 2018, the median annual wage for someone employed as an *aircraft structure, surfaces, rigging, and systems assembler* was $53,340. (Italics indicate official Labor Department job categories.) For comparison, the median annual wage was $40,070 for a *computer-controlled machine tool operator (metal and plastic)*, $35,430 for a *foundry mold and core-maker*, $31,540 for an *assembler and fabricator, all other (including team assemblers)*, and $28,780 for a *textile bleaching and dyeing machine operator/tender*.[84]

Wages for different manufacturing occupations also display variation based on education requirements and geographic locations, as well as industry type. For example, a *textile bleaching and dyeing machine operator/tender* in Rhode Island earned 31 percent more in annual wages than a counterpart in California, whereas someone employed in this occupation in the *textile furnishing mills* industry earned 27 percent more in annual wages than a worker in the *apparel knitting mills* industry.[85]

Of the approximately one million people employed in the *computer and electronic product* manufacturing industry in 2018, 29 percent worked in production occupations for which a high school education is sufficient, and for which median annual pay was $36,240.[86] However, 21 percent of this industry's employees were in architecture and engineering occupations, with median annual pay of $86,960, whereas 13 percent were in computer and mathematical occupations with median annual pay of $106,930.[87] These higher-paying jobs not only require higher education levels, but they also inflate the overall average for manufacturing wages.

The *churn rate* is another statistic that suggests manufacturing does not provide uniquely stable employment. This metric, reported by the Department of Labor's Bureau of Labor Statistics, is the sum of both *hires* and *separations*, where separations include both employees who quit and those who are fired.[88] Although the annual churn rates for manufacturing durable goods (3.8) and nondurable goods (4.7) are among the lowest reported, the rates are similar to those of other industries, such as educational services (4.7), wholesale trade (4.9), and finance and insurance (4.2).[89] Moreover, when considering both churn and the number of job openings, manufacturing's combined durable and nondurable ranking is very similar to the ranking of educational services, wholesale trade, finance and insurance, and even construction.[90]

Evidence also shows that higher churn rates exist in jobs with younger workers, less-educated workers, and male workers, and that employer-specific characteristics—rather than industry-level factors—explain much of the variation in churn rates and, by extension, job stability.[91] Thus, any attempt to push more people into manufacturing jobs would be, at best, an overly broad policy based on a widespread myth of manufacturing job stability.

Given these wage and stability statistics, as well as the long-term trends toward higher specialization and a more highly educated workforce, it is difficult to see how forcing more people into manufacturing jobs would provide abundant future opportunities for those with low education levels. To be successful by the critics' standards, industrial policy would have to—at minimum—force people to produce things that are not currently being produced, force manufacturers to hire people who currently make up a small part of the workforce, and force people to pay higher prices than they currently pay for all kinds of products (either directly, indirectly through higher taxes to pay for subsidies, or both).

Of course, if industrial policy were to accomplish these tasks, it is difficult to describe such a process as merely redirecting the market. On the contrary, it would supplant the market by subjugating both employers' and consumers' needs to the desires of a small group of people, such as those in charge of a government agency. Put differently, it would empower a small group to decide what is best for everyone else, even though this group cannot possibly know more about everyone else's needs than those individuals themselves. This sort of policy amounts to telling Americans that they can do just fine with paper and pencil instead of a computer because, after all, some people do not have the skills to design, build, or even use computers. Worse, it tells American workers that they need not worry about competing with anyone or gaining more high-level skills and education because "the government" will take care of them.

In the long run, this type of industrial policy would leave even more people unprepared to deal with the changing life circumstances that they regularly face, many of which make it more difficult to support families and build thriving communities. Perhaps in anticipation of this critique, many industrial policy advocates want to implement training and education programs for American workers—particularly those without a college education—like the ones used in Germany and Japan. The next section examines these policies.

Training and Apprenticeships Have Not Been a Cure-All

A key part of German industrial policy involves a formal apprenticeship system (*Ausbildung*) that includes both on-the-job training and theoretical learning. In 2017, 52.9 percent of "young people" from the resident population in Germany started an apprenticeship program. In 2018, the share increased to 54.5 percent, but the number of trainees has been on a downward trend since 2010, when the number was more than 1.5 million.[92] Historically, few of these apprenticeships had been provided to people pursuing university degrees, but the share of apprentices enrolled in college has been rising steadily, increasing by more than 43 percent from 2009 to 2017.[93] Long before the recent increase in college-educated apprentices, evidence suggested that the German apprenticeship system does not create the lifelong employment relationship that the popular press often suggests.[94]

One study reports that approximately 70 percent of apprentices left their training enterprise within five years of completing their program, and that those apprentices who did stay with their training firm earned less than those who left.[95] The study also reports that German apprentices earned more than less-educated Germans to a degree that is close to the rate at which American high school graduates out-earned Americans who did not finish high school. American high school graduates, who complete a similar number of education years as newly minted German apprentices, earned 23 percent more than those without a high school diploma, whereas German apprentices earned 19 percent more than a similar (lower-education) group of Germans.[96]

Separately, a 1996 study of the German labor market reports that apprentices "experienced fewer unemployment spells in the transition to their first full-time employment" relative to nonapprentices and that those trained in the largest firms had the smoothest transition.[97] However, the study shows that once they were employed, apprentices had similar job tenures to nonapprentices (regardless of whether they stayed with their training firm).[98] The study also reports that job changes for apprentices were frequent and "contributed to a retention rate of apprenticeship graduates of about 30 percent after five years," a finding consistent with other empirical work.[99]

Although newer research supports the finding that German vocational training may help transition younger people into the workforce, it also shows that any such advantage is offset as workers get older. In particular, lifetime-earnings calculations show that the average net effect can become negative as workers age, a pattern most pronounced in Denmark, Germany, and Switzerland, countries with well-developed apprenticeship programs.[100] A 2009 OECD study also reveals that in most countries with formal apprenticeship systems, people have created various institutional arrangements to settle problems with those programs, such as "low educational content, free riding, and undertraining."[101]

Despite these problems, and the United States' own history with apprenticeships,[102] many US officials for decades have called for the creation of some type of government-supported apprenticeship program. Such programs, supposedly, would improve workers' employment prospects and help build a more skilled labor force.[103] The US government has never created such a system, though the National Apprenticeship Act of 1937 directed the Department of Labor (DOL) to "formulate and promote the furtherance of labor standards necessary to safeguard the welfare of apprentices."[104] Using this authority, the DOL developed the Registered Apprenticeship system, in which federal and state agencies register individual apprenticeship programs as meeting federal or state standards.

In 2016, the Obama administration set a goal to double the number of registered apprenticeships in the United States, arguing, "Training programs like apprenticeships are a clear path to shared prosperity."[105] These actions have not satisfied proponents of industrial policy, most of whom favor government-subsidized apprenticeship and training programs. Some even support *tracking*, a system used in Germany and Japan, whereby students are preselected for certain types of education—and therefore careers—at a young age.

In Germany, students are typically selected by age 10 for one of three different tracks based on academic performance and on whether a school will accept the student: *Gymnasium* (eight years of university-prep school), *Realschulen* (six years of education with an apprenticeship as the ultimate goal), or *Hauptschulen* (the lowest track, for slower learners).[106] In Japan, at the end of middle school (ninth grade), young students must decide whether to advance to a vocational school or to a general high school with college as the ultimate goal. Japanese students' prior academic achievement is a major criterion for the post–middle school track, and middle school teachers actively steer students into different tracks—immediate employment, vocational high school, or general (academic) high school. Japanese teachers actively discourage poorly performing students from pursuing higher education.[107]

Although Oren Cass does not call for the complete adoption of the German or Japanese system, he does call for the "tracking of less academically talented students toward vocational training."[108] He provides the following details:

> An alternative to the current approach would be to accept instead that students' roads to the future will inevitably diverge and to help each excel on her trajectory. This requires the reintroduction of tracking, a term with various definitions in education-reform circles but used here to denote the separation of high school students into educational programs that seek different outcomes. One could lead toward college enrollment, another toward occupational training that leaves a twenty-year-old with serious work experience, a marketable skill, and $30,000 in a savings account.[109]

This type of system would empower a small group of people to limit what others might achieve in academics and their careers, a drastic departure from both American culture and the existing American education system.[110] This elitist approach also appears to conflict with Americans' constitutional rights. As one recent court case noted, "The right of citizens to support themselves by engaging in a chosen occupation is deeply rooted in our nation's legal and cultural history and has long been recognized as a component of the liberties protected by the Fourteenth Amendment."[111]

Regardless, although there is clearly a growing sentiment that a four-year college degree is not for everyone, it does not follow that the federal government should subsidize any education programs, much less ones that make it easier to remain in the low-education portion of the labor force.[112] In fact, given that the federal government has increasingly subsidized higher education during the past several decades, particularly after the 1965 Higher Education Act, failures of the current system provide a cautionary tale against providing new subsidies.[113] Indeed, these subsidies played a role in pushing so many young people into college at the cost of not pursuing other types of training.[114] In general, these policies have created a higher-education system that devalues a college degree, enriches school officials, needlessly buries students in debt while raising the cost of tuition, and exposes Americans to more financial risk.[115]

Still, critics such as Cass complain, "No workforce-based programs are eligible for support, while tens of billions of dollars flow to ineffective classroom-based programs on college campuses."[116] This statement is inaccurate in that many formal vocational training programs have existed in the United States for decades, often subsidized through federal and state grants. Not all these programs may fit Cass's definition of "workforce-based programs," but the focus of vocational education has always been to provide the skills that workers need. It is surely worth debating whether these efforts have been successful and whether they need to be improved, but the programs—and the federal subsidies—have existed for many years.[117]

Some statistics indicate that the federal government recently cut back on efforts to provide job training; however, that conclusion is incorrect. For instance, in 1996, the House Ways and Means Committee identified 154 federal employment and training programs, but in 2011, the US Government Accountability Office identified only 47 federally funded employment and training programs.[118] Despite this apparent decline in federal programs, the overall history of federal job training shows an almost constant reshuffling and consolidation of programs and a general expansion of training efforts (and federal funding) since the New Deal era.[119]

After World War II, the first big push to federally fund job training came in 1962, when Congress passed the Manpower Development and Training Act (MDTA).[120] The MDTA allocated federal funds to local communities on the basis of various population and poverty characteristics. One of its main goals was to provide training to workers displaced by technological advancement.[121] In 1973, the Comprehensive Employment and Training Act (CETA) sought to improve on the original program by providing local officials with more decision-making authority. CETA ultimately allocated funds to almost 500 "prime sponsors" to oversee job training for low-income groups and disadvantaged youths.[122] The Job Training Partnership Act of 1982 (JTPA), the next major effort to improve worker training, delivered both classroom and on-the-job training to low-income and dislocated workers through more than 600 local "service delivery areas."[123]

By the end of the 20th century, Congress believed that there was too much overlap and inefficiency among the many federal workforce programs, so it passed the Workforce Investment Act of 1998 (WIA),[124] which repealed the JTPA and consolidated many of its programs by creating a "one-stop" employment assistance system for workforce development.[125] Today, this system includes nearly 3,000 one-stop development centers administered by the Department of Labor's Employment and Training Administration.[126]

It is not the case that there has been no federal funding—or even a drastic cut in federal funding—for workforce development programs in recent years.[127] Aside from an additional $4.2 billion authorized by the 2009 American Recovery and Reinvestment Act, Congress appropriated an average of $5.2 billion per year for Title I WIA programs from 2000 to 2013 (only for these WIA programs, not *all* the federal workforce development programs).[128] It is extremely difficult to construct a comparable series of appropriations before the year 2000 because the WIA (and previous legislation) changed and consolidated so many programs, but this $5.2 billion figure is a slight increase from the 1998 appropriation for similar JTPA programs.[129]

The annual amounts appropriated by Congress between 1962 and 2013 indicate that the federal government spent almost $400 billion (adjusted for inflation) on the MDTA, CETA, JTPA, and WIA.[130] That's approximately $7.5 billion per year on just these workforce programs.

It is also difficult to get a consistent data set for federal programs and spending on just apprenticeships. However, a 1984 appraisal by the National Council on Employment Policy reports that the Labor Department funded "an action-oriented organization to assist minority workers in learning about the apprenticeship system and prepare them for apprenticeship examinations," and that this effort was responsible for "tripling the proportion of minority workers in apprenticeship programs between 1967 and 1980."[131] In 2016, the Obama administration awarded $50 million in apprenticeship grants, and the United States added more than 125,000 apprenticeships.[132] Not to be outdone, the Trump administration, in 2019, announced more than $300 million in grants for various apprenticeship programs.[133]

Despite the difficulty in constructing a long-term series of federal funding for occupational training grants, the evidence clearly shows that such funding has occurred for years through many different avenues. For instance, the federal School-to-Work program, created by the School-to-Work Opportunities Act of 1994, "attempts to bring together existing programs, such as technical education, school-based enterprises, youth apprenticeships, and job training initiatives."[134] Similarly, the 3,000 "one-stop" workforce development centers authorized by the WIA provide, among other services, occupational skill training, classroom training, and on-the-job training.[135]

When it comes to strictly vocational training, critics have no case. For instance, President Trump signed the reauthorization for the Carl D. Perkins Career and Technical Education Act in 2018, a bill that provides $1.2 billion for Career Technical Education (CTE) programs and job training. But this act simply reauthorized the Vocational Education Act, which was first enacted in 1963 to provide annual vocational education grants to states.[136] The CTE grant total has exceeded $1 billion per year since at least 1997.[137] The amount of CTE grants disbursed to each state varies considerably based, in part, on population.[138] For instance, in 2018, California received 10 percent of the total grants, whereas Alaska received 0.39 percent of the total.[139]

Many people have taken advantage of these vocational training opportunities. For instance, enrollment in community colleges (public two-year institutions) has been on a largely upward trend since the 1960s, so it is not only four-year institutions that have seen an influx of students. Although total enrollment for two-year public colleges dropped from 2012 to 2019, it was more than 5.6 million in 2019, almost 1 million more than the total enrollment in all public degree-granting institutions—both two- and four-year—in 1967.[140] For all two-year degree-granting institutions, both public and private enrollment stood at 5.9 million students in 2017.[141] Moreover, in academic year 2016/17, 78 percent of students enrolled in two-year degree-granting institutions received financial aid, and a large portion of those students received federal Pell Grants.[142]

Billions of dollars, including direct federal grants to students, have been flowing annually to community colleges that teach vocational skills. As of the 2011/12 academic year, 38 percent of students at two-year public institutions received Pell Grants, with an average award of $3,000. Both this percentage and the dollar amount are nearly twice as high as their respective figures from the 1999/2000 academic year, when 17 percent of students at two-year public institutions received Pell Grants and the average award was $1,700.[143] The latest statistics show that in academic year 2015/16, the most recent year available, 34 percent of students at two-year public institutions received Pell Grants, with an average award of $3,300.[144]

Although it makes sense to evaluate whether these funds could be spent more wisely and whether the US education system could be improved, it is not the case that the United States has been devoid of federally supported vocational training or workforce development. Given that many tradesmen, including welders, plumbers, and electricians, happily take on apprentices without subsidies, one must ask why the government should fund such training in the first place. Regardless, xpanding these subsidies to implement industrial policy would threaten economic opportunity for many Americans by fostering a closer relationship between government officials and the most politically connected individuals and companies.

Even without formal industrial policy, the federal government (a) hands out roughly $100 billion per year in direct corporate welfare payments to various businesses, (b) guarantees trillions of dollars in loans for favored firms and financial institutions, (c) bails out some businesses while allowing others to fail, and (d) interferes in international trade on behalf of certain companies at the expense of others.[145] As of 2023, the total number of federal subsidy programs was up to 2,418, more than double the total from 1990.[146] State governments also hand out billions of dollars in subsidies and tax breaks to attract companies, sometimes giving billions to single companies, such as Amazon.[147] Regardless of the level of government—state or federal—economists call this activity "rent seeking," a term that describes any efforts to obtain economic benefits through the political arena.[148]

Implementing a formal industrial policy would breed rent-seeking behavior and cronyism like never before seen in the United States, an outcome that some industrial policy advocates would happily accept.[149] The current system is not ideal, but purposely expanding cronyism will degrade the status quo because cronyism reduces opportunity and spurs some of the biggest economic problems that Americans face.[150] It isolates the winners of special political favors from having to compete with other firms, ultimately raising consumer prices and providing fewer opportunities for other entrepreneurs and workers. Industrial policy exacerbates these problems because, by design, it seeks to eliminate more productive economic behavior to accomplish politically predetermined outcomes.[151]

Research shows that policies that increase competition and efficiency lead to higher productivity.[152] In contrast, industrial policy and other government efforts to direct the economy ultimately harm individuals and businesses by isolating them from the many changes—both positive and negative—that occur in a dynamic free-enterprise system. Industrial policy rejects the more productive economic activities that win out through the competitive process in favor of the less productive activities preferred by those implementing the industrial policy.

A free society that respects people's right to improve their lives by making their own economic decisions—free from government-guaranteed privileges—maximizes its citizens' opportunities to improve their living standards. Yet critics of free enterprise insist that they can better provide such opportunities by redirecting the market, pushing people to make decisions that conform to the critics' own views. As always, recent critics are especially interested in using trade, technology, and immigration policy to redirect people's choices. The next chapter looks more closely at whether technological progress—especially through automation—positively affects opportunity and prosperity.

3

PRODUCTIVITY INCREASES FROM TECHNOLOGY
INCREASE LIVING STANDARDS

Fear that technology will lead to massive job losses has existed throughout the industrial age, with the infamous Luddites serving as perhaps the best-known early example. In 1812, a mob in Nottingham, England, supposedly taking orders from a mythical General Ludd, smashed new knitting machines that could produce the same amount of knitted goods as nearly 100 textile workers.[1] To some extent, it makes sense that this fear persists because the very purpose of such technology is to substitute machines for human labor.

In fact, even the fear of substituting machines for service-oriented tasks is quite old. In 1964, against a backdrop of rapid productivity growth, Congress created the National Commission on Technology, Automation, and Economic Progress.[2] The commission's final report, published in 1966, noted:

> Technological change is exemplified by the automation of a machine tool, reorganization of an assembly line, substitution of plastics for metals, introduction of a supersonic transport, discovery of a new method of heart surgery, teaching of foreign languages by electronic machines, introduction of self-service into

retailing, communications by satellite, bookkeeping by electronic computer, generation of electricity from nuclear energy, introduction of frozen foods and air conditioning, and the development of space vehicles and nuclear weapons.[3]

Thus, even in the 1960s, people were concerned with machines taking over service industry and clerical jobs, as well as manufacturing jobs.

In the 1980s, Apple Computer cofounder Steve Jobs tried to allay concerns regarding technology-related job losses by pointing to the less obvious benefits that arise when technology increases productivity. He nicely articulated the kinds of benefits that economists have been attributing to technological improvements for centuries. As a profile of Jobs in *Inc.* magazine reported:

> As for worker fears that office automation may lead to greater unemployment, he [Jobs] insists the opposite is true, with personal computers opening up jobs for Apple employees. He singles out an area associate outside his office, a young woman with no previous computer experience, who was hired three months ago and was given an Apple II with which to familiarize herself. "In another month, she should be able to take on other functions within the company. There's a special relationship that develops between one person and one computer that improves productivity on a personal level."
>
> His own productivity has been enhanced not only by Apple products, but also by those of the nearly 200 companies offering hardware and software for Apple systems.[4]

Jobs also spoke of the decision to put a computer on every desk as part of his mission "to institute a more humane workplace" and to give workers "the freedom to do more rewarding, enriching tasks."[5]

Technological advances such as the personal computer are labor-saving devices that increase productivity, both directly and indirectly. Accountants can use computers—instead of multiple assistants with typewriters, pencils, and hardback ledgers—to do the same amount of work in less time. They can then expand their business, work on other tasks, or enjoy more leisure time. Either way, the technology provides new job opportunities as people discover new ways to use the new technology, possibly further increasing their productivity gains.

As with other labor-saving mechanisms, these beneficial effects do not occur instantly, and new technologies do cause some jobs to disappear. Still, economic theory is clear on why technological advances do not lead to permanently lower employment—machines both substitute *and* complement labor.[6] The historical evidence is also clear: technological advances have led to higher demand for new products and services, and they have not caused large-scale or permanent unemployment.[7] The strong interdependence between automation and labor tends to increase productivity, raise earnings, and boost labor demand.[8] Technological improvements and automation have also made the workplace—and life in general—safer and more enjoyable.[9]

Still, as a 2016 *New York Times* article shows, the age-old debate over labor-saving technologies killing jobs rages on. It chronicles the troubles of 56-year-old Sherry Johnson, who claims to have lost multiple factory jobs. According to the *Times*: "Donald J. Trump told workers like Ms. Johnson that he would bring back their jobs by clamping down on trade, offshoring, and immigration. But economists say the bigger threat to their jobs has been something else: automation."[10] Essentially, all that is new in this debate is the term "offshoring."

Often lost in debates on whether technology kills jobs is the fact that public policies should not simply focus on increasing the number of jobs in the economy. One reason the debate has raged on, though, is that automation—like trade, offshoring, and immigration—does eliminate jobs. But there's a catch. Although economists generally acknowledge that machines eliminate jobs, they also point out that labor-saving phenomena have multiple effects that offset those job losses. Because these offsetting effects tend to boost welfare so much, most economists recognize that labor-saving phenomena—especially automation—are good for society even though they cause some jobs to disappear.

A chainsaw, for example, enables fewer people to harvest a forest in less time, so there will be fewer jobs requiring people to cut down trees with handsaws. The idea that chainsaws—specifically designed to do work for people—reduced the number of lumberjack jobs is uncontroversial. However, the invention of the chainsaw also created offsetting effects because it expanded the number of jobs for people to make and fix chainsaws and increased the demand for other types of jobs, especially those related to products made from lumber.

These offsetting effects are often harder to see, but they are just as important as the direct job-displacing effects of new technology because they create new opportunities and yield important benefits, including higher productivity (producing more goods per hour of work) and lower prices. Because chainsaws enable people to greatly increase the amount of available lumber—which lowers prices for lumber and related products—they provide new job opportunities for companies that sell lumber and related products. It becomes less costly to produce everything from cabinets to buildings.

The new machines also provide more employment opportunities because they free up time for people to do other things. This advantage may be hard to fathom in 21st-century America, but that's largely because machines have ensured that every man, woman, and child in the United States no longer has to engage in constant backbreaking labor to survive.

Few politicians would admit to advocating for policies that are tantamount to outlawing mechanical saws and requiring all lumber to be manufactured with hand tools. Yet many elements of industrial policy amount to just that. In the lumber example, such industrial policy would certainly provide more jobs, but it would also result in higher consumer prices and very little time for people to do anything other than produce lumber. There would be little point in worrying about how much paid vacation or family leave employers offer. People would be worse off because they would be less productive. They would have a much harder time achieving the same standard of living that they can attain when they employ technological advancements and use labor-saving machines.[11]

Eschewing the use of labor-saving technology leads to people working at tasks that take longer than necessary, while wasting resources that could be put to better use elsewhere. Business owners earn fewer profits, so they are less able to hire workers, expand production, provide on-the-job training, invest in new businesses and ventures, and buy consumer goods for themselves. People have less time available for leisure. Each of these forgone activities results in fewer employment opportunities and lower living standards. The same dynamic applies to training and education as well: people acquire more skills and education so that they can be more productive and thus command a higher wage.

Before the 1970s, many economists argued that automation was the main culprit behind job losses in manufacturing, and trade was a relatively unimportant component of the US economy.[12] In the 1990s, a few researchers suggested that trade was a bigger cause of manufacturing job losses than originally thought. But by the early 2000s, a broad consensus had emerged among economists: manufacturing job losses had been primarily due to technological changes, many of which required workers to have higher skills.[13] A brief manufacturing employment revival in the 1990s quelled the debate for a while, but then a sharp manufacturing employment drop starting in 2000, along with increased trade with China, renewed interest in the debate over trade's effects on the labor market.[14] Nonetheless, productivity increased throughout the past several decades, meaning that, holding all other factors constant, the number of manufacturing jobs should have declined. And as seen in figure 3.1, changes in manufacturing productivity and employment were mirror images of each other during the past few decades—meaning that fewer workers can produce more.

Manufacturing now relies so heavily on automation for this higher productivity that, unless machines are strictly outlawed, no amount of industrial policy can restore the number of US manufacturing jobs to its pre-1980s peak. As Donald Allan Jr., CEO of Stanley Black & Decker Inc., recently told the *Wall Street Journal*, "You've gone from a situation where if you did a power tool assembly in China or Mexico, you might have 50 to 75 people on a line. The automated solution that we've created in North Carolina, current version, has about 10 to 12 people on that line because of the high level of automation, and the 2.0 version looks like it's going to get down to two to three people on the line."[15]

FIGURE 3.1

Manufacturing productivity and employment share, 1987–2022

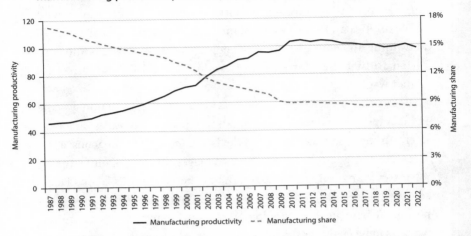

Source: US Bureau of Labor Statistics, "Manufacturing Sector: Labor Productivity [MFGOPH]"; US Bureau of Labor Statistics, "All Employees, Total Nonfarm [PAYEMS]."

✴ ✴ ✴

Millions Gain—and Lose—Jobs Throughout the US Economy

Every month, the Bureau of Labor Statistics (BLS) releases US employment data in what is frequently referred to as "the jobs report." It typically begins with a statement such as "Total nonfarm payroll employment rose by 128,000 in October, and the unemployment rate was little changed."[16] In a nation of more than 300 million people, with more than 160 million employed, an increase of 128,000 might seem rather small. It is, in fact, rather small. The reason is that it is a *net* number, calculated by comparing the nation's gross job gains with its gross job losses.

Both the gross job gains and losses in the US economy, on an annual basis, are regularly in the tens of millions. In 2018, for example, private employers added 13.5 million jobs and eliminated 11.4 million, for a net annual gain of approximately 2 million jobs. These dynamics have been present in the United States during the past several decades, for as long as the BLS has reported the data. From 1994 to 2018, the country had annual average gross job gains of 13.8 million and gross job losses of 12.5 million, figures that were very close to 10 percent of the total number of jobs in the economy.[17]

*   *   *

Some recent debates over technology's effects on labor markets are centered on robots and artificial intelligence (AI).[18] As with older technologies, recent studies suggest that AI boosts productivity, often by complementing existing technology for workers. For instance, a 2023 National Bureau of Economic Research paper reports that customer service agents using AI tools increased the number of customer queries they were able to resolve per hour by "14% on average, including a 34% improvement for novice and low-skilled workers."[19] Two additional 2023 papers find that using AI can result in even larger productivity enhancements. The first paper, by MIT economists Shakked Noy and Whitney Zhang, shows that ChatGPT improves business professionals' writing productivity by 59 percent.[20] The second, by researchers from MIT, Microsoft, and GitHub, shows that computer programmers using AI can code 126 percent more projects per week.[21]

Other researchers have fueled the debate by suggesting automation could drastically reduce the number of jobs in the United States. The largest estimates originate with a 2013 study by University of Oxford's Carl Benedikt Frey and Michael Osborne, in which they claim that "47 percent of total US employment is in the high risk category, meaning that associated occupations are potentially automatable over some unspecified number of years, perhaps a decade or two."[22] Frey and Osborne are careful to point out that they are not trying to forecast the future composition of the labor market or even how many jobs might actually be automated.[23] Furthermore, their study is largely based on subjective assessments of the potential for occupations to be automated.[24]

Still, some researchers have ignored these caveats and used the paper's automation figures to estimate employment losses.[25] Unsurprisingly, Frey and Osborne's predictions have proved unhelpful in forecasting actual job changes. For instance, the paper predicts that personal care aides are at high risk of having their jobs fully automated, but employment in this occupation increased by nearly one million jobs between 2013 and 2018.[26]

Additional research suggests that similar assessments of the likelihood of automation of certain types of jobs are much too high because tasks vary considerably within occupations. In other words, jobs are typically a bundle of tasks, with some of those tasks more amenable to automation than others. One 2017 study suggests that controlling for task variety in the workplace reduces the probability that US jobs will be automated from 38 percent to 9 percent.[27]

Other studies report small employment effects from automation. For instance, a 2017 paper by Daron Acemoglu and Pascual Restrepo reports that the increase in the stock of industrial robots in the United States from 1993 to 2007 reduced the employment-to-population ratio in "a commuting zone with the average US exposure to robots by 0.37 percentage points, and average wages by 0.73 percent, relative to a commuting zone with no exposure to robots."[28]

Other automation research demonstrates the offsetting positive effects of technological advancements. For instance, a 2018 study of 17 countries, also using data from 1993 to 2007, found that more rapid increases in robot use were associated with larger gains in labor productivity, and that the increased use of robots: (a) lowered output prices, (b) boosted total factor productivity, (c) boosted average wages, and (d) reduced the share of hours worked by low-skilled workers relative to higher-skilled workers.[29] Furthermore, a 2019 study of the Japanese labor market reports that AI reduces the number of hours worked by 17.2 minutes per day, and *increases* the number of "regular employees" by 2.4 percent.[30]

Some economists have also pointed to the fact that several countries with a higher share of their workforce employed in manufacturing—including Japan, Germany, and South Korea—use more industrial robots than do US manufacturers.[31]

Aside from specific empirical estimates, the consensus in the economics literature matches the anecdotal evidence: technological advances over the past two centuries have not resulted in net aggregate job losses.[32] Technological advances, including automation, have reduced labor requirements per unit of output produced, which suggests that offsetting forces have overcome this job-displacing tendency over time.[33] In fact, automation *complements* many tasks. In other words, automation displaces jobs for performing certain tasks, but it also allows people to allocate time and effort more effectively, thus increasing productivity and the demand for workers to perform other tasks.

This increased labor demand can be viewed as a *reinstatement* effect, whereby technological advances lead people to create new jobs.[34] Overall, this reinstatement effect has counterbalanced the job displacement effect of new technology. Moreover, technological advances can lead to increased trade, and vice versa, thus magnifying all these effects—and making it difficult to parse out the magnitude of "trade" or "technology" on employment.[35] Aside from these complicated scenarios, there are many clear illustrations of technological advancements leading to both displacement and reinstatement effects in the United States.[36]

In the financial industry, for example, technology has both displaced and created countless jobs. Municipal bond traders no longer sell paper bonds from the trunks of their cars, and the days of a mob-like trading pit in the New York Stock Exchange are gone. Still, at the end of 2018, the BLS reported that 6.3 million people were working in the *financial activities* sector, up from 5 million in 1990.[37] Similar trends can be seen in specific financial industry job categories—between 2000 and May 2018, the number of people employed as *financial analysts* went from 159,490 to 306,200, while those employed as *personal financial advisors* went from 77,420 to 200,260.[38]

An analogous episode took place in the banking industry after ATMs were developed in the 1970s. ATMs automated some of the basic tasks that bank tellers performed and lowered the cost of running a bank branch, which allowed banks to open more branches.[39] Thus, ATMs displaced some bank tellers but also helped increase the demand for other bank tellers and other bank employees. From 1990 to 2010, the number of ATMs installed in the United States went from 100,000 to more than 400,000, and the number of bank tellers employed rose from about 500,000 to almost 600,000.[40]

Not only did ATMs directly boost productivity by automating some basic tasks, but they also boosted it by freeing up bank employees to interact with customers on a personal level for other services, such as those related to investment and retirement accounts.[41] As a result, bank tellers became part of the "relationship banking teams" that provide bank customers with additional services.[42] The net result was an increase in employment. Throughout the financial industry, technology created a feedback effect, both democratizing investment opportunities for consumers—virtually anyone can now invest in the stock and bond markets, a vast difference from even the 1980s—and creating new employment opportunities in the process.

*　*　*

The United States Absorbed More People—and People Created More Jobs

The US labor market has been extremely dynamic in its overall size and share of the population working. In 1970, just shy of 71 million people, or 57 percent of the population, were employed in the United States.[43]

FIGURE 3.2
Working population and share of population employed, 1970 versus 2019

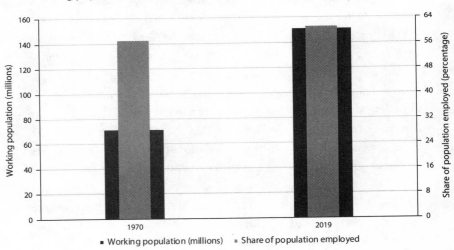

■ Working population (millions)　■ Share of population employed

Source: World Bank, "Population, Total for United States [POPTOTUSA647NWDB]"; US Bureau of Labor Statistics, "Employment-Population Ratio [EMRATIO]."

By December 2019, more than 151 million people, or 61 percent of the US population, were employed. Thus, the number of workers more than doubled by 2019, and a higher percentage of the population found work (see figure 3.2). Just as remarkable, the total US population increased from 205 million people in 1970 to 328 million people in 2019 (60 percent), whereas manufacturing employment fell by 34 percent from its peak in 1979.[44]

*   *   *

Though technology has changed over the centuries, the current arguments surrounding technological advances are virtually identical to those heard in the early industrial period. In both cases, labor-saving inventions displace some jobs and make people more productive.

Interestingly, one prominent critic of recent US economic policy, Oren Cass, vigorously argues that the United States should embrace the productivity gains that arise from automation.[45] He correctly notes that the same principles apply to both education and technology. That is, people acquire more skills and education so that they can be more productive, which enables them to command higher wages. Cass points out:

> In either case, with training or technology, the effect is to improve productivity—the amount of output per unit of work. Such productivity gains, whatever the mechanism, are the key to rising wages for workers and rising material living standards for society as a whole.[46]

Cass correctly points out that productivity gains, whatever the mechanism that spurs them on, are precisely what allows people to increase their living standards. Productivity in the United States has steadily increased since the end of World War II, both broadly and in specific sectors and by multiple metrics. For instance, aggregate hourly productivity and manufacturing output per person have both been increasing.[47] Net productivity in nonfinancial industries increased by 341 percent between 1947 and 2023.[48] As figure 3.3 shows, real hourly output per *manufacturing* employee has been on an upward trend since

FIGURE 3.3

Real annual output per employee: Manufacturing, 1959–2021

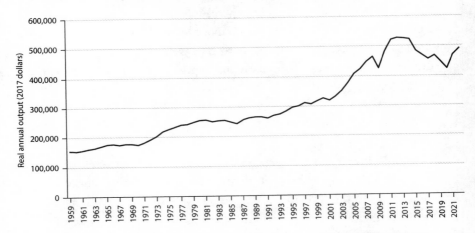

Source: US Bureau of Economic Analysis, "Gross Output by Industry"; US Bureau of Labor Statistics, "All Employees, Manufacturing [MANEMP]"; US Bureau of Economic Analysis, "Personal Consumption Expenditures Excluding Food and Energy (Chain-Type Price Index) [PCEPILFE]."

1959—it was 189 percent higher in 2019.[49] And whereas it took 12 work-hours to produce a ton of steel in 1980, it took approximately 0.6 work-hours as of 2018, a 20-fold increase.[50] Put differently, in 1980, one steelworker could produce 0.083 tons of steel in an hour, whereas in 2018, one steelworker could produce 1.67 tons.

These trends mean that fewer employees are needed to produce the same quantities of goods and services in all sectors of the economy, including in well-established industries. It would be impractical for US firms to employ as many people as they once did in, for example, steel production, even if most other countries stopped producing steel. A rough estimate shows that, at these higher productivity levels, with 1980 levels of employment, the United States would produce approximately two-thirds of the world's steel, far surpassing the share it produced in the aftermath of World War II—when most other industrialized nations were unable to produce steel because their industrial capacity had been severely damaged or destroyed during the war.[51] For anyone who doesn't want their child to spend 30 years working in a steel factory, this higher productivity is great news.

Nonetheless, many critics of US economic policy fail to see the upside of fewer people being needed to manufacture products, including steel, and instead bemoan a loss of jobs. Moreover, many critics, including Cass, do not attach the same importance to the productivity increases derived from trade and immigration. Yet each of these phenomena increases productivity and creates new employment opportunities through multiple channels. New technology requires more people to build and repair new machines, and it allows people to specialize in new tasks that they previously did not have the time or financial resources to undertake. New specialization and labor-saving capabilities make it—literally—easier to work.

Though it may not seem obvious, the same effects help explain why trade and immigration have also enhanced productivity. The next chapter looks more closely at trade.

4

PRODUCTIVITY INCREASES FROM TRADE
INCREASE LIVING STANDARDS

Trade, much like automation, is a labor-saving activity. Although trade eliminates some jobs, it also results in higher productivity and creates opportunities for people to improve their living standards. Restricting trade, much like restricting technological progress, isolates and harms workers by denying them access to new choices and opportunities that trade provides. It weakens the forces of competition and scale that help people become more productive.[1] An open society that exposes people to competition and that embraces technological change and trade creates more commerce, prosperity, and opportunities for people to move further away from poverty.

A closed society achieves the opposite. It impoverishes people by isolating them as if they were castaways forced into a subsistence lifestyle. Much like a group of castaways, a city whose citizens must produce all the consumer products they desire, from start to finish with no outside help, would be flush with jobs, but virtually everyone would be employed in nonproductive ways. Its citizens would work long hours doing routine tasks that could be done more easily with machines and with tools made outside the city. In many cases, they would be making products that could be acquired more easily and at less cost from elsewhere. The same logic applies to all the people within a state's borders, as well as a region's borders, and even a nation's borders. The only question people need to figure out is which products to produce on their own rather than buy from someone else. That decision, it turns out, is rather easy.

The basic case for free trade is straightforward: it is in society's best interest for people to have the choice to buy goods at the lowest possible cost.[2] Adam Smith, writing in the 18th century, was one of the first to express this idea. He did so in response to businessmen of his day who sought to keep less expensive competing products out of domestic markets. Smith argued:

> In every country it always is and must be the interest of the great body of the people to buy whatever they want of those who sell it cheapest. The proposition is so very manifest that it seems ridiculous to take any pains to prove it; nor could it ever have been called in question had not the interested sophistry of merchants and manufacturers confounded the common sense of mankind. Their interest is, in this respect, directly opposite to that of the great body of the people. . . .
>
> Hence the high duties and prohibitions upon all those foreign manufactures which can come into competition with our own. Hence, too, the extraordinary restraints upon the importation of almost all sorts of goods from those countries with which the balance of trade is supposed to be disadvantageous; that is, from those against whom national animosity happens to be most violently inflamed.[3]

Smith was reacting to the rent-seeking businessmen of his day, namely merchants and manufacturers, who won restraints to isolate their domestic markets, thus protecting their own businesses from foreign competition. These arguments were nearly identical to those used by today's critics of free trade, and the basic case against them has remained largely unchanged for centuries—they hurt consumers and reduce our standard of living.

In modern times, it is undeniable that America's trade policies currently impose unduly high costs on consumers, including agricultural price supports and volume controls, as well as tariffs on trucks and various items of food and clothing.

For instance, as of 2017, Americans paid a 20 percent import tariff on some dairy products, a 132 percent import tariff on certain peanut products, and up to a 35 percent import tariff on canned tuna.[4] As of 2015, before the Trump administration, tariffs on imported clothing were nine times as high as the average tariff for all imported goods.[5] Americans have paid a 25 percent tariff on pickup trucks—which dates back to a 1960s trade dispute with Europe involving chickens—that has resulted in higher prices and fewer vehicles available for sale in the United States.[6] Americans also pay tariffs of at least 10 percent and face tariff rate quotas (whereby once a specific quantity of a good is imported, it faces a higher tariff) on food products, including, among others, cantaloupes, apricots, various meats, sardines, spinach, soybean oil, watermelons, carrots, celery, okra, artichokes, and sweet corn. These trade policies cost Americans billions of dollars each year.[7]

Worse, these costs are especially burdensome for lower-income workers and families because they spend a relatively larger share of their income on necessities like food and clothing. As of 2019, those in the lowest quintile spend about 36 percent of their after-tax income on food and approximately 7 percent on clothing. In contrast, households in the highest quintile spend about 8 percent of their after-tax income on food and roughly 2 percent on clothing (see figure 4.1).[8] These statistics highlight the extremely regressive nature of these trade policies—Americans with higher incomes can more easily afford food and clothing so they suffer much less than lower-income Americans.

The existence of these tariffs and other trade barriers is typically due to lobbying by self-interested parties (e.g., companies, unions) trying to stave off foreign competition or misguided fears about imports leading to a trade deficit or job losses. Interestingly, Adam Smith dealt with many of the same anti-trade sentiments found today—pleas for the government to implement tariffs and trade restrictions and prohibit low-cost competitors, as well as fears over balance-of-trade problems with certain nations.[9]

Adam Smith also pointed out that trade provides additional benefits because it is a labor-saving (i.e., productivity-enhancing) activity.

FIGURE 4.1

Share of after-tax income spent on goods by income quintile, 2015

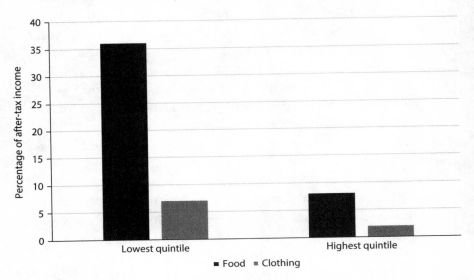

Source: Daren Bakst and Patrick Tyrrell, *Big Government Policies That Hurt the Poor and How to Address Them* (Washington: Heritage Foundation, 2017).

Smith knew, for instance, that it would be harmful for a family to try to make all the items they need rather than buy some of those goods. They would be much better off if instead they focused on producing only those goods in which they had some advantage.[10] He expanded:

It is the maxim of every prudent master of a family, never to attempt to make at home what it will cost him more to make than to buy. The tailor does not attempt to make his own shoes, but buys them of the shoemaker. The shoemaker does not attempt to make his own clothes, but employs a tailor. The farmer attempts to make neither the one nor the other, but employs those different artificers. All of them find it for their interest to employ their whole industry in a way in which they have some advantage over their neighbors, and to purchase with a part of its produce, or what is the same thing, with the price of a part of it, whatever else they have occasion for. What is prudence in the conduct of every private family can scarce be folly in that of a great kingdom. If a foreign country can supply us with a commodity cheaper than we ourselves can make it, better to buy it of them with some part of the produce of our own industry, employed in a way in which we have some advantage.[11]

The arguments for and against free trade have changed so little since Smith's time that his words apply just as easily in the 21st century. Voluntary trade is a mutually beneficial activity that enhances the welfare of both parties. Smith made a valiant effort to debunk the idea that trading with a foreign nation for certain goods results in one nation losing something, but that perception persists.[12]

A recent Economic Policy Institute (EPI) paper, for example, claims, "A rising trade deficit indicates that US manufacturers are losing business to manufacturing industries in other countries like China and Japan, who manipulate their currency to make their goods cheaper and therefore more appealing to consumers in the United States and elsewhere."[13] Possible currency manipulation aside, the premise behind this statement is faulty because no companies have any particular right to a given customer—the essence of a market economy is that *everyone* must compete to satisfy consumers' needs. To be sure, the only reason to produce something is so that it can be consumed; thus, it would have made just as much—perhaps more—sense for the EPI paper to claim that US manufacturers are failing consumers.

Concerns over trade deficits—the amount by which a country's imports exceed its exports—are similarly misplaced. In fact, a trade deficit is not even an economic concept but rather part of a national accounting system called the balance of payments.[14] This payments framework tracks the flow of money, so when imports exceed exports, it means that the amount of money leaving the United States to buy imports is larger than the amount of money coming in from selling exports. The balance-of-payments framework refers to this scenario as a trade deficit.

However, if the accounting framework were designed instead to track the quantity of goods, this same situation would be referred to as a "goods surplus." In other words, a trade deficit does not indicate that anyone has lost anything, or that anyone is owed anything.[15] It is simply one way of explaining the flow of imports and exports. Other methods could work just as well using opposing terms.

Additional details of the national accounting system further bolster this point. For instance, the balance-of-payments framework includes a current account and a capital account. The current account measures the flow of goods and services—that is, trade—and the capital account tracks all the inflows of investment dollars into America from foreigners. By definition, when the United States runs a current account deficit—which is virtually identical to a trade deficit—it must also run a capital account surplus so that all international payments balance—that is, the overall balance of payments is zero.[16] When foreigners sell their consumer products to Americans, they must do something with all the dollars they receive. They can either buy American products or invest in American assets (both real and financial). Thus, to the extent that Americans continue to import more than they export, a surplus must arise in the trading of American assets. That is, a US trade deficit must be paired with a US capital surplus.

Any nation that has a trade deficit must also have a capital surplus, a situation that is inherently neither good nor bad. In contrast, any nation that has a trade surplus must also have a capital deficit, a situation that is also neither inherently good nor bad.[17]

For most of its history, the United States has had a trade deficit, including during prosperous periods.[18] During the 1930s, however, the country had a trade surplus for 102 of that decade's 120 months.[19] Still, as miserable as the 1930s economy was, the fact that the United States mostly ran a trade surplus in a decade gripped by the Great Depression does not indicate that trade surpluses are inherently bad. Economies are too complex to draw such broad conclusions about trade deficits and surpluses, both of which originate in a specific national accounting framework. The trade deficit, as noted, simply is not an economic concept, much less one that policymakers should target.

Congress has dealt with this deep misunderstanding of trade deficits and surpluses throughout the post–World War II period, but it persists nonetheless. In 1965, for example, a congressional committee named the Review Committee for Balance of Payments Statistics released a report that explicitly rejected the idea that people should view the balance of payments as represented by the concept of a surplus or deficit.[20] Although the balance-of-payments framework may simplify reality, many economists acknowledge that it also complicates explaining the gains from trade precisely because of the negative connotation of the phrase "trade deficits." Yet the national accounting framework that gives rise to this deficit/surplus calculation tells us little about why people should, or should not, trade with others rather than make a product on their own.

Like their predecessors, recent critics of US economic policy have exploited the negative sounding "trade deficit" to argue for tariffs and restrictions to "protect" American workers and industries from foreign competition and related job losses. A large body of evidence, however, shows that trade deficits were not the culprit behind the decline in US manufacturing employment, which was far from unique. Like the United States, most industrialized countries experienced a downward trend in manufacturing jobs after 1970. Trade deficits could not have caused these declines, though, because many of these countries consistently had trade surpluses.[21] Yet the same employment downturns are found in countries including Germany, Japan, and Italy—all of which had trade surpluses that averaged 7.6, 6.2, and 4.2 percent of their GDPs, respectively, between 1973 and 2010.[22] Adam Posen of the Peterson Institute for International Economics demonstrated that, beginning in 1992, similar employment declines occurred in North Rhine-Westphalia, a German industrial hub, which had trade surpluses, and the state of Ohio, which had trade deficits.[23]

Internationally, no clear relationship exists between a trade imbalance and a nation's manufacturing employment. From 1994 to 2019, in a nine-country sample of both developed and developing nations, some with trade surpluses and others with trade deficits, all but India displayed a decline in the percentage of their population employed in manufacturing.[24] In the United States, as international trade increased in the 1980s, the share of manufacturing employment fell at nearly the same rate (0.4 percentage points per year) as it did in the 1960s and 1970s, when trade accounted for a much lower share of the economy.[25] Meanwhile, the respective shares of imports and exports to GDP rose almost in tandem from 1960 to 2019. That's hardly surprising, as most

FIGURE 4.2

Export and import shares of GDP, 1960–2015

Source: US Bureau of Economic Analysis, "Gross Domestic Product [GDP]"; US Bureau of Economic Analysis, "International Trade in Goods and Services."

of the country's largest importing firms are also some of its largest exporters.[26] Thus, US manufacturing employment has fallen while *both* imports and exports, as a share of the economy, have been rising at nearly the same rate (see figure 4.2).

Separately, the annual US trade deficit as a percentage of GDP has varied little since the end of World War II. Rather, it has fluctuated within a roughly five-percentage-point band from 1960 to 2019.[27] From 1979—when manufacturing employment began a pronounced downward trend—to 2019, the trade deficit as a percentage of GDP was slightly larger and less variable than it was during the period 1960–2019. It averaged 3 percent, with only a 1 percent variation from 1979 to 2019, compared with an average of 2 percent, with 2 percent variation, from 1960 to 2019.[28] Therefore, if trade deficits had any causal effect on anything—and there is no economic reason to think so—the effect should have been smaller after 1979.

Another major strike against the idea that the trade deficit (or even increased trade) has been a major contributor to job losses in manufacturing is that manufacturing employment for 2010 can be precisely forecast without using any data beyond 1980.[29] In fact, said forecasting can be done using only total manufacturing employment data that predate China's economic rise, the formation of the World Trade Organization, China's permanent normal trade relations status, and the North American Free Trade Agreement. In other words, a forecaster in 1980 could ignore all these trade-related events—which supposedly decimated manufacturing employment—and still accurately predict manufacturing employment for 2010.[30]

Using the same statistical method with different data further weakens the idea that post-2000 changes in trade—or automation, offshoring, or immigration, for that matter—caused males to drop out of the labor force. For instance, labor force participation for males can be almost perfectly predicted for 2018 using only labor force participation data from 1948 to 1999.[31] If these post-2000 factors had been particularly important for the decline in the labor force, it would be impossible to accurately predict the 2018 rate without incorporating them into the forecast.

Still, it is true that increased international trade that replaces domestic manufacturing can cause some jobs to disappear. If Americans only import door hinges, for example, then few Americans would have jobs making door hinges. For economists, there isn't much controversy; they support free trade despite the negative job effects because the evidence overwhelmingly supports the net positives of free trade.[32] As a result, most recent research focuses on very narrow questions, such as the amount by which increased trade with China might have caused manufacturing employment to decline.

*   *   *

Displaced Workers in the United States Find New Jobs Quickly

Displaced American workers are generally able to find new employment relatively quickly. For instance, from January 2015 through December 2017, three million workers were displaced from jobs that they had held for at least three years, and 66 percent of those workers were reemployed by January 2018.[33] The displaced workers who were not reemployed represent only 0.6 percent of the labor force.[34]

These displacement and reemployment rates have been typical in the United States for decades. For instance, from January 2001 to December 2003—a period that includes a recession—5.3 million workers were displaced from jobs they had held for at least three years, and 65 percent were reemployed by 2004.[35] From 1991 to 1992, another period that includes a recession, 2.8 million workers were displaced from jobs they had held for at least three years, and 75 percent were reemployed by 1994.[36] Although the number of displaced workers was higher in the 1991–1992 period than from 1981 to 1982, the displaced worker share of the labor force was essentially the same for both periods.[37] Additionally, the percentage of people reemployed without taking a lower-paying job has gone up over the past few decades. Between 1991 and 1992, only one-third of the reemployed earned as much or more than they did in their previous job.[38] However, this figure rose to 43 percent between 2001 and 2003, and to 51 percent between 2015 and 2017.[39]

The share of displaced workers from manufacturing jobs relative to total job displacements was much higher in earlier periods—50 percent from 1981 to 1982[40]—than in later periods—33 percent from 2001 to 2003,[41] and 16 percent from 2015 to 2017.[42] And throughout much of the 1990s, roughly half of all reemployed displaced workers found jobs in the same industry.[43] Yet in 2010, shortly following the Great Recession, displaced workers in virtually all industries were likely to have new jobs in different industries.[44]

Differences in reemployment rates across racial categories have also declined—the 2018 rate was virtually identical for blacks (65.9 percent) and whites (65.3 percent), and higher for both Asians (69.9 percent) and Hispanics (68.6 percent).[45] Between 1979 and 1983, the difference in reemployment rates between black men and white men was 15 percentage points; between 1984 and 1986, the gap had closed to 10 percentage points (black males had a lower reemployment rate). Between 1979 and 1983, the difference in reemployment rates between black women and white women was 9 percentage points; between 1984 and 1986, the gap had closed to 2 percentage points.[46]

These figures are not indicative of a systemic job-loss crisis in the United States during the past few decades—the raw numbers of displaced workers are too low, and the reemployment rates are too high. The data also demonstrate that the labor dynamics in manufacturing are not unique—even displaced workers in leisure and hospitality are likely to find new jobs in a different industry, a phenomenon that occurred, to an above-average degree, in the wake of the COVID-19 pandemic.[47]

*   *   *

Several researchers have studied the "China Shock," a reduction in US manufacturing employment after 2000 that was supposedly caused by increased trade with China.[48] One problem with this story is that, although Chinese imports did increase in 2000, they largely replaced imports from other Pacific Rim countries. As a Congressional Research Service paper points out, Pacific Rim countries, including China, accounted for 47.1 percent of all US manufactured imports in 1990, the same share they had in 2017. All that changed is the share of the 47.1 percent accounted for by Chinese imports—it was just 7.6 percent in 1990, but it was 55.4 percent by 2017.[49]

Nonetheless, the paper that essentially kicked off this research effort is a 2013 study by economists David Autor, David Dorn, and Gordon Hanson, published in the *American Economic Review*. They report:

> We more conservatively estimate that Chinese import competition explains 16 percent of the US manufacturing employment decline between 1990 and 2000, 26 percent of the decline between 2000 and 2007, and 21 percent of the decline over the full period. For the mainland US working-age population, these estimates imply a supply-shock driven net reduction in US manufacturing employment of 548,000 workers between 1990 and 2000 and a further reduction of 982,000 workers between 2000 and 2007.[50]

Even the larger of these figures—122,750 per year from 2000 to 2007—represents only 1 percent of the typical job loss in the United

States annually. In another paper, one that popularized the term "China Shock," Autor, Dorn, and Hanson estimate that trade with China from 1999 to 2011 caused cumulative US manufacturing job losses of 985,000, and economy-wide US job losses of two million.[51] These figures average about 76,000 and 154,000 jobs per year, respectively—no more than roughly 1 percent of the typical annual job loss in the United States. Importantly, the authors' work shows that the effects are geographically concentrated, and that the so-called shock ended around 2008, when current account balances between China and the United States reversed.[52] Furthermore, of the papers that study the China Shock, Autor and his coauthors find the largest negative effects on US manufacturing employment.[53]

Just as important, even some of these narrowly focused studies find a net positive effect from trade, while other research is even more positive.[54] For instance, like Autor and his coauthors, a group led by Stanford University economist Nicholas Bloom reports a concentrated loss of employment associated with increased Chinese imports in areas with low levels of human capital. However, they report that the China Shock had a "significant positive effect on US nonmanufacturing employment concentrated in areas with high initial levels of human capital," and that this positive effect "more than offset" the negative manufacturing employment effects.[55]

Other economists find even more positive effects from increased trade with China. For example, George Mason University economist Zhi Wang and his coauthors report that the overall impact of the China Shock was an increase in both local employment and wages.[56] Specifically, the authors report that "the total effect for an average region is a net job increase of 1.27 percent," and that "75 percent of the workers in an average region experience a real wage growth as a result of exposure to the China trade."[57] They report a net increase in service jobs even in those regions where manufacturing jobs fell the most.

Although none of these papers report a China shock that persists beyond 2010, Autor and his coauthors state that the regions most affected by increased Chinese imports had not fully recovered by 2019. Interestingly, US manufacturing employment increased by more than 1.3 million jobs (11.17 percent) between 2010 and 2019, a period when

FIGURE 4.3

Change in Chinese imports and US manufacturing employment, 2010–2019

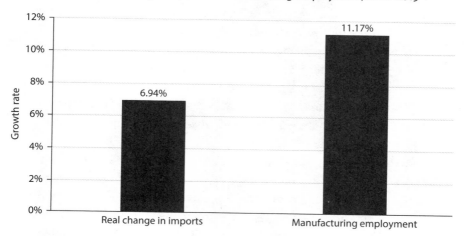

Source: US Bureau of Labor Statistics, "All Employees, Manufacturing [MANEMP]"; US Bureau of Economic Analysis, "Personal Consumption Expenditures Excluding Food and Energy (Chain-Type Price Index) [PCEPILFE]."

Note: The real value of Chinese imports refers to the value of US imports from China as reported on the United Nations Comtrade Database, adjusted for inflation with the PCE price index.

the nominal (real) value of Chinese imports increased 23.37 percent (6.94 percent) (see figure 4.3).[58] Regardless, none of these researchers recommend implementing higher tariffs to address the trade shock, a policy that would make little sense given that its impacts have already dissipated.[59]

Relatedly, some observers have called for government assistance to help displaced workers; however, such policies would not be new. For example, Autor and his coauthors report that American workers affected by the so-called China Shock took advantage of government grants provided under the Trade Adjustment Assistance (TAA) program. Specifically, they report that the largest "proportionate increase" in government transfer payments for locations with high import exposure was for TAA payments, though other types of transfers (such as Social Security Disability Insurance benefits and benefits from

Supplemental Security Income) were larger in absolute terms.[60] Notably, a separate 2013 study pointed out that more than 845,000 US workers in the manufacturing sector were certified for TAA since the North American Free Trade Agreement's 1994 implementation because they lost their jobs owing to imports from Canada and Mexico or from the relocation of factories to those countries.[61] This figure, however, works out to only 42,000 jobs per year, less than 1 percent of the typical annual job loss in the United States.[62] (For a brief discussion of how trade might indirectly cause job losses, see the appendix section titled "Trade Research Overview.")

It might be surprising, but trade can lead to more US manufacturing jobs as firms shift industries to provide services to other manufacturing firms, such as product design. In fact, the service component of manufacturing companies throughout the developed world has been growing for decades, leading to higher demand for different types of manufacturing jobs, for companies as diverse as Apple, Xerox, Medtronic, and Rolls-Royce.[63] Thus, trade can indirectly lead to higher productivity and to more jobs. To whatever extent such effects occur, the singular focus on total manufacturing employment overstates the negative effects on society from the recent decline in US manufacturing employment.[64] Even though some studies of the wage or employment effects ignore these offsetting positive effects (often out of necessity), both theory and evidence confirm their importance.[65]

Another beneficial aspect of trade is that imported products provide competition for domestic firms, pushing companies to innovate and improve their products. In the absence of such pressures, companies can more easily fall behind, producing inferior products—in quality or price—that consumers eventually stop purchasing. This lack of competitive pressure could also contribute to some workers failing to improve their own skill levels. To the extent that such negative incentives take hold, isolating people from competition with foreign workers fosters Rust Belt–like conditions with dying industries and an aging population ill-prepared for the types of jobs needed to improve living standards.[66]

Much like using new technology, purchasing goods produced by others saves labor. It enhances productivity by allowing people to take on new tasks for which they previously did not have the time or resources. Though it may not seem obvious, the same principle helps explain why immigration is productivity enhancing. The next chapter looks more closely at immigration, perhaps the most controversial of the productivity-enhancing activities discussed in this book.

5

PRODUCTIVITY INCREASES FROM IMMIGRATION
INCREASE LIVING STANDARDS

n the 1840s, a virulent anti-immigrant attitude coincided with the creation of one of the United States' earliest populist political parties, the anti-immigrant Know-Nothing Party. During this time, many US citizens expressed concerns that the new arrivals—especially the nearly two million Irish willing to accept labor-intensive jobs at low pay—would put excessive downward pressure on wages and take jobs from US-born workers.[1] The anti-Irish-immigrant sentiment was so strong that it even inspired a scene in the 1974 movie *Blazing Saddles*, Mel Brooks's satirical western film, and was central to the plot of Martin Scorsese's 2002 film, *Gangs of New York*.

This sentiment may have lessened among Americans today, but it certainly has not disappeared. In a 2017 Gallup poll, when asked, "Do you think immigrants: mostly help the economy by providing low-cost labor, (or) mostly hurt the economy by driving wages down for many Americans?," 40 percent of respondents answered, "mostly hurt."[2] This finding seems to support the narrative surrounding the Trump campaign's success, but other findings reveal a more complicated picture. For instance, *The Great Revolt* describes the story of Erie County, Pennsylvania, a stereotypical Trump town beset by recent job loss. It turns out that the county has been pinning its revival strategy on "bringing in refugees to help rebuild the dwindling population"—not exactly the approach one might expect from residents that fear immigrants will take their jobs or decrease their income.[3]

Although offshoring—moving jobs to an overseas affiliate—no longer attracts as much media attention as immigration, it was a major issue during the 2004 presidential campaign because, much like immigration, offshoring stokes fears of Americans "losing jobs" to other workers.[4] It is difficult to get reliable offshoring statistics, but there is no shortage of immigration data.[5] To put US immigration flows in perspective, the share of foreign-born individuals in the population has steadily increased from about 5 percent in 1970 to 13.7 percent in 2019. The 2019 share is near the historical record, 14.8 percent, reached in 1890.[6] Although the United States generally welcomes more immigrants per year than any other country, it does not allow a particularly large portion of immigrants to enter each year relative to its total population.

Using this relative measure, the United States ranks 33rd out of the 35 Organisation for Economic Co-operation and Development member countries, and the top 10 of these OECD countries all allow immigrant inflows of more than 1 percent of their population, whereas the United States allows inflows of 0.31 percent of its population (see figure 5.1).[7] Perhaps more relevant to labor market studies, the number of foreign workers coming into the United States each year is a small percentage of the total labor force. On an annual basis, the combined total of all the major categories of temporary foreign workers and legal permanent residents (including family members not eligible to work) allowed into the United States has averaged less than 1 percent of the labor force for the past 21 years (see figure 5.2).[8] (Also see figures 5.3 and 5.4 for additional visualizations on legal permanent residents.)

Focusing only on the major temporary work visa categories for lower-skilled workers paints a similar picture. For instance, the H-2A and H-2B visa categories are for temporary workers performing agricultural services and temporary workers performing other services, respectively.[9] Although it is less meaningful to compare these smaller categories with the overall labor force, the total number of H-2A and

FIGURE 5.1

Immigration inflow as a percentage of population, 2019

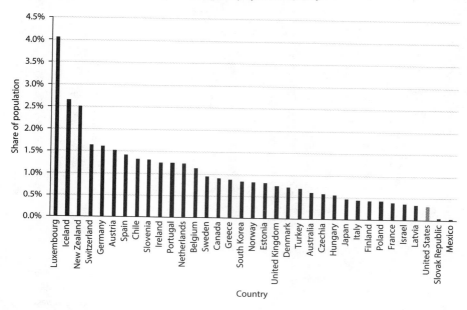

Source: Organisation for Economic Co-operation and Development, "OECD International Migration Statistics."

FIGURE 5.2

H and L visa holders, plus legal permanent residents, as percentage of labor force, 1998–2018

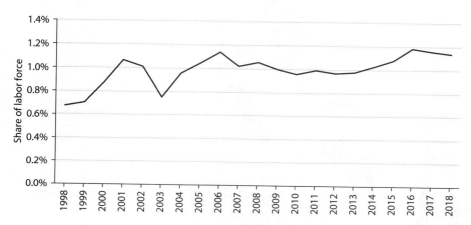

Source: US Department of State, *"*Nonimmigrant Visa Statistics," "Table 1. Persons Obtaining Lawful Permanent Resident Status: Fiscal Years 1820 to 2018"; Office of Homeland Security Statistics, *2018 Yearbook of Immigration Statistics*; US Bureau of Labor Statistics, "Civilian Labor Force Level [CLF16OV]."

FIGURE 5.3

New US legal permanent residents by broad type, FY 2001–FY 2020

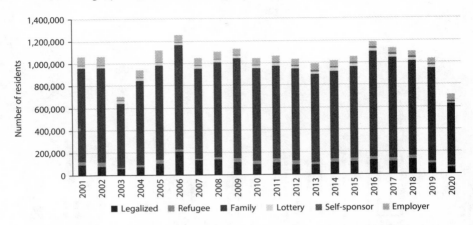

Source: Freedom of Information Act request COW2020000194, "Count of Form I-140 National Interest Waivers," US Citizenship and Immigration Services, 2020.

Note: "Family" includes dependents of nonfamily. "Refugee" includes primaries under the Refugee Act and Iraqis and Afghans. "Employer" includes primaries under EB-1B, EB-1C, EB-2, EB-3, and EB-4 (except for Special Immigrant Juveniles) minus the number of EB-2 national interest waivers (NIWs). "Self-sponsor" includes NIWs and primaries under EB-1A and EB-5, the 2011–2019 average number of NIWs was used for 2020. "Legalized" refers to non-family-based applicants in which physical presence in the United States is required.

H-2B visas issued each year is relatively small compared with the lower-skilled labor pool, a subcategory of the overall labor force. Using the total number of people age 25 and older without a high school degree as a proxy for this subcategory of the labor force, the total number of H-2A and H-2B visas issued annually showed an upward trend, though it was under 1 percent for 11 of the previous 14 years (see figure 5.5).[10]

Even though annual US immigrant inflows are relatively small as a share of the population, it is easy to "see" that an influx of immigrants (or offshoring) might cause a decline in some job opportunities or wages, especially as the total number of immigrant workers rises. If, for instance, employers tend to favor immigrant workers willing to work for lower wages, then competing workers might be unable to fill those same jobs. Indeed, they might even face pressure to accept lower wages for similar jobs. In a basic supply-and-demand framework

FIGURE 5.4

Diversity lottery entrants and share receiving green cards, 1995–2021

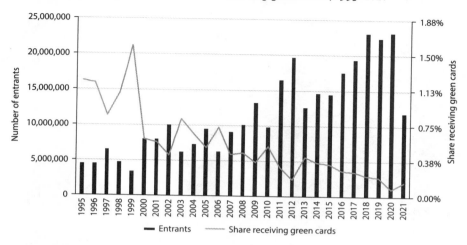

Source: US State Department Bureau of Consular Affairs, "Diversity Visa Program Statistics," Travel .State.Gov; "2006 Diversity Visa Lottery Registrations," US State Department, archived; US State Department, "Results of the Diversity Immigrant Visa Program (DV-99)," press statement by James B. Foley, May 6, 1998; Rachel L. Swarns, "A Futile Rush in Desperation for Green Card," *New York Times*, January 31, 1996.

FIGURE 5.5

Total H-2 visa holders as a percentage of lower-skilled labor, 2006–2019

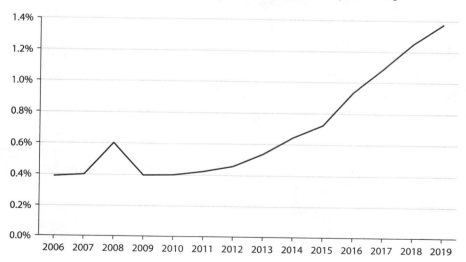

Source: Author's calculations using the annual number of H2-A and H2-B visas issued as reported by the Department of State, relative to the number of people (25 years and older) without a high school diploma as reported by the Census Bureau, from 2006 to 2019. See "Nonimmigrant Visas Issued by Classification," US Department of State, various years; and US Census Bureau, "CPS Historical Time Series Tables, Table A-1, Years of School Completed by People 25 Years and Over, by Age and Sex: Selected Years 1940 to 2019," 2023.

FIGURE 5.6
Supply and demand of the labor market

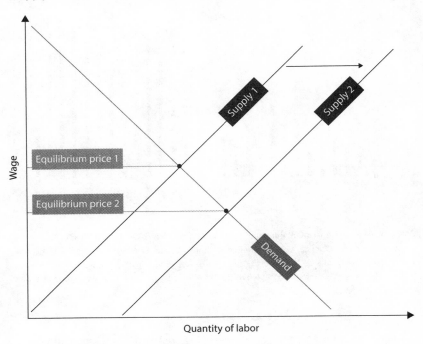

Source: Author's illustration.

(shown in figure 5.6), as the number of immigrant workers increases (the labor supply curve shifts right), market wages will drop, holding all other relevant factors constant. Just as with trade and automation, though, there are many other relevant factors to consider that can off-set this negative wage effect.

First, immigrants are also consumers, so an influx of immigrants increases the demand for goods and services, and for the labor and cap-ital needed to produce those additional goods and services. An influx of immigrants, therefore, also increases the demand for other types of labor and puts upward pressure on wages. Moreover, productivity is partly a function of human capital, so immigration can enhance pro-ductivity as people bring new knowledge (including tacit knowledge and skills that people learn through experience) into the economy. In one of the first major economic studies of immigration, the economist Julian Simon pointed out, "It is a simple fact that the source of improvements in productivity is the human mind, and a human mind is seldom found apart from a human body."[11]

Bringing more people into an economy increases human ingenuity, thus increasing opportunities for improving specialization and division of labor.[12] It can lead to improvements in productivity as people with complementary skills work together. Increased immigration can also boost a country's exports as migrant networks generate lower transaction costs and help transfer product-specific knowledge, both of which increase productivity.[13] Just as important, increased immigration can bring noneconomic benefits to a country, such as enriching the existing culture, cuisine, and knowledge of other places and people.

Although increasing the pool of workers increases competition in the labor market, a free-enterprise system depends on competition because competitive market forces—including between people competing for jobs—push people to improve and expand their economic opportunities. Restricting labor competition, on the other hand, provides incentives against constantly improving skills.

It is also not the case that workers compete for a fixed number of jobs, or that the amount of capital in an economy is fixed. Instead, employers and investors regularly adjust the types of jobs they offer and the type of capital they employ to take better advantage of changing productivity. Losing out on a given job, therefore, does not relegate a worker to long-term unemployment.

Additionally, employers generally do not view all workers as perfect substitutes because people have different attributes and skills that often complement those of other employees. To whatever extent workers are complementary, as opposed to substitutes, the basic prediction that an increase in immigration will decrease jobs and wages no longer holds. In fact, the opposite holds. That is, both immigration and offshoring lead to greater demand for workers to the extent that they reduce costs and complement existing capital and workers' skills.[14]

As with trade and automation, the evidence generally shows that immigration and offshoring have net positive effects on employment.

Several researchers have examined whether increased immigration and offshoring caused the decline in US manufacturing employment from 2000 to 2007, a time that saw one of the largest historical employment declines. During this period, manufacturing employment fell by 20 percent, from 17.3 million employees in January 2000 to 13.8 million by December 2007.[15] One such study reports that the overall share of immigrants in the United States increased from 12.8 percent to 14 percent from 2000 to 2007, whereas the share of offshore employment in total manufacturing employment increased from 22.3 percent to 29.3 percent.[16] The study also reports a great deal of variation in immigration and offshoring across industries from 2000 to 2007.[17]

The authors of that study report that immigration had a positive net effect on the employment of US-born workers, and offshoring had no net effect. The study's results are also "consistent with the existence of a positive productivity effect" from immigration and offshoring "within manufacturing industries."[18] The authors also find that immigrant workers typically specialize in manual tasks and do not compete with native workers, and that offshore workers tend to compete more directly with native-born employees. The results suggest that an increase in offshoring tends to push native workers into jobs that require more cognitive-intensive tasks, and that the productivity effect of offshoring offsets any negative effect on native employment.[19]

Another paper, by Williams College economics professor William Olney, studies the employment decline between 2000 and 2007 and finds that the "productivity effect [of immigration and offshoring combined] is large enough to compensate for the labour supply effect [lost jobs in the United States] and causes offshoring to actually increase the wages of low-skilled native workers."[20] Olney reports, "Offshoring has a more positive impact on the wages at the low end of the distribution than immigration, but this gap decreases as the wage deciles increase."[21] The results suggest that a one percentage point increase in the share of offshoring *increases* low-skilled workers' wages by 4.4 percent, whereas a one percentage point increase in the share of foreign-born workers *decreases* low-skilled workers' wages by 0.1 percent.[22] For immigration, these results suggest a very small wage effect—a one percentage point increase in the share of immigrant workers decreased low-skilled workers' wages by $1 for every $1,000 they earned.

Beyond this brief period, the bulk of the evidence suggests that other factors, such as higher productivity and increased consumer demand, tend to outweigh the downward pressure that new immigrants place on wages. One major piece of evidence is the fact that most US wage categories—including those employing lower-educated workers—have displayed upward trends over the past few decades as immigration numbers climbed. More importantly, most of the detailed empirical studies support this position, with one notable exception being the work of Harvard economist George Borjas.

For instance, using results from his paper published in the *Quarterly Journal of Economics*—results that stood in contrast to most earlier studies—Borjas made the following argument:

> Wage trends over the past half-century suggest that a 10 percent increase in the number of workers with a particular set of skills probably lowers the wage of that group by at least 3 percent. Even after the economy has fully adjusted, those skill groups that received the most immigrants will still offer lower pay *relative* to those that received fewer immigrants.[23]

One often overlooked aspect of this empirical result—and of most results in this body of economic research—is that it does not refer to an absolute decline in wages. Borjas's results, instead, refer to a relative decline in wages, suggesting that wages for a particular skill group are 3 percent lower than they would have been in the absence of higher competition with immigrants. Put differently, Borjas's result does not imply that low-skilled workers competing with immigrants saw their wages decline. Given that wages generally increased over this period, the study suggests that wages went up less for those workers who had to compete with more immigrants than for workers who did not have to face the same competition.

Additionally, University of California economists David Card and Giovanni Peri have demonstrated that Borjas's result hinges on how employers view high school dropouts versus high school graduates in the lower-educated labor pool. If, for example, employers of lower-educated workers tend to view high school dropouts and high school graduates as perfect substitutes, Borjas's main results are severely attenuated, so much so that there is almost no relative wage effect on high school dropouts.[24] Separately, economists at the International Food Policy Research Institute have shown that adding data from the 2010 decennial US Census, which captures a decade when the immigrant supply shock accelerated, decreases Borjas's original relative wage effect estimate by one-third. Even under Borjas's most pessimistic assumptions, this smaller wage effect would mean that the overall welfare gain of immigration is positive (by $3.1 trillion) rather than zero.[25]

Even if one ignores these critiques of Borjas's work, the overall evidence on the relative wage question suggests that any negative effects from immigration on wages and employment, where they do exist, are quite small. Several meta-analyses, for instance, examine the findings of numerous studies and find very small wage and employment effects.[26] One such study analyzes 129 estimates taken from published studies and finds "small wage and employment impacts, even smaller than have been detected in previous metaanalytic research."[27] The authors report that a "1 percentage point increase in the share of immigrants in a local labor market of the typical host country decreases wages of the native born by 0.029 percent [30 cents for every $1,000 earned] . . . and decreases employment of the native born by 0.011 percent."[28]

A similar study looks at more than 1,500 published estimates and reports that "the impact of immigration on the labor market of the native-born population is quantitatively very small and estimated coefficients are more than half of the time statistically insignificant."[29] In other words, more than half the time that these researchers estimated the effect of immigration on the labor market, they were unable to say that the effect was any different than zero. Separately, several comprehensive reviews of the economics literature report that the effect of immigration on labor markets, particularly wages, is negligible. One of these reviews reports, "Most empirical analysis of the United States and other countries finds that a 10 percent increase in the fraction of immigrants in the population reduces native wages by *at most* 1 percent."[30] The paper concludes:

> Despite the popular belief that immigrants have a large adverse impact on the wages and employment opportunities of the native-born population, the literature on this question does not provide much support for this conclusion. Economic theory is equivocal, and empirical estimates in a variety of settings and using a variety of approaches have shown that the effect of immigration on the labor market outcomes of natives is small. There is no evidence of economically significant reductions in native employment.[31]

A 2016 National Academy of Sciences (NAS) report affirms these findings. Chapter 5 of the report reviews the empirical literature and discusses the wide range of estimates for the wage impact of immigration on certain subgroups of the population, such as high school dropouts. The NAS chapter reports:

> As noted . . . , some studies have found sizable negative short run wage impacts for high school dropouts, the native-born workers who in many cases are the group most likely to be in direct competition for jobs with immigrants. Even for this group, however, there are studies *finding small to zero effects*, likely indicating that outcomes are highly dependent on prevailing conditions in the specific labor market into which immigrants flow or the methods and assumptions researchers use to examine the impact of immigration. The literature continues to find less favorable effects for certain disadvantaged workers and for prior immigrants than for natives overall.[32]

A close review of the studies discussed in the NAS report suggests that the range of estimates for these wage effects on certain subgroups is even wider—and less certain—than the preceding passage implies. Table 5-2 in the NAS chapter covers 10 empirical studies and reports wage effects that range from −1.7 percent to 0.3 percent.[33] In fact, several of the studies that report negative wage effects for some subgroups also report positive, or zero, wage or employment effects for other subgroups, thus mitigating any negative findings.[34] One of the studies, by Joan Monras of Sciences Po, concludes, "Thus the US labor market for low-skilled workers adjusts to unexpected supply shocks [an influx of immigrants] quite rapidly."[35]

Some of the strongest evidence showing that an influx of immigration does not lead to large negative effects in the labor market—even for lower-skilled workers—comes from two separate immigration events, one during 1980 and another in 1964.[36] These events provide what economists refer to as "natural experiments" because they effectively represent random events, thus approximating a statistically "clean" economic change, as if someone had set up a purely random experiment. The first of these events is the Mariel boatlift, the arrival of approximately 125,000 low-skilled Cuban immigrants in Miami from May through September 1980.

In 1990, economist David Card published the first major economic study of the boatlift, an event that created "a 7% increase in the labor force of Miami and a 20% increase in the number of Cuban workers in Miami."[37] Card compared low-skilled workers' wages and employment in the Miami area to those in Atlanta, Houston, Los Angeles, and Tampa–St. Petersburg, cities that did not have a similar spike in immigration.[38] To identify "less-skilled" workers, Card used a statistical procedure that controlled for, among other factors, education, potential experience, and variables for each gender and race group.[39] The main findings of the paper are as follows:

a. Real wages for whites in both Miami and the comparison cities were fairly constant between 1979 and 1985;
b. Real wages for blacks in Miami were roughly constant from 1979 to 1981, fell in 1982 and 1983 during a recession, and rose to their previous level in 1984;
c. Real wages for blacks in the comparison cities showed a steady *downward* trend between 1979 and 1985;

d. Real wages for non-Cuban Hispanics in Miami were stable between 1979 and 1985, with only a slight dip in 1983 during the recession; and

e. Non-Cuban Hispanic wage rates in the comparison cities fell by approximately six percentage points.[40]

Card's paper concludes:

> The influx of Mariel immigrants had virtually no effect on the wage rates of less-skilled non-Cuban workers. Similarly, there is no evidence of an increase in unemployment among less-skilled blacks or other non-Cuban workers. Rather, the data analysis suggests a remarkably rapid absorption of the Mariel immigrants into the Miami labor force, with negligible effects on other groups. Even among the Cuban population there is no indication that wages or unemployment rates of earlier immigrants were substantially affected by the arrival of the Mariels.[41]

This research inspired many economic studies that tried to explain Card's findings because the large—much larger than the norm—and sudden influx of unskilled labor into the United States created such a high potential for observing negative short-run wage and employment effects. Though the debate became somewhat technical, the most recent research definitively affirms Card's original findings. Economists Michael Clemens and Jennifer Hunt bolster these results, showing that there was no decline in wages for low-skilled labor in Miami during this period. Indeed, if anything, wages actually rose for this group after 1980.[42]

The second event was a 1960s policy change that, unlike the Mariel boatlift, *removed* low-skilled workers from the US economy. Between 1942 and 1964, the United States and Mexico had agreed to a set of three bilateral agreements to allow manual laborers (braceros) from Mexico to work in the US agriculture sector.[43] The bracero program eventually supplied the United States with nearly 500,000 Mexican workers per year, and the program's economic effects became increasingly controversial.

In the early 1960s, President John F. Kennedy publicly stated that the program had an adverse effect on "the wage and employment conditions of domestic workers."[44] The Johnson administration terminated it on December 31, 1964, with the explicit goal of boosting US farm workers' wages. According to multiple reports, the main reason offered for discontinuing the bracero program was that it "depressed the wages of native-born Americans in the agricultural industry."[45] Supporters of the program argued that shutting it down would have no lasting effects on domestic farm workers' wages because farmers would simply substitute more workers with machines.[46] By all accounts, the bracero exclusion is one of the largest—if not *the* largest—known attempts in the United States to increase a narrowly targeted group's wages by restricting immigration.

A 2018 study published in the *American Economic Review* reports that the bracero exclusion failed to increase domestic farm workers' wages.[47] The study finds that farm wages in states with *some exposure* to bracero workers—both high and low exposure—rose *more slowly* after the bracero exclusion than wages in states with *no exposure* to bracero workers. If discontinuing the program had worked as designed, wages in the states with exposure to bracero workers would have risen more quickly. The study's results are also consistent with the rapid adjustment of capital and technology mitigating any possible wage effects. Overall, the evidence shows that one of the largest-known attempts to raise the wages of low-skilled domestic US workers by restricting immigration failed.[48]

Separate from the isolated effects of immigration on labor markets, the evidence overwhelmingly shows that immigration has positive overall economic effects. For example, one review of recent studies suggests that removing restrictions on immigration worldwide would increase global income in the range of 67 to 147 percent of gross domestic product, likely dwarfing the gains from removing restrictions on trade or capital flows.[49] Broadly, whereas isolating people in one geographic location would be expected to produce a stagnant economy, an influx of people would be expected to give an economy a "shot in the arm."[50] Essentially, more people translates into a bigger market, with more consumers and more workers with more and different skills, and therefore, more economic opportunities.

The results from one recent macro-level study suggest that each immigrant generates, on average, 1.2 jobs for local workers, and that an annual influx of immigrants of 1 percent of the population increases total employment by between 1.2 percent and 3.5 percent, with native employment rising between 0.9 percent and 2.5 percent.[51] The paper also presents evidence that US workers move into areas that receive higher immigrant inflows, suggesting that immigration does not crowd out native employment.[52] Many other macro-level studies find positive economic effects from immigration, including greater investment, per capita income, and productivity.[53]

These types of positive economic effects are also consistent with experience in many rural US towns, where immigrants have been responsible for most of the population growth during the 2000s. In fact, without an influx of Hispanic immigrants, 221 nonmetropolitan US counties would have experienced an absolute population decline between 2000 and 2005.[54] In rural Iowa towns such as Storm Lake, Perry, and Marshalltown, immigrants have helped satisfy a well-documented labor shortage and prevented economic decay that can dramatically lower people's living standards.[55]

The population of Perry, for instance, grew by nearly 33 percent during the 2000s mainly owing to immigrants working at a Tyson Foods plant, and the town has "experienced an economic revitalization that has invigorated the local housing market and downtown business district."[56] Perry is not an isolated case. Since the 1970s, the Rust Belt town of Erie, Pennsylvania, has actively sought refugees to revitalize its economy. Refugee workers now account for almost 20 percent of the city's population, making Erie a city with one of the largest concentrations of refugees in the United States.[57]

There are obvious economic benefits from adding high-skilled workers to a geographic location; however, it is also the case that skill diversity broadens opportunities for people to specialize and fosters the spread of knowledge.[58] Adding lower-skilled workers to a well-developed economy can increase productivity because those individuals complement the existing knowledge base, enabling employers to better match capital and workers. This phenomenon partly explains the "place premium," the fact that being in America allows low-skilled workers to quickly build skills and use productive capital in ways that they would not be able to in their home country.[59]

In more developed countries, even immigrants who possess little formal education or few skills at their time of entry can eventually become—or parent—high-skilled workers who contribute enormously to the American economy.[60] For example, economist George Borjas, a Cuban immigrant, came to the United States with his mother when he was only 12 years old, long before anyone could have predicted he would become a PhD economist at Harvard.[61] Similar stories abound in American culture:

- Amazon founder Jeff Bezos's father, Mike Bezos, immigrated to the United States from Cuba when he was 16, alone and unable to speak English.[62]
- Known mostly for her roles in Hollywood films, Hedy Lamarr also invented frequency-hopping, a method of transmitting radio signals by rapidly changing the carrier frequency. Her invention helped the American military defeat the Nazis in World War II, and it essentially formed the basis of modern wireless communication technology. Born in Vienna in 1914, Lamarr emigrated to America in 1937.[63]
- Richard Montañez, the Frito-Lay executive who helped develop Flamin' Hot Cheetos, a multibillion-dollar snack product, is a first-generation Mexican immigrant who grew up in a migrant labor camp in California, dropped out of high school, and worked as a janitor at Frito-Lay.[64]
- Ray Kroc—the man who transformed McDonald's from a local chain restaurant into one of the world's most recognizable businesses—was born in Illinois in 1902 to parents of Czech origin.[65]
- Born in 1925 to Jewish immigrants from Russia, Evelyn Berezin founded Redactron, a company that developed the

first computerized word processor, which was introduced in 1971. She also designed one of the first computerized reservation systems for airlines.[66]

- Jerry Yang, the founder of Yahoo!, was born in Taiwan and moved to the United States with his family at the age of 10.[67]
- Steve Chen, cofounder of YouTube, was born in Taiwan and immigrated to the United States with his family when he was only eight years old.[68]
- Esther Sans Takeuchi, born to immigrant parents who fled Soviet-occupied Latvia for Germany in 1945 and arrived in the United States in 1951, invented the tiny batteries that power implantable cardiac defibrillators for millions of heart patients.[69]
- Dr. David D. Ho, born in Taiwan, immigrated to the United States when he was 12 years old; he went on to conduct breakthrough research in the treatment of AIDS.[70]
- Donald Trump's grandparents came to the United States from Germany in the late 19th century; his grandfather was a 16-year-old barber who wanted to escape compulsory military service.

All these examples, and countless similar stories that would no doubt include people whose contributions to America go unnoticed by most, demonstrate how difficult it is to discern anyone's skill and potential before observing what they accomplish. This applies equally to individuals with formal education. So restricting immigration based solely on education level is likely to prevent high-skilled individuals from contributing to the US economy *and* produce shortages of people to fill jobs with lower skill requirements. Though it is tempting to argue that the United States has always absorbed new immigrants of various skill levels into its labor force so effectively because it has such a strong and dynamic economy, it could also be the case that the US economy is so strong and dynamic because it absorbs immigrant labor so effectively.[71]

The economic case for restricting immigration is very weak. If anything, the full body of evidence suggests that immigration is an overall economic benefit, meaning that it helps people. The evidence does not support the notion that an influx of immigrants puts excessive downward pressure on wages and harms employment—not even among some lower-educated segments of the population. Overall, the evidence suggests that any negative wage effects from immigration, where they do exist, are quite small and short lived, as should be expected in any well-developed dynamic economy.

As with trade and technology, isolating American workers from competition with foreign-born workers is likely to leave them ill-prepared for the many economic challenges they will regularly face. Policies that isolate people, even when they are well-intentioned, blunt the competitive processes that help people quickly and effectively build skills and develop better opportunities. Implementing policies that expand economic freedom by empowering more people to pursue their own material gain, with others working toward the same purpose, magnifies everyone's opportunity to improve their lives.

Empowering, instead, a small number of officials to subjectively se- lect how people organize their lives—whom they can work with, whom they can trade with, what they can purchase, and so forth—only serves to enrich a handful of individuals at the expense of others. Such a framework results in fewer opportunities for most Americans because it erects artificial barriers that prevent people from improving their living standards. During the past five decades—and even the first 25 years of the post–World War II period—there has been near constant growth in these government-erected barriers. Critics love to blame Americans' economic problems on policies informed by strict ideolog- ical adherence to free markets, but it is difficult to find such an eco- nomic system in the United States.

6

CRITICS' FREE-MARKET PARADISE IS A STRAW MAN

Critics have convinced many Americans that income has stagnated, and that only the wealthiest Americans have done well during the past few decades. They've also convinced many Americans that strict adherence to free-market policies, particularly through free trade, open immigration, and unrestricted technology, caused many of these problems. But as the preceding chapters have demonstrated, the critics miss the mark on trade, immigration, and technological progress. These three phenomena have been a net positive for Americans' living standards, even though each causes some negative outcomes.

As this chapter demonstrates, the critics have also missed the mark on free markets in general. Expansive government-created barriers—not free markets—worsen Americans' inequality of opportunity. Unfortunately, policymakers have been erecting more of those barriers for decades. Although Congress has not implemented industrial policy to direct entire economic sectors, these expansive regulatory barriers have made it more difficult for Americans to improve their living standards through trade, immigration, and technological progress.

It is true that the United States remains one of the freest and most open economies in the world compared with most other developed nations. It is by far the largest economy.[1] And it has some of the strongest and most reliably protected personal and property rights of any country. The United States ranks seventh on the Fraser Institute *Economic Freedom of the World* index.[2] It would be strange to refer to the United States as an autocratic country, or as a Soviet-style command-and-control economy, but it would be just as strange to refer to America as a purely free-market economy. It is a relatively open free-enterprise economy, but virtually no sector of the American economy is unregulated.

In fact, the full scope of federal regulation and intervention in the US economy is so staggering that it is difficult to comprehend why critics blame Americans' socioeconomic problems on blind faith in free-market ideology.[3] More than 250 federal agencies now impose regulations related to activities that include "occupational health and safety, environment, wages and overtime, health and retirement benefits, family leave, workplace harassment and discrimination, disability, immigration and employment eligibility, labor unions, privacy, antitrust, truth in advertising, foreign trade, and many other areas."[4] It is true that the types of government regulations and interventions have changed throughout America's history, but those changes have not altered the overall trend toward increased government regulation and intervention.

Federal economic intervention greatly expanded during and after the New Deal, with much heavier direct government involvement in the economy through activities like price and wage controls.[5] Near the end of the 20th century, the federal government backed away from price controls and rate-of-return regulation in industries such as banking, transportation, and telecommunications, but simultaneously expanded social regulation in areas such as consumer affairs and environmental protection.[6] Overall, federal intervention has continued to expand, transforming the American economy into a less pure free-enterprise system.

Although many critics associate this supposed shift to a free market with the Reagan administration's deregulatory efforts, the Reagan administration did not permanently reduce federal intervention in the economy, and it did not create an unencumbered free market in the United States, not during that decade or beyond.[7] Despite popular myths, scholars and practitioners have long acknowledged the Reagan administration's failure to make any kind of long-lasting deregulatory change.[8]

Scholarly research affirms that the Reagan administration did not achieve lasting deregulatory change. As one in-depth study notes:

> While the Reagan administration achieved significant successes in its first three years in terms of budgetary cutbacks, reductions in enforcement actions, and the near-elimination of new regulations, the institutions and policies of the public lobby regime held firm. The successes appear to be a series of pyrrhic victories that provided temporary regulatory relief rather than lasting regulatory change, and resulted in serious political losses for the administration.[9]

The authors explain that "despite all of the positive institutional change of the 1970s," after eight years of the Reagan administration's efforts, there were "more federal programs, more government bureaucracy, and a policymaking process that hardly could be called broadly democratic or egalitarian."[10] One of the main reasons that the Reagan administration failed to bring about lasting regulatory change was that its efforts consisted almost entirely of agency-level directives that were easily altered and reversed in later years. That is, instead of working with Congress to implement a longer-lasting set of legislative reforms, the Reagan administration relied on executive branch actions to pursue its goals.[11]

Regardless of the reasons, growth in government employment, total government spending, the size of regulatory agency budgets, and staff at various regulatory agencies—all of which take money, people, and physical resources out of the private sector—have remained on an upward trend since at least 1960.[12] Though it is a crude measure of regulation, the number of pages in the *Federal Register* increased from 60,000 pages in 1969 to more than 70,000 by 1977.[13] In 2020, the page count was 186,000.[14] In the 1960s, the page count *per decade* was 170,325, a figure that increased to 450,821 in the 1970s, and has already exceeded 800,000 pages during the 2020s (see figure 6.1).[15]

FIGURE 6.1

Federal Register pages per decade, 1940s–2020s

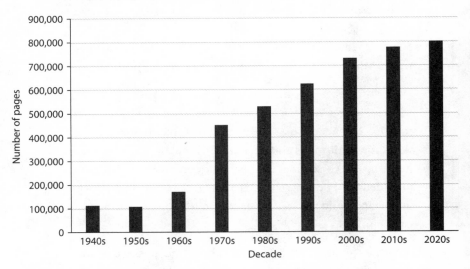

Source: Clyde Wayne Crews Jr., *Ten Thousand Commandments: An Annual Snapshot of the Federal Regulatory State* (Washington: Competitive Enterprise Institute, 2023), p. 35, figure 11.

Although the long-term average is approximately 3,000 new regulations or "final rules" each year, federal agencies published more than 70,000 final rules in the *Federal Register* between 2000 and 2018, averaging more than 10 *per day*.[16] The *Code of Federal Regulations*, the repository for all general and permanent federal regulations, now contains more than 100 million words, approximately three times its size in 1970.[17] It is difficult to reconcile these trends with the idea that the US economy is based on strict adherence to free-market policies.

The conventional financial deregulation story also fails on more technical grounds because it mischaracterizes much of the supposed deregulation that occurred. For instance, the Depository Institutions Deregulation and Monetary Control Act (DIDMCA) of 1980 did phase out the interest rate ceiling on deposit accounts. However, that change merely removed one price control. It did not allow banks to offer unregulated deposit accounts. Moreover, the rate ceiling, in place since the 1930s, had little impact because it was kept above short-term market rates until the 1960s. Then Congress tried to use the price control to stop broader interest rates from rising and to expand mortgage credit. The policy failed to achieve either objective, as acknowledged in the 1980 DIDMCA itself, and interest rates rose sharply during the 1970s.[18]

Similarly, the Riegle-Neal Interstate Banking and Branching Efficiency Act of 1994 allowed banks to open branches in other states, but those branches did not operate as unregulated (or even less regulated) banks. Some critics claim that the 1999 Gramm-Leach-Bliley Act (GLBA) deregulated financial markets because it repealed the Glass-Steagall Act, thus leading to excessive risk-taking by US financial firms.[19] Aside from the fact that the GLBA did not fully repeal the Glass-Steagall Act, the GLBA unambiguously did not deregulate financial activities. The GLBA did allow financial firms to engage in some activities from which they had been previously restricted; however, all those activities remained highly regulated at the federal level and, in some cases, they became even more regulated.[20] This reality has not stopped critics, especially politicians, from perpetuating the deregulation myth.

Shortly after the 2008 crisis, House Speaker Nancy Pelosi (D-CA) leveled a broader critique, claiming, "The Bush Administration's eight long years of failed deregulation policies have resulted in our nation's largest bailout ever, leaving the American taxpayers on the hook potentially for billions of dollars."[21] Congress invoked this narrative when it passed the 2010 Dodd-Frank Wall Street Reform and Consumer Protection Act, a major expansion of the existing financial regulatory framework.[22] But this broader critique is also wrong. The Bush administration did not deregulate financial markets. Neither, for that matter, did any previous administration during the 20th century.

US financial firms have always been highly regulated, and their overall regulatory burden did not decline during the past few decades. Between 1999 and the Lehman Brothers failure in 2008, federal financial regulators issued 7,100 pages of regulations for more than 800 separate rules (see figure 6.2).[23] That record is not deregulatory, and it reflects the long-run trend in US financial regulation during the past 100-plus years.[24] Congress has consistently expanded both the size and scope of the financial regulatory framework, increasing the volume of regulations and shifting away from a disclosure/fraud prevention–based

FIGURE 6.2

Cumulative pages added to the *Federal Register* from 2000 to Lehman Brothers collapse (2008)

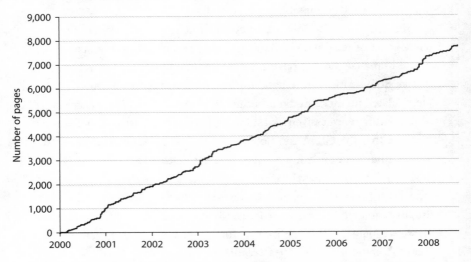

Source: Norbert Michel and Tamara Skinner, "The Popular Narrative about Financial Deregulation Is Wrong," *Daily Signal,* July 29, 2016.

regime toward one focused on actively managing firms' decisions.[25] For decades, Congress has increasingly empowered regulators to micromanage risks at financial firms.[26] At the same time, Congress has regularly increased expectations for federal bailouts, socializing many firms' losses.[27]

This approach has been disastrous. The United States has experienced 15 banking crises since 1837, a total that ranks among the highest of all developed countries.[28] Among severe economic downturns in six developed nations from 1870 to 1933, they were accompanied by banking crises only in the United States.[29] More recently, the United States is one of only three developed countries with at least two banking crises between 1970 and 2010.[30] This shift to heavier government involvement in financial markets has also failed outside the United States. As federal interventions such as central banking, deposit insurance, and loan guarantees became more widespread internationally, banking crises have occurred relatively more frequently.[31]

The federal government is heavily involved in the US housing finance system, more so than in most segments of the economy. The idea that housing finance in the United States resembles a free market is, to say the least, mistaken. In addition to a dizzying array of both bank and nonbank regulations, housing finance includes a federal government mortgage insurer, government guarantees of mortgage securities, and government-sponsored enterprises that dominate mortgage lending. Yet the volatility of home prices and home construction from 1998 to 2009 in the United States was among the highest in the industrialized world.[32]

Before the 2008 financial crisis, the federal government controlled a dominant share of the US housing finance system, and that share expanded right up to, and through, the COVID-19 pandemic. As of December 31, 2020, Fannie Mae and Freddie Mac—both of which have been in government conservatorship since 2008—had combined total assets of $6.6 trillion, representing approximately 42 percent of the nation's outstanding mortgage debt.[33] From 2008 to 2019, the annual market share of mortgages for the Federal Housing Administration (FHA) ranged from 16.49 percent to 32.6 percent.[34] From 2009 to 2020, Fannie and Freddie's annual share of the total mortgage-backed security (MBS) market averaged 70 percent. Including Ginnie Mae securities (those that are backed by FHA mortgages), the federal share of the MBS market averaged 92 percent per year.[35] Moreover, from 2008 to 2020, the Federal Reserve went from holding no MBSs to holding more than $2 trillion in MBSs (combined Fannie, Freddie, and Ginnie MBSs).[36]

This expansive federal role in housing finance has done little to expand homeownership. Outside of the temporary increase that preceded the 2008 financial crisis, the US homeownership rate has changed little since the 1960s. As of December 2019, the rate was 65 percent, versus 64 percent in 1968, the year Fannie Mae became a publicly traded government-sponsored enterprise and Congress created Ginnie Mae.[37] In fact, robust mortgage financing exists in virtually every developed nation, without the high degree of government involvement found in the United States. Yet the overall US homeownership rate (65 percent) is below average among developed nations (68.1 percent for Organisation for Economic Co-operation and Development [OECD] member countries).[38]

More broadly, as of 2019, Americans shouldered more than $25.5 trillion in potential losses due to federal loans, loan guarantees, and subsidized insurance (provided by close to 150 federal programs).[39] Again, these facts and figures are wholly inconsistent with the notion that the US economy is anything close to an unencumbered free market.

A similar critique applies to claims that greater trade liberalization led to practically unfettered free trade during the past few decades. Although tariffs have generally decreased, this decline coincided with an increase in nontariff trade barriers. For instance, average tariff rates declined from 10 percent in 1997 to 4 percent in 2015, but the average for nontariff trade barriers generally increased through the period, from 22 percent in 1997 to as high as 51 percent in 2009.[40] Moreover, several instances remain of particularly harmful tariffs and nontariff barriers. These include a 25 percent tariff on imported pickup trucks, the Jones Act (a law that requires that ships engaged in transporting goods be built in the United States, crewed by US citizens, owned by US citizens, and registered under the US flag), an average tariff rate on imported clothing and footwear of 13.9 percent (as of 2020), and volume restrictions on imported sugar that cause Americans to pay double the average global price for refined sugar.[41]

The scope of government regulation and intervention in the economy goes well beyond financial markets and international trade. The American immigration system, for example, is highly regulated and extremely restrictive.[42] Education and health care are two of the most heavily subsidized and regulated sectors of the US economy. They do not even remotely resemble free markets.[43] In the US energy sector, federal intervention has regularly delayed projects, restricted consumer access, subsidized wasteful projects, and imposed harmful mandates, all resulting in less affordable and reliable energy for American households.[44] Aside from countless state and local laws, approximately 30 federal laws governing employment in the United States raise the cost of providing jobs and reduce workers' wages.[45]

Across all industries, excessive government regulation and other types of intervention, such as subsidies and tariffs, harm the ability of people to adapt successfully to changing economic conditions and create sustained improvements in their living standards.[46] Often, well-established firms support federal intervention and regulation because it protects them against losses and keeps competitors at bay by raising the cost of starting and operating a business.[47] Broadly, evidence shows that this high cost has negative effects on entrepreneurship and new business formation, both of which are vital sources of innovation and job growth in the United States.[48] And the rate of entrepreneurship in the United States has essentially been on a downward trend from 1987 to 2016.[49] Business "exits" exceeded new startups for several years after the 2009 recession, and the share of firms 16 years old or older has increased by 50 percent over the past two decades.[50] The hardships on new businesses have been the result of many harmful public policies, including an immigration system that makes it difficult for firms to gain access to talented foreign workers and for immigrant-entrepreneurs to enter the United States to start businesses.[51]

Overall, the cumulative weight of many bad incentives and economic barriers created by government programs, regulation, and crowding out have made it more difficult for people to develop economic opportunities and improve their living standards.[52] It is remarkable how Americans have prospered despite these bad incentives and regulatory barriers. Yet the evidence suggests that removing such hurdles would allow them to prosper even more. Had policymakers done a better job of removing government barriers to opportunity over the past few decades, instead of erecting more of them, the typical American could have reached even higher living standards.

The truth is, in too many cases, government barriers both crowd out opportunities for private businesses to provide services *and* diminish incentives for individuals to contribute to a productive economy.

For instance, rising participation in the Social Security Disability Insurance (SSDI) program explains a significant portion of the decline in labor force participation among 45- to 54-year-old men (though it explains little of the drop in labor force participation for younger males).[53] In fact, the long-term decline in male labor force participation that began in the 1950s coincides with the expansion of federally provided welfare programs that served to replace work, particularly the SSDI program.[54] Although an aging population accounts for some of the increased participation in the SSDI program during the past few decades, shifts in the program's eligibility criteria in the 1980s—Congress expanded the ways in which workers could qualify for SSDI—explain a large portion of the increased SSDI enrollment.[55]

*   *   *

Some Safety Net Programs Produce Perverse Incentives

Many people simply may not want to work very much, and if friends, neighbors, or relatives make not working easy enough, they might end up working very little. And although very few politicians would openly acknowledge it, many of the public policies that make up the so-called social safety net in the United States, such as means-tested welfare and Social Security disability payments, can have the same effect on work–leisure choices. They can even have the same effect on education choices. In 2012, *New York Times* journalist Nicholas Kristof visited Appalachia, where he was shocked to see parents take their children out of literacy classes to keep from losing welfare benefits:

> Many people in hillside mobile homes here are poor and desperate, and a $698 monthly check per child from the Supplemental Security Income program goes a long way—and those checks continue until the child turns 18.
>
> "The kids get taken out of the program because the parents are going to lose the check," said Billie Oaks, who runs a literacy program here in Breathitt County, a poor part of Kentucky. "It's heartbreaking."[56]

While social safety net policies such as these are surely well-intentioned, they often overlook the factor that many populists overlook: the people.[57]

*   *   *

A great deal of evidence suggests that the SSDI program has long served as a replacement for employment, which helps explain at least part of the decline in male labor force participation during the past few decades.[58] Even evidence surrounding the Great Recession affirms that SSDI can function as an unemployment insurance program—the Great Recession produced an unexpected spike of almost one million SSDI applications, of which 42 percent were awarded benefits.[59]

Other social safety net programs, such as unemployment insurance, wage subsidies, and other means-tested income transfers, also produce economic incentives that induce people to work less than they would in the absence of such programs.[60] As University of Chicago economist Casey Mulligan points out, "Decades of empirical economic research show that the reward to working, as determined by the safety net and other factors, affects how many people work and how many hours they work."[61] Mulligan demonstrates that an expansion of the social safety net programs that began in 2007—particularly expansions in unemployment insurance, the Supplemental Nutrition Assistance Program (SNAP), and Medicaid—explains at least half of the reduced labor hours in the United States during the 2008–2009 recession.[62]

In general, all social safety net programs that provide resources to low-income individuals face a basic tradeoff that can lead to a reduction in work: the programs raise an individual recipient's standard of living, but they also provide a disincentive to raise one's own standard of living at the expense of losing benefits. Thus, social safety net programs that cannot overcome this tradeoff, no matter how well-intentioned, are likely to lead to some combination of fewer individuals in the workforce and more people working fewer hours than they would otherwise. This problem is caused, in part, by the fact that program benefits generally must be taken away as the recipient earns higher income, a feature shared by many wage subsidy proposals.[63]

The United States does not have a formal wage subsidy program, but the nation's second-largest means-tested cash welfare program, the earned income tax credit (EITC), subsidizes wages to encourage low-income people to work. Although the EITC may have merits as a welfare program, its deficiencies have important implications for broader wage subsidy and universal basic income policies.[64] For instance, as workers earn more money, the EITC subsidy begins to phase out and, eventually, goes to zero. Thus, the EITC suffers from a built-in inducement to quit working before benefits decline.

In general, the EITC program creates complex incentive structures among different groups. A 2015 National Bureau of Economic Research review of the EITC notes, for instance, "The EITC's structure can be expected to encourage labor force participation among single parents, but to discourage it for many would-be secondary earners in married couples," and "some [workers] face incentives to work more, while many more face incentives to work less" because of the EITC.[65]

A large body of evidence suggests that the expansion of the EITC in the 1990s increased employment rates for single mothers (with multiple children) in the lower-skilled labor force, and that the EITC has had relatively small effects on hours worked.[66] However, a 2020 National Bureau of Economic Research study suggests that the labor-inducing effects reported in earlier studies were due mainly to the confounding factors of welfare reform and the booming macro economy.[67] Separately, recent evidence from random assignment experiments in New York City and Atlanta cast doubt on the EITC's ability to induce work. These experiments showed that quadrupling the maximum value of the EITC for childless adults (from $500 to $2,000) and doubling the point at which the EITC phased down to zero (from $15,000 to $30,000) had virtually no discernible effect on employment or earnings among the eligible group.[68]

Another possible shortcoming—which is applicable to wage subsidies in general—is that the EITC might actually cause employers to reduce wages.[69] For instance, some research shows that employers pay low-skilled workers less than they would in the absence of the EITC subsidy, capturing $0.36 per dollar spent on the EITC program. Moreover, it appears that this reduction is not uniform across workers, with employers capturing $0.55 of every EITC dollar for single mothers, and $0.18 for single childless women.[70] Other evidence indicates that expansions in the EITC have no effect on the wages of college graduates, but that a 10 percent increase in the credit reduces hourly wages for high school dropouts by 5 percent and for those with only a high school diploma by 2 percent.[71]

In general, it is uncontroversial that social safety net programs, including SSDI, various means-tested income transfers, and wage subsidies, create harmful work disincentives because they make it more costly to earn more income. As the authors of one recent study explain:

> Earn $1 too much two years back and your Medicare Part-B premiums will rise by close to $800. Earn $1 too much and, depending on the state, lose thousands of dollars in your own or your family's Medicaid benefits. Hold $1 too much in assets and forfeit thousands in Supplemental Security Income. . . . Earn $1 too much and lose 22 cents, in the Earned Income Tax Credit and the list goes on.[72]

The authors demonstrate what they characterize as a "potential poverty trap" that arises from this system by estimating the marginal tax rates for low-income earners that earn an additional $1,000. They report that, for those near the top (the 75th percentile) of the lowest quintile, depending on age, marginal tax rates range from 67.4 percent to 76.5 percent.[73] Put differently, as benefits phase out, earning an additional $1,000 provides three times more to the government than to the worker. Similar research has shown that benefit reductions combined with higher income and payroll taxes can raise marginal rates for some workers up to 95 percent.[74]

It is incumbent on critics who decry the long-term decline in labor force participation to address these kinds of disincentives. Means-tested transfers now boost income for some in the lowest quintile by more than 66 percent (see figure 6.3), so it is at least plausible that many in the lowest quintile actively choose to remain in the lowest quintile to avoid losing that income.[75] Doing so would be a perfectly rational response to the tradeoffs such individuals face. An example from a Pennsylvania Department of Welfare study puts these disincentives in very stark terms: "The single mom is better off earning gross income of $29,000 with $57,327 in net income and benefits than to earn gross income of $69,000 with net income and benefits of $57,045."[76]

Although it does not follow that *all* means-tested welfare programs should be eliminated, it is obvious that many of these programs create

FIGURE 6.3

Average household income of lower quintile before and after taxes and transfers, 2016

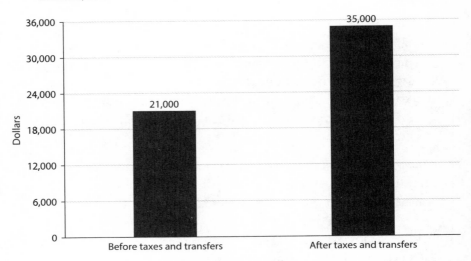

Source: Congressional Budget Office, "The Distribution of Household Income, 2016," July 9, 2019.

the incentive to work less.[77] Just before the COVID-19 pandemic, for instance, Bureau of Labor Statistics data show that three-fourths of the decline in prime-age male labor force participation is accounted for by men who say they do not want a job.[78] Anyone who wants to see higher income mobility for people in the lower income quintiles—especially those who have dropped out of the labor force because they do not want a job—must address why people might not want to work.

Government Policies Crowd Out Private Solutions

Countless federal government programs and policies intervene in markets in the name of improving living standards but in fact create perverse incentives and detract from the benefits that private markets can provide. For instance, millions of people annually receive federal income transfers to assist with paying for housing.[79] While surely well-intentioned, federal public housing and voucher programs are open-ended transfers that contribute to trapping people in poverty and offer few incentives for upward mobility.[80] But government intervention in housing goes well beyond that.

More generally, the federal government has become increasingly involved in the housing market since the 1930s, and the perceived success of this involvement has led many people to suggest that the private housing market cannot properly function without a broader government guarantee. Evidence shows, however, that these expanding policies harm consumers and mainly shift financial risks from borrowers (and lenders) onto taxpayers, thus contributing to a financially unsustainable increase in homeownership in the 2000s.[81]

For instance, in the residential real estate market, federal policies that increase high-risk debt through Fannie Mae and Freddie Mac—the two housing finance giants under government control since 2008—and the FHA have made entry-level homes *less* affordable by allowing buyers to bid against each other for the same (restricted) stock of housing.[82] The above-average price growth for entry-level homes has had a disparate impact on minority homebuyers because they are disproportionately represented in the entry-level price tier.[83] These federal policies have also removed many of the incentives to regularly save money for a down payment, and also created the incentives to take on more debt.

Just as important, when government agencies provide services that private companies can provide on their own, the government crowds out private businesses and reduces economic opportunities for entrepreneurs and their potential employees and customers. For instance, fewer private companies provide mortgage insurance because the FHA provides mortgage insurance at below-market prices. The same concept applies to the Federal Deposit Insurance Corporation—few private companies provide deposit insurance because the government provides it at such a low price.[84]

Federal programs also crowd out private charities that are critical to civil society. In many cases, federal welfare programs subsidize physical needs, thus creating dependence and paternalism.[85] According to

James Whitford, the cofounder and executive director of Watered Gardens Gospel Rescue Mission and the True Charity Initiative:

> Recent research that argues against a crowd-out condition fails to control for the disenfranchising effect of regulatory requirements and not-for-profits that masquerade as true charities but spend more time at state capitols lobbying for funds than they do at churches and civic groups recruiting for volunteers.
>
> Finally, most researchers have not stood where I do to experience it firsthand. For nearly two decades, I have witnessed crowd-out clearly tied to government entitlements.
>
> Jon [a former homeless man in a yearlong recovery and work-ready program] was offered quite an entitlement package: HUD [Department of Housing and Urban Development] housing, early SSI [Supplemental Security Income] disability, food stamps. He was enticed to settle into a workless and dependent life. He admits that turning that down for a life of work and self-reliance instead was one of the hardest things he has ever done.[86]

Many private charities, such as those that help former prisoners find employment and build a life in mainstream society, critically depend on volunteers.[87] Because federal welfare policies can make people less likely to volunteer, they make it more difficult for private charities to help people.[88] Ultimately, these crowding-out effects undermine the civil institutions that enhance and increase the economic gains people can create in a system of free enterprise.[89]

At their core, expansive government policies make it more difficult for Americans to improve their lives because they diminish economic freedom, thus reducing the benefits inherent to a free-enterprise system. Long after scholars such as Adam Smith and Milton Friedman made this type of argument, empirical research has bolstered the point. For example, the third chapter of the Fraser Institute's *Economic Freedom of the World* examines more than 1,300 peer-reviewed journal articles, of which, more than 700 "looked at the impact of economic freedom on the human condition."[90] From this body of research, most of the articles "find a link between high or increasing levels of economic freedom with gains in prosperity and other measures of well-being; less than one in 20 find negative consequences."[91] Similarly, the *Wall Street Journal*/Heritage Foundation's *Index of Economic Freedom* has consistently shown that "the most critical variable in sustaining the economic dynamism and wealth of nations is economic freedom, which is really about dispersing economic power and decision-making throughout an economy and—most important—empowering ordinary people with greater opportunity and more choices."[92]

Had policymakers done a better job of removing government barriers to opportunity during the past few decades, instead of erecting them, Americans could have reached even higher living standards. Fortunately, Americans still experienced robust income growth during the past several decades, much larger than what supporters of restricting automation, trade, and immigration would have the public believe.

7

CRITICS MISS THE MARK ON AMERICANS' INCOME GROWTH

The economic plight of Americans, especially people living in Rust Belt and Appalachian towns, was a popular explanation for Donald Trump's 2016 electoral victory. Supposedly, Trump's America First message on trade and manufacturing resonated with many Americans because their ability to earn a living had been severely hampered by free-market policies, especially those that promoted free trade.[1] Believing that these policies had led to income stagnation, many conservatives joined progressives in championing various aspects of industrial policy, including tariffs, government-funded research and development, and manufacturing subsidies.[2]

Aside from whether Americans' income truly stagnated, which this chapter delves deeper into, there are good reasons to doubt this explanation. For instance, the authors of the 2018 book *The Great Revolt* surveyed so-called Rust Belt Trump voters and found that 84 percent "were actually optimistic about their own future career path or financial situation, regardless of how they felt about their community's prospects as a whole."[3] The authors also tell the story of Sally Tedrow, a resident of Lee County, Iowa, who says that she "didn't vote for Donald Trump," but that she "voted against Hillary Clinton."[4] Exit polling suggests Tedrow's view was widespread and instrumental in the outcome—voters did not like Trump or Clinton to a larger degree than "any major-party candidate who had come before them," and the 18 percent of voters who viewed both candidates unfavorably seem to have voted for the candidate "who was newer to the political scene."[5]

Another problem with this explanation is that decaying towns are nothing new. The Midwest and western United States are both littered with ghost towns that people abandoned between the Civil War and the 1950s. Typically, these towns sprang up, flourished, and decayed around a single industry, such as mining—for resources including coal, oil, gold, and lead—or agriculture.[6]

In *Big White Ghetto: Dead Broke, Stone-Cold Stupid, and High on Rage in the Dank Woolly Wilds of the "Real America,"* author Kevin Williamson describes the story of Garbutt, New York, founded in 1804 by settler Zachariah Garbutt.[7] When digging the foundation for a grist mill, Garbutt discovered a vein of gypsum, a mineral used as a fertilizer. After the gypsum industry ran its course, Garbutt died out, much like the typical Rust Belt or Appalachian town central to Trump's victory. In 1908, a local historian wrote of Garbutt:

> As the years passed away, a change came over the spirit of their dream. Their church was demolished and its timber put to an ignoble use; their schools were reduced to one, and that a primary; their hotels were converted into dwelling houses; their workshops, one by one, slowly and silently sank from sight until there was but little left to the burg except its name.[8]

Jumping ahead to 1964, *Life* magazine published "The Valley of Poverty," a special feature described as "one of the very first substantive reports in any American publication on President Lyndon Johnson's nascent War on Poverty."[9] The magazine informed readers:

> President Johnson, who has declared "unconditional war on poverty in America," has singled out Appalachia as a major target. . . . Appalachia stretches from northern Alabama to southern Pennsylvania, and the same disaster that struck eastern Kentucky hit the whole region[—]the collapse of the coal industry 20 years ago, which left Appalachia a vast junkyard.[10]

According to this account, Appalachia was already a "vast junkyard" 20 years before Johnson's efforts. The date is driven home in a photo caption that reads: "All over Appalachia the ruins of trestles jutted from deserted hillside coal mines. This mine had once offered workers a good living, but it closed in 1945."[11]

Not only are recent critics mistaken about when the industrial collapse started in these regions, but they're also mistaken about the level of government intervention in the Appalachian economy. In 1964, President Johnson began promoting his War on Poverty by touring parts of Appalachia, and he began working with Congress to craft a bill designed to aid the Appalachian economy.[12] Those efforts ultimately resulted in the passage of the Appalachian Regional Development Act, the first significant Great Society legislation, which Congress passed and Johnson signed into law on March 9, 1965.

The act created the Appalachian Regional Commission to oversee economic development projects in Appalachia, including the construction of the Appalachian Development Highway System to connect isolated areas with larger national markets.[13] The 1965 act authorized (a) the formation of local development districts, (b) grants for research and economic development demonstration projects, (c) grants for demonstration health projects, (d) grants for job training programs, and (e) federal assistance for proposed low- and middle-income housing projects, among other initiatives.[14] These provisions, and the broader concept of government-supported economic development in the region, were not short-lived—the Appalachian Regional Commission still exists today.[15]

The rise and fall of towns tied to discrete industries is not a new phenomenon that took hold in the "past few decades," as advocates of the recent stagnation story would have us believe. Rather, change has long been the norm in the American economy. In fact, the United States was a net importer of manufactured goods for most of the 19th century, shifted to being a net exporter of manufactured goods between 1890 and 1913, and then underwent drastic economic changes again before and after World War II. America even became a net importer of steel in 1959, long before the recession that ran from November 1973 to March 1975.[16]

The new stagnation critics—even though they have convinced many people that Americans did not prosper during the past several decades—not only have been wrong on these facts, but also have their income statistics wrong, as the remainder of this chapter demonstrates. Specifically, a general stagnation—or decline—in Americans' income did not occur during the past several decades. More broadly, many different measures of welfare demonstrate that Americans have improved their living standards during the past few decades.

How could the critics be so wrong? As a starting point, this chapter evaluates the opening lines of Oren Cass's book: "Yet while gross domestic product tripled from 1975 to 2015, the median worker's wages have barely budged."[17] It is very easy to verify GDP growth for this period, so that's not where the problem with the stagnation story lies. Yet evaluating the "median worker's wages" is not so straightforward.

There simply is no single way to define the median (or typical) worker. The term "median worker" could reference, for example, someone who earns the median wage of all US employees. Instead, it could reference the median wage of all private employees, or the median wage of all production and nonsupervisory employees (excluding managerial staff).[18] Arguably, the term should exclude all part-time workers or all workers under the age of 16. This basic problem is magnified by multiple definitions of "income," including wages, total compensation (wages plus fringe benefits, such as health insurance), and household income (both before and after taxes and transfers).

Additionally, adjusting any given income measure for inflation with different price indexes results in large disparities in real income growth over long periods. Two commonly used measures of inflation are the consumer price index (CPI), published by the Bureau of Labor Statistics, and the personal consumption expenditures (PCE) price index, published by the Department of Labor's Bureau of Economic Analysis.[19] The two measures differ because they are constructed using different weights and different formulas and measure somewhat different goods and services. Moreover, both indexes suffer from biases that tend to overstate inflation, and that the CPI tends to overstate inflation more than the PCE.[20] As a result, using either index to adjust for inflation tends to make older incomes appear larger than they really were, thus artificially suppressing real growth rates. Over very short periods, the differences between the CPI and the PCE tend not to matter, but that's not the case for long periods, such as, for example, 40 years.

Separately, choosing different periods from within the overall length of a data series can easily produce a deceptively low or high growth rate. These problems are all further complicated because the "typical" household from distant decades is no longer the typical American household—aside from multiple other demographic changes, more household income is now typically spread over fewer family members.

It is straightforward to use Cass's example to illustrate some of these points. For instance, using the CPI to adjust average hourly earnings of production and nonsupervisory employees suggests that real wages have grown by less than 1 percent from 1975 to 2015, consistent with Cass's statement.[21] However, adjusting the same data with the PCE index indicates that real wages were not stagnant—they grew by 22 percent.

It is also easy to show that using either a longer or shorter time frame provides a very different growth figure from Cass's 1975–2015 period. First, examining the same income series from 1964—the first year the data are available from the Bureau of Labor Statistics—to 2015, while adjusting for inflation with the CPI, shows that real wages increased by almost 9 percent. Using the PCE, instead, shows that real wages grew by more than 39 percent from 1964 to 2015. Separately, using the same CPI-adjusted income series from 1991 to 2015 (both 1975 and 1991 mark the end of a recession) shows that income grew by almost 15 percent. Using the PCE, instead, shows that income grew by 27 percent for this shorter period.

As these statistics demonstrate, just these two variables—the chosen inflation metric and the starting point for the period of analysis— heavily influence the growth rate. In fact, using 1975 as the starting point for this analysis, with CPI-adjusted income, produces the lowest possible (positive) growth rate of any of the years that could have been

FIGURE 7.1

Real wage growth in the United States from varying start year (1964 to 2000) to 2015

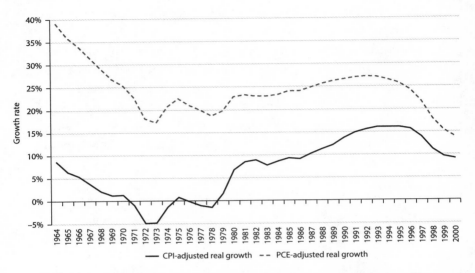

Source: Federal Reserve Bank of St. Louis, FRED Economic Data, "Average Hourly Earnings of Production and Nonsupervisory Employees, Total Private (AHETPI)."

Note: CPI = consumer price index; PCE = personal consumption expenditure.

TABLE 7.1

Real wage growth in the United States from start year to 2015

Start Year	PCE-Adjusted Real Growth	CPI-Adjusted Real Growth
1964	39%	9%
1991	27%	15%

Source: Federal Reserve Bank of St. Louis, FRED Economic Data, "Average Hourly Earnings of Production and Nonsupervisory Employees, Total Private (AHETPI)."

Note: CPI = consumer price index; PCE = personal consumption expenditure.

chosen between 1964 and 2000 (see figure 7.1 and table 7.1).[22] Essentially, the only way to give the impression that real income was stagnant is to use the method that Cass uses while ignoring all the others. However, all the other methods show that stagnation is a false impression—real income was not stagnant over the past 50 (plus) years.

FIGURE 7.2

Real income growth for each decile, 2007–2019

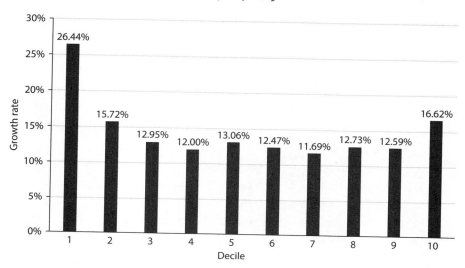

Source: US Department of Labor, "2019 Current Population Survey March Supplement."

Notwithstanding Cass's focus on the median worker, some of the highest income growth during the past few decades occurred among some of the poorest American workers. For instance, the annual (wage and salary) incomes of full-time workers in the bottom 10 percent of earners saw an increase of 39 percent between 1980 and 2000, more than the increases at the mean, the median, the 25th percentile, the 75th percentile, or even the 90th percentile. From 2000 to 2006, just before the Great Recession, all groups saw an increase in their hourly earnings.[23]

Although the Great Recession produced a temporary slowdown, income across all 10 deciles (10 equal increments from the income distribution) grew from 2007 to 2019 (see figure 7.2).[24] In fact, the bottom 10 percent saw cumulative income growth of 26 percent from 2007 to 2019, significantly more growth than either the second decile (16 percent growth), third decile (13 percent), fourth decile (12 percent), or fifth decile (13 percent).[25] The 2007 to 2019 growth figures for the 7th through 10th deciles averaged 13 percent. Full-time workers in all deciles realized at least 10 percent real growth from 2007 to 2019 (the top decile realized 16.62 percent growth).[26]

*   *   *

Wage Growth for High School Dropouts Is High Starting in the 1990s

Because of the general increase in Americans' education levels during the past few decades, many researchers have focused on income for subgroups of the population with lower levels of education. For instance, University of Michigan economists Ariel Binder and John Bound estimate that *real hourly earnings* for the typical 25- to 54-year-old male with only a high school diploma fell by almost 20 percent from 1973 to 2015 (from $21.40 to $17.50), whereas real hourly earnings for college-degreed men ages 25 to 54 increased by approximately 11 percent (from roughly $27 to $30).[27] These statistics appear to show poor income growth for less-educated males, but the downward trend is largely due to measuring growth from the 1970s through 2015. Binder and Bound also report, across all demographic groups, "Since the early 1990s, cumulative wage growth appears to be higher for high school dropouts than for high school graduates or those with some college education."[28]

*   *   *

Another important factor in considering whether living standards have improved over the past several decades is that workers' total compensation has increased because of higher nonwage benefits, including, among others, health insurance, retirement benefits, and paid leave. In 1973, nonwage benefits accounted for 13 percent of employee compensation, a figure that steadily rose to 30 percent by December 2019 (see figure 7.3).[29] This shift toward more nonwage compensation, along with rising health care and education costs, has likely contributed to the perception that income has stagnated, but the fact remains that wage income alone paints an incomplete picture of how workers' compensation has changed.

FIGURE 7.3

Nonwage benefit share of total compensation, 1973 versus 2019

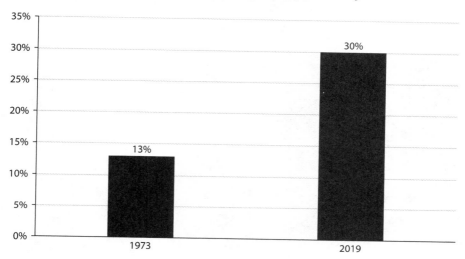

Source: James Sherk, "Productivity and Compensation: Growing Together," Heritage Foundation Backgrounder no. 2825, July 17, 2013; US Bureau of Labor Statistics, "Employer Costs for Employee Compensation—December 2019," news release, March 19, 2020; in the national income accounts, using different definitions of income, the figure is 23 percent. See US Bureau of Economic Analysis, "Gross Domestic Product, Fourth Quarter and Year 2019 (Second Estimate)," news release, February 27, 2020, p. 13.

Even if the long-term trend in average wages had been flat, workers' total compensation still would have increased because of higher non-wage benefits. Using the BLS index of total hourly compensation, a metric that the BLS adjusts for inflation using the CPI, real total compensation increased almost 50 percent from 1975 to 2015 (see figure 7.4).[30] Even though 50 percent growth is far from stagnant, some analysts harp on the fact that it represents slower growth compared with the first two decades after World War II.[31] It is true that, from 1947 (the earliest date of the total compensation series) to 1974, total real compensation growth was 100 percent. But this period included the largest two-quarter increase in nominal GDP in the entire historical record (before 2020), an anomaly that occurred during the recovery from World War II, when American companies faced little

FIGURE 7.4

CPI- and PCE-deflated total hourly compensation, 1959–2022

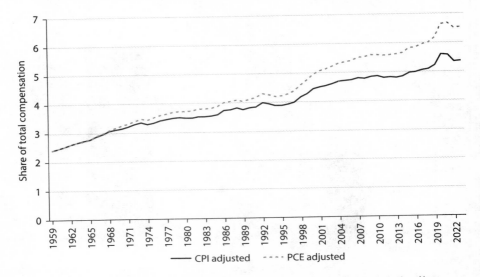

Source: US Bureau of Labor Statistics, "Labor Productivity and Real Hourly Compensation, Non-farm Business Sector since 1973," n.d.; US Bureau of Economic Analysis, "Personal Consumption Expenditures: Chain-Type Price Index [PCEPI]."

Note: CPI = consumer price index; PCE = personal consumption expenditure.

international competition. In other words, that high growth period was outside the norm.

Moreover, measuring total compensation growth from an alternative start date provides a very different result. Arbitrarily starting one decade later, for example, shows that total compensation growth from 1957 to 1974 was only 44 percent. Compared with this period, total compensation growth did not slow down from 1975 to 2015—it increased (see figure 7.5).[32]

Other critics have made stagnation claims using household income data. For instance, using the official household income statistics published by the Census Bureau, Brookings Institution scholars Eleanor Krause and Isabel Sawhill claim, "American households in the middle of the distribution have experienced very little income growth in recent decades."[33] Krause and Sawhill bolster their claim with a graph of

FIGURE 7.5

Real compensation growth by period, 1957–1974 versus 1975–2015

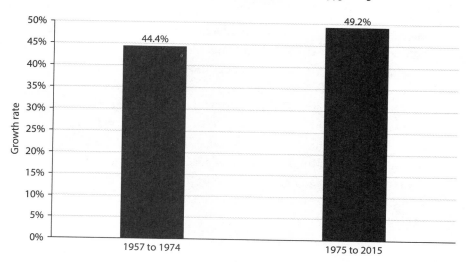

Source: US Bureau of Labor Statistics, "Labor Productivity and Real Hourly Compensation, Non-farm Business Sector since 1973," n.d.

annual median household income from 1967 to 2015 (adjusted for inflation, as reported by the Census Bureau). Although the line on the Brookings chart looks relatively flat from 1967 to 2015, indicating very little growth, it shows that median household income grew from $44,895 in 1967 to $57,230 in 2015, an increase of 27 percent in real (inflation adjusted) income.

Krause and Sawhill view this increase as "very little income growth," but this increase—more than 25 percent real growth—indicates that the median household gained more than 25 percent in purchasing power. It would certainly be better if this growth had been even higher, but is it really accurate to refer to 25 percent real growth as "very little" income growth?

Additionally, these median income figures understate how well *people* have done over this period. One reason is that the official income figures are not adjusted for demographic changes over time. These official figures are median *household* incomes, as opposed to per-person incomes, a particularly important caveat because average household size has been falling for decades. As a result, as real incomes have increased for households, they have been spread among fewer people in each household, meaning that per-person incomes have been growing faster than the official household income figures indicate. On a per-person basis, the increase in household income from 1967 to 2015 was 64 percent, more than twice as high as the raw household figure.[34]

Another problem is that the Census Bureau adjusts income data using the CPI, an adjustment that, although perfectly legitimate, artificially suppresses the reported long-term growth rate. Adjusting the entire household income series for inflation with the PCE instead of the CPI, and adjusting for household size, show that per-person median income grew 140 percent from 1967 to 2019.[35] It is difficult to describe either of these per-person income growth figures as "very little" or stagnant.

FIGURE 7.6

CPI- and PCE-adjusted per-person income growth and number of households over time, 1967–2019

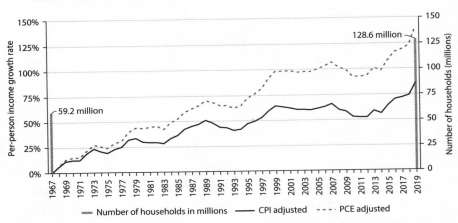

Source: US Census income and household size data: US Census Bureau, "Table A-2. Households by Total Money Income, Race, and Hispanic Origin of Householder: 1967 to 2019"; US Census Bureau, "Table HH-4. Households by Size: 1960 to Present"; US Bureau of Labor Statistics, "Consumer Price Index for All Urban Consumers: All Items in U.S. City Average [CPIAUCSL]"; US Bureau of Economic Analysis, "Personal Consumption Expenditures: Chain-type Price Index [PCEPI]."

Note: CPI = consumer price index; PCE = personal consumption expenditure.

To give these growth figures even more context, there were only 59.2 million US households in 1967, but the total had climbed to 128.6 million by 2019 (see figure 7.6).[36] The fact that median per-person income growth in the—extremely large—US economy was anywhere near 100 percent from 1967 to 2019 is nothing short of amazing.

Income in a Market Economy Is Not Fixed

The income statistics discussed in this chapter paint a picture of widespread prosperity in America during the past several decades. Still, some proponents of the stagnation story are so concerned with income inequality that they often miss this prosperity. For instance, in a 2017 article in *The Atlantic* on the US Census Bureau's 2018 report *Income and Poverty in the United States*, the author was so focused on the middle class and unequal outcomes across demographic groups that she downplayed—perhaps subconsciously—the obvious increase in prosperity in the data.[37] She noted: "Around 13 percent of households made more than $150,000 last year; a decade ago, by comparison, 8.5 percent did. While that's something to cheer, without a solid middle class, it's not indicative of an economy that is healthy and stable more broadly."[38]

At best, the author is guilty of a major understatement. The Census report shows that more than five million households—not individuals, but families—moved into the high-earning category. That shift is surely something to cheer about, but these numbers hardly support the "disappearing middle class" narrative. The same Census report shows that the share of households earning between $35,000 and $100,000 (adjusted for inflation with the CPI) fell from more than 53 percent in 1967 to 42 percent in 2018, whereas the share of households earning more than $100,000 essentially tripled, from less than 10 percent in 1967 to more than 30 percent in 2018.[39]

Perhaps this rising share of higher-income families coincides with a rising share of families earning even lower income? It turns out that's not the case. The article largely ignores it, but the share of households earning less than $35,000 fell, from approximately 36 percent in 1967 to less than 28 percent in 2018.[40] Together, these statistics show a broad increase in prosperity, one that is even more impressive considering that the number of American households essentially doubled from 1970 to 2018.

It also makes sense to ask whether a larger "middle class" is necessarily a good public policy goal. One major problem with this approach is that the term "middle class" has no objective definition. The article in *The Atlantic* implies that anyone earning more than $150,000 is no longer in the middle class, so let's assume that number is the correct upper limit. Using this logic, one might think that all those families who earned more than $150,000 would have been better off if they had, instead, earned $140,000, thus preserving a larger middle class. The same would be true even if the upper limit were $100,000, $50,000, $35,000, or any other number. If the goal is simply to preserve a larger middle class, for any fixed range of income, it amounts to telling poorer folks that they should try to earn more money, but not too much more, lest they earn above the "middle class" threshold. If, on the other hand, the public policy goal is for people to move out of poverty by earning more, then the broad-based prosperity that the Census reported in 2018 (and in many other recent years) is something to celebrate, regardless of the size of "the middle class."

Still, even many people who acknowledge the general rise in prosperity throughout the United States bemoan income inequality, a separate issue that refers to how much more income some people have compared with others. The previously referenced *Atlantic* article, for example, states:

> Despite the improvements in poverty and income across ethnic groups, the American economy is still characterized by significant income inequality; while the poor are finally finding more stable footing following the recession, the rich have been doing well for quite some time now.[41]

The *Atlantic* author uses the official Census Bureau income distribution to explore the issue of inequality, but doing so badly distorts the underlying trends in both inequality and general prosperity.

As mentioned previously, the Census reports income for households rather than for individuals or workers. The failure to account for that fact tends to exaggerate economic differences among demographic groups because households consist of different numbers of people, some of whom do not work. In the best-case scenario, simply comparing household incomes in the official Census income distribution omits important information. In the worst case, it artificially magnifies inequality.[42]

A quick explanation demonstrates this potential problem. The distribution is not designed to describe income for the typical American worker. To compile the official reports, the Census Bureau sorts households from the lowest reported income to the highest, and then divides them into five equal increments (quintiles) of 20 percent. As a result, each household income quintile contains the same number of households, but not the same number of people, or even the same number of people working.

It turns out that these different factors explain a great deal of the supposed income inequality, as well as the apparent stagnation, that appears in the Census Bureau's income distribution.[43] For instance, whereas the lowest quintile contains only 14 percent of the population, the top quintile contains 25 percent.[44] There are 82.1 million people in the top quintile, but there are only 45.7 million in the bottom quintile. The fact that almost twice as many people are in the top quintile as in the bottom—but the same number of households—means that the income in the top quintile supports almost twice as many people as the income in the lowest group. Simply looking at the income in the two quintiles ignores this and mistakenly implies that inequality is much worse than it really is.

Separately, adjusting for the number of workers in each household mitigates the inequality in the household income distribution. For instance, whereas some households consist of a 40-year-old part-time worker living with her retired grandparents, others consist of dual-earning 40-year-old attorneys with no children. In the former case, a small amount of income would be divided among three people. In the latter case, a larger amount of income would be divided between two (working) household members.

The fact that the top two quintiles of the population contain 54 percent of the prime-working-age adults and perform 61 percent of the total hours worked in the economy is important by itself, but it is critical when making a comparison with other quintiles.[45] The lowest quintile, for instance, contains only 12 percent of working-age adults, who perform just 5 percent of the hours worked. Only about half of the households in the lowest quintile contain at least one adult of prime working age.[46] From both an economic and statistical standpoint, it would be strange if the incomes of these two groups were not radically different.

Together, these statistics demonstrate that basic demographic differences, particularly in the number of prime-working-age people earning income in each household, explain a large part of what appears to be a supposedly unequal annual income distribution. These figures also suggest that it is difficult to use a single annual income distribution to gain a true understanding of inequality, stagnation, or mobility, because demographic factors tend to change over time.

* * *

It Is Far from Clear That Income Inequality Causes Income Growth to Decline

The question of whether income inequality reduces economic growth has been researched heavily since the 1970s, when Yale economics professor Arthur M. Okun argued that policies that reduce income inequality would also reduce growth.[47] Yet after decades of research, there is still no clear evidence that inequality harms economic growth. Many of the studies that find income inequality reduces economic growth are based on data in developing countries, making their results largely inapplicable to the United States.

Several studies even report evidence that income inequality is positively related to economic growth. For instance, a 2011 study shows that within both the United States and other developed nations, there is no relationship between changes in income inequality and economic growth for the period 1905–2000, as well as a small positive relationship after 1960 between growth and the top decile's income share.[48] In other words, as the highest income earners did better or worse, the broader economy did better or worse. Additionally, political science professor Lane Kenworthy reports that, across 13 different countries, there is "a modestly strong positive association between change in the top 1 percent's share of income and change in GDP per capita."[49] As Kenworthy points out, though, even these results do not suggest that higher inequality causes higher economic growth. Instead, the results merely identify a correlation. Separately, research by economist Alan Reynolds shows that the poverty rate and the unemployment rate tend to fall when the top 1 percent's share rises, and that both rates tend to rise when the top share falls.[50]

*   *   *

All the evidence discussed so far suggests that income in the United States has not stagnated during the past few decades. However, a more robust way to study income mobility is to use data that follow the same individuals through time.[51] Such data are referred to as "longitudinal" (or "panel") data.[52] Studies that use these kinds of data consistently reveal that a great deal of income mobility occurs in the United States, quite the opposite of most Americans being "stuck" at one income level for prolonged periods.

Many workers, in fact, move up from lower income quintiles into higher quintiles, and many move down from higher to lower quintiles. Such mobility is even normal for those in the lowest and highest quintiles. Despite what many critics claim, Americans display both a great deal of *absolute mobility*, meaning that their income changes over time, as well as *relative mobility*, meaning that their income tends to change relative to the income of others. The following list provides highlights of the evidence from those research papers. (A review of studies using these types of data is provided in the appendix.)[53]

- Following the same taxpayers across nearly two decades shows that 54 percent of the taxpayers in the lowest quintile in 1979 had moved into a higher quintile by 1995, and 47 percent of those in the highest quintile in 1979 had moved into a lower quintile by 1995.

- Following the same working-age taxpayers (25 and older) from 1987 to 1996 shows that, of the entire group of filers in 1987, only 11 percent were in the lowest quintile by 1996. Separately, more than 61 percent of those in the lowest quintile in 1987 had moved into a higher quintile by 1996, with 28 percent moving into the second quintile and 7 percent moving to the highest group. Similar findings hold when studying 1996 through 2005.

- Almost one-third of those in the top quintile in 1987 had dropped to a lower quintile by 1996, and 54 percent of those in the top 1 percent in 1996 were not in the top 1 percent a decade earlier. Similar findings hold when studying 1996 through 2005.

- Tracking the same Americans from 1968 to 2011 shows that remaining in either the bottom 10 percent or 20 percent of the income distribution for 10 or more years is practically unheard of in the United States. Almost 95 percent never spend 10 or more consecutive years in the bottom 20 percent, and nearly 99 percent never spend 10 or more consecutive years in the bottom 10 percent.

- Very few Americans spend 10 consecutive years in the top 1 percent of the distribution, with only 0.6 percent of the population earning such a distinction. Still, over the past 40 years, 70 percent of working-age adults spent at least one year in the top income quintile, and 80 percent never spent more than two consecutive years in the bottom 10 percent of the income distribution.

Critics of the US economic system blame income inequality for a long list of problems, including harm to the poor and the middle class, financial crises, and reduced economic growth.[54] The empirical evidence aside, the theoretical case is very weak for a causal link between inequality and these various ills. A market economy does not function with a fixed pool of income for people to compete over, so the fact that some people earn relatively high incomes does not prevent others from earning higher incomes. More broadly, inequality and mobility metrics on their own tell us little about people's economic opportunities, or what roadblocks might prevent workers from taking full advantage of, or expanding, those opportunities. They also tell us little about the choices people make to earn more—or less—as their lives change.

In a free-enterprise economy, business owners ultimately earn high incomes by making consumers happy, not by harming or exploiting them. Unless they win special government privileges—a harmful defect rather than an inherent feature of a market economy—business owners can only make more money by providing more customers with better products at lower cost. This relationship also applies to employment because employers need to attract workers by providing them relatively good compensation and opportunities for advancement. So in theory, making large amounts of money—high profits—in a market-based economy helps promote economic growth and opportunity.[55]

A careful review of the empirical evidence provides no basis for the idea that income inequality is at the root of America's economic problems, or that reducing inequality would increase economic growth, improve mobility, stave off financial crises, or fix the myriad other problems that critics attribute to inequality. Most of the research fails to support any causal link between inequality and the various socioeconomic ills that critics often attribute to it.[56]

Poor-Quality, Low-Paying Jobs Are Not the Norm

The evidence reviewed in this chapter so far is not a mixed bag—it demonstrates solid growth throughout the income distribution during the past few decades. It clearly runs counter to the narrative of a weakening American middle class, a weakening working class, or even stagnating incomes. Nonetheless, many critics of free markets argue that too many low-quality, low-paying jobs have replaced higher-paying jobs that disappeared during the past few decades.

A recent Bloomberg editorial suggests that the "quality of the jobs being created does leave much to be desired," and Cornell law professor Daniel Alpert believes the United States "has been creating an overabundance of low-quality service jobs."[57] Some of the critics also insist that increasing the minimum wage will help the workers in these low-paying jobs. Sen. Bernie Sanders (I-VT), for example, claims, "In order to rebuild the American middle class and boost the economy, the federal minimum wage should be a living wage."[58]

It may be surprising but, despite popular myths, relatively few Americans work for minimum wage. BLS data show that, as of 2019, 82 million US workers were paid hourly rates, and the median hourly wage rate was $19.14.[59] Of this group, only 1.6 million workers earned at or below the federal minimum wage of $7.25 per hour.[60] This total represents 1.9 percent of all hourly paid workers, and barely 1 percent of the overall labor force.

This 2019 figure is not an anomaly. The percentage of hourly workers earning at or below the minimum wage has trended downward for at least 40 years. The 2019 figure (1.9 percent) is well below the 13.4 percent recorded in 1979, when the BLS began regularly reporting the statistic, and the percentage of hourly workers earning at or below the minimum wage has averaged just 3.5 percent for the past two decades.[61] Thus, even as service-sector jobs have represented a larger share of total jobs in the United States, minimum-wage jobs have remained a relatively small part of the economy (see figure 7.7).

Not only are minimum-wage workers relatively scarce in the labor force, but comparatively few rely solely on their minimum-wage job to support themselves or their families. Most are young, work part time, and are single without children. Workers under age 25 represent about 25 percent of all hourly paid workers; however, they make up more than half of those earning at or below the minimum wage.[62] Almost 60 percent of those earning at or below the minimum wage work part time, and 78 percent are unmarried.[63] Using 2016 data, single parents supporting their children while earning at or below the minimum wage

FIGURE 7.7

Workers at or below minimum wage as share of hourly workers and labor force, 1979 versus 2019

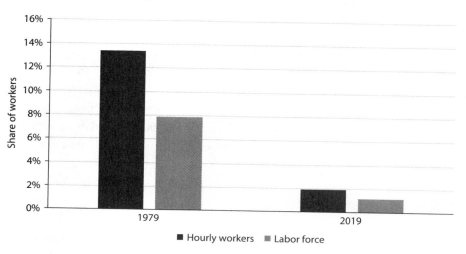

Source: Bureau of Labor Statistics, "Characteristics of Minimum Wage Workers, 2019," April 2020, Table 10.

represent an almost imperceptible share of the labor force—222,000 out of 163 million workers.[64]

BLS data also show that nearly 75 percent of people earning at or below minimum wage are employed in the service sector. Within this broad category, 61 percent work in the *leisure and hospitality* industry, where tips frequently supplement hourly wages.[65] Of the 61 percent working in leisure and hospitality, the average age is 29.5. So even though the economy has continued to shift toward a service-based workforce as manufacturing jobs have disappeared, those ostensibly higher-paying manufacturing jobs could not have simply shifted to minimum-wage service jobs.[66] The typical service-sector worker is too young for that explanation to hold up.

Still, it is possible that boosting the minimum wage could help more people than it harms, so it would be premature to dismiss the idea before looking at the evidence. Though here again, the critics' hopes are dashed. Although there has been some recent controversy over the effects of minimum-wage laws, a large body of research suggests that they have done virtually nothing to help alleviate poverty or to raise the incomes of most low-income families.[67]

The evidence also indicates that legally mandating higher wages, despite the good intentions behind such efforts, hurts the most economically vulnerable members of the population.[68] Naturally, the least-skilled members of the labor market tend to work for the lowest wages in jobs at which they are easily replaced, which means that the lowest-skilled workers have the most to lose from minimum-wage laws. Members of minority groups, as well as younger workers and those with relatively few skills, are among those most disproportionately harmed by minimum-wage laws.[69]

A minimum-wage law is a price control that dictates what employers must pay, so it forces employers to adjust job quality along nonprice dimensions because they can't pay certain workers the lower wages they would otherwise pay. As a result, employers tend to offer fewer minimum-wage jobs. Employers are also more likely to upgrade their hiring standards, and to reduce benefits, including job training, for those low-paying jobs that they do offer.[70]

Unions have historically supported minimum-wage laws, which make higher-skilled and more experienced workers relatively more attractive to employers. That is, they make it comparatively less burdensome to pay for the higher-skilled worker. Similarly, minimum-wage laws make investing in labor-saving technology more attractive than paying lower-wage workers.[71]

Ultimately, the mandates make it harder for those with the fewest skills to get jobs and to acquire the human capital necessary to move up the income scale. A comprehensive review of the evidence through the early 2000s concludes that minimum-wage laws have a particularly negative effect on job training for workers in their early 20s, and that such laws mainly result in a redistribution of income among lower-income workers.[72] In other words, because of minimum-wage laws, some lower-income workers earn a higher income, but it comes at the expense of others because of fewer employment opportunities, or reduced hours. The bottom line is that minimum-wage laws result in (a) fewer job opportunities and reduced income for lower-skilled workers, (b) no net reduction in poverty, and (c) a long-term reduction in the acquisition of skills. Fortunately, relatively few—though still too many—US workers are directly harmed by minimum-wage laws.

*   *   *

Consumption–Based Measures Demonstrate Steady Declines in Poverty

Relatively few people had telephones, typewriters, or automobiles in the late 19th century, and hardly anyone in the early 20th century had automatic dishwashers and washing machines in their homes. All these items were quite common among US households by the 1970s; however, not many people in 1975 had home computers or automobiles with airbags, cameras, or GPS. No matter what their income level, people in the early 1900s simply could not buy iPhones or iPads. Similarly, people in the 1970s could not equip their homes with wireless internet networks, space-saving microwaves, computerized ovens, flat-screen high-definition televisions, printers, or video baby monitors that fit in a shirt pocket and work from across the street.

Because it is so difficult for a simple price index adjustment to adequately describe these types of differences, consumption-based measures of well-being tend to provide a clearer picture of long-term changes in individuals' standard of living.[73]

Although the official US poverty rate suggests that poverty displayed no clear trend after the 1960s—in 2017, the rate was 12.3 percent, the same as in 2006, and only one percentage point higher than in 1973—one widely used consumption-based measure shows a steady decline in the poverty rate.[74] This metric, which uses a broad measure of consumption, shows that the poverty rate declined from more than 30 percent in 1960 to just 13 percent in 1980. It then fell to 6.2 percent in 2000, and to only 2.8 percent in 2017.[75] It also shows that consumption for the lowest 10 percent of income earners grew 54 percent from 1980 to 2009, more than 22 percent above what inflation-adjusted income measures imply.[76]

*   *   *

Despite how few Americans depend on minimum-wage work, it is still possible that critics are right about lower-quality jobs replacing those that have disappeared during the past few decades. Is it true, for instance, that the US economy has been creating too many low-quality service jobs?

One major problem with this proposition is that virtually all the job growth in the United States since the 1990s has been in the service sector. In fact, an even bigger problem is that most of the job growth throughout the full post–World War II era has been in the service sector. Yet looking at either of these periods, Americans' incomes, by various measures, dramatically increased.

In 1939, the first year for which the BLS reported the data, 62 percent of the US economy's jobs were in the service-providing industries, and 38 percent were in the goods-producing industries. By 1970, 69 percent were in the service category, with only 31 percent in the goods category. This trend continued and, by 1990, 78 percent of all jobs were in the service category—only 22 percent were in the goods-producing industries. As of 2019, just 14 percent of US workers had jobs in the goods-producing category.[77] Yet during this entire period, the total number of jobs in the United States steadily increased, from 30.6 million in 1939 to 109.5 million by 1990 and to 151 million by 2019 (see figure 7.8). Thus, by 2019, there were 130 million service jobs in the United States, more than a fourfold increase from total employment in 1939.

Maybe, as several other critics have claimed, the problem is simply that manufacturing jobs have disappeared. Conceivably, those were the better-paying/higher-quality jobs.[78] It is hardly scientific evidence, but it is very easy to find former manufacturing workers who balk at this suggestion. Chuck Almdale, for instance, recently sent a letter to the editor of the *Los Angeles Times* in which he states:

> In the fall of 1967, I worked in "the pit" at a Chrysler assembly plant in Michigan. Every 45 seconds a car rolled on tracks overhead

FIGURE 7.8

Goods and services sector shares of employment and total nonfarm employment, 1939–2023

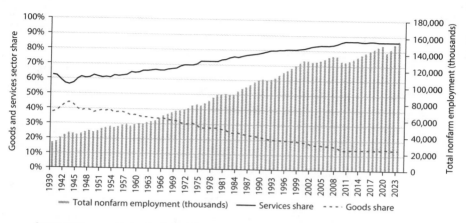

Source: US Bureau of Labor Statistics, "All Employees, Service-Providing [SRVPRD]"; US Bureau of Labor Statistics, "All Employees, Goods-Producing [USGOOD]"; US Bureau of Labor Statistics, "All Employees, Total Nonfarm [PAYEMS]."

while our three-man team inspected several essential items. . . . My next job was making wheels for cars, which included painting, pressing, hole punching, weld stripping and sheet metal cutting. A friend lost his thumbs to a 100-ton press. Flakes of metal embedded in my eyes, I breathed paint and fumes, and my hearing was damaged because of continuous mechanical thunder. I eventually quit and went to college. A "golden age?" Baloney. No sane worker wants a job like this; necessity forces him into it.[79]

Of course, Almdale's opinion is just that—it is simply his opinion, not empirical evidence. However, it is possible to examine some of the facts on wages and job safety, as well as fringe benefits, all factors that contribute to job quality.

For starters, there is currently little difference in average earnings among workers in goods-producing and service-providing industries. As of December 2019, average hourly earnings for production and nonsupervisory employees in goods-producing industries was

$25.07, whereas the average for those in the service-providing industries was $23.58.[80] It is true, though, as critics such as Cornell Law School's Daniel Alpert point out, that average wages are much lower among two main sectors in the service industry: *retail* and *leisure and hospitality.*

It is also true, though, that most minimum-wage workers are employed in these sectors. In 2019, average hourly earnings for nonsupervisory employees in *retail* and *leisure and hospitality* were $16.90 and $14.77, respectively.[81] Yet from 1990 to 2019, employment in the *retail trade* rose from 13.2 million to 15.6 million, whereas it rose from 9.3 million to 16.6 million in *leisure and hospitality.* Combined, this increase of 9.7 million jobs accounts for roughly 25 percent of the increase in total nonfarm employment from 1990 to 2019.[82]

Perhaps more importantly, these average wage and job growth figures tell us very little about who is taking these jobs. As with household income, the demographics tell the real story. It turns out that most of these jobs are going to younger folks. For example, the average age in the lower-income deciles (for all workers) is much lower in the service and sales sectors (31.8 and 31.9, respectively) than in the production sector (37.8) (see figure 7.9).[83] In fact, the data show that 44 percent of the full-time workers in the first decile of service jobs, and 40 percent in the first decile of sales jobs, are between 16 and 25 years old. Thus, accounting for just age makes it clear that there is an abundance of newly created jobs in the service sector for younger people. The data also show that lower-paying service jobs are not typically filled by parents supporting their families or by older people who used to work in manufacturing jobs.[84]

There are many other reasons to believe that these service jobs are, in fact, *high-quality* jobs. For instance, among the first decile of earners, 81.7 percent of full-time workers in the service industry and 86.1 percent in the sales industry have health insurance coverage, compared with 78.9 percent for production workers.[85] Furthermore, the University of Michigan's Health and Retirement Study shows that many of the service jobs created in the past few decades are less physically strenuous and more mentally demanding, a change that many people

FIGURE 7.9

Average age of first decile workers by sector

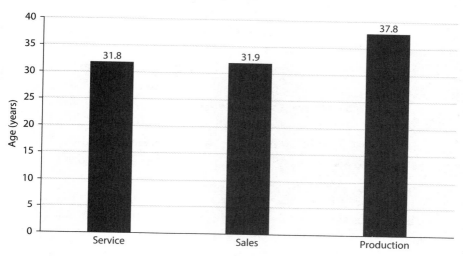

Source: Author's calculations using 2019 Current Population Survey Data.

Note: The statistics for full-time workers include those who annually worked at least 1,250 hours.

see as positive. This improvement has especially been the case for jobs in the service sector and in public administration, and those "in occupations such as management, professional specialty, sales, administrative, and technical support."[86]

The shift out of heavier industrial work also coincides with a steady decline in workplace injuries and deaths. This shift is not surprising, since heavy industrial work is more physically demanding and dangerous than other types of occupations. The US Department of Labor estimates that approximately 14,000 employees were killed on the job in 1970, a total that fell to 4,340 by 2009.[87] The rate of nonfatal workplace injuries and illnesses has also declined, from 11 per 100 workers in 1972 to 2.8 in 2019.[88] Similarly, the rate of fatal workplace injuries per 100,000 workers has been falling, from 5.2 in 1992 to 3.5 in 2019.[89]

The data are clear. Based on several job traits, including wage growth, most of the job growth in recent decades did *not* consist of low-quality jobs.

Time and Work Needed to Purchase Goods Have Fallen Dramatically

One consumption-based measure of well-being is the number of work-hours needed to purchase the same goods at two different points in time. If the amount of time someone would need to work to buy the same bundle of consumer goods in 1975 is no different from that in, for example, 2019, then real income has stagnated. On the other hand, if the required work time to purchase the same goods has fallen, then real income has increased. Using a sample of 400 consumer products, one researcher reports that only one good—men's work boots—costs more in work time in 2019 than in 1975.[90]

In *Myths of Rich and Poor: Why We're Better Off Than We Think*, Michael Cox and Richard Alm use this method.[91] They report that the affordability of most goods and services has increased since the 1970s, and that poor Americans are now more likely to own many consumer products than were middle-income Americans in the 1970s.[92] The Simon Project, an endeavor of HumanProgress.org, formalized these ideas by creating an index based on the "time price" (how long someone must work to acquire a good) of 50 basic commodities.[93] The index shows that the average time price of these 50 commodities fell more than 74.2 percent between 1980 and 2019.

In practical terms, this figure means that if it took one hour of work to buy a commodity—such as sugar, coffee, pork, or lumber—in 1980, it took only about 15 minutes of work to buy that commodity in 2019. Put differently, if it took one hour of work to buy an item in 1980, that same hour of work would buy about four units of the same good in 2019. This improvement represents a more affordable lifestyle, with the ability to produce and acquire more goods and services while using fewer resources.

8

CONCLUSION

What most people really object to when they object to a free market is that it is so hard for them to shape it to their own will. The market gives people what the people want instead of what other people think they ought to want. At the bottom of many criticisms of the market economy is really lack of belief in freedom itself.

—Milton Friedman, from "The New Liberal's Creed: Individual Freedom, Preserving Dissent Are Ultimate Goals," *Wall Street Journal*, May 18, 1961

M any recent critics of US economic policy blame elected officials' supposed overreliance on free-market ideology—derisively termed "market fundamentalism"—for all sorts of economic problems. A major flaw in this story is that elected officials have been moving the United States further away from a pure free-enterprise system for decades, steadily producing a more heavily regulated economy and increased government intervention. Health care and education— two areas of the economy that elicit some of Americans' most vigorous complaints—are now so heavily subsidized and regulated that they look nothing like free markets. Even the supposed deregulatory years of the George W. Bush administration included some of the highest levels of new regulatory burdens seen up to that time, and they unambiguously did not include the deregulation of financial markets.

Much to the detriment of the common American, increased government regulation and other types of economic intervention have consistently shaped the current US version of free enterprise. Damaging regulations and harmful public–private business relationships are responsible for some of the largest economic problems Americans have faced in the past 50 years. Capital regulations and bankruptcy rules that were designed in collaboration with large financial institutions—along with perverse financial incentives propagated throughout the economy via Fannie Mae and Freddie Mac (both government-sponsored enterprises)—were primary causes of the 2008 financial crisis.

Expansions of government-provided unemployment and disability insurance prolonged the Great Recession that followed. Outside the financial industry, the cumulative weight of countless economic barriers created by government programs, trade barriers, regulation, and the crowding out of private businesses have made it more difficult for people to develop economic opportunities and improve their living standards. Naturally, people earning lower incomes feel the brunt of these barriers more sharply than the highest-earning Americans.

There are literally hundreds of ways in which Congress could reverse these trends and remove government-created barriers to economic opportunity for millions of people, but critics would prefer to continue expanding the federal government's involvement in the economy. These critics base their proposals on their own definition of the common good, insisting that if the government forces people to cooperate in a certain way everyone will be better off. Of course, this type of social cooperation is not really cooperation at all, but coercion. Critics who are dissatisfied with America's free-enterprise economy reject the notion that people's voluntary associations in markets, civil society, and families benefit the common good. By implication, these critics want whoever is in power politically to define the common good.

On the other hand, a true free-enterprise system that maximizes people's ability to freely cooperate to improve their lives produces the closest to a broadly agreed-upon version of the common good. One of the main reasons that the critics' approach has repeatedly failed is that it denies this reality. Instead, it empowers one small group of people to define the common good for everyone else. Tragically, supporters of this scheme ignore the evidence that more economic freedom leads to more opportunity and more prosperity, and that government barriers to economic freedom reduce people's ability to improve their lives. They insist that the US economy must be "redirected" because it is no longer providing the goods and services that Americans want and need. Yet they ignore the fact that virtually all consumption-based metrics clearly demonstrate that Americans have improved their material well-being throughout the post–World War II era.

Some argue that elected officials should ignore the clear success as measured by consumption, and instead focus on the supposed failures on the production side of the economy. This prescription is faulty for several reasons, not least of which is because production and consumption are merely two sides of the same coin. Simply put, there is no reason to produce other than to consume, and there is no reason to produce anything that people do not want to consume. Failure to recognize this relationship has produced countless harmful government policies that enrich well-connected groups at the expense of others.

Frequently, the poor results of such government policies have provided further impetus for Congress to expand the government's role in the economy. It is hardly surprising that most recent policy proposals that restrict economic freedom are recycled versions of ones that have been tried out for decades and, in some cases, centuries. Among the oldest of these notions is that the government needs to restrict trade and immigration, provide subsidies, and increase tariffs, all to isolate certain industries from "unfair" competition and to "save" domestic jobs. These arguments play to people's fears and ignore that changing economic conditions equate to new opportunities for people to better their lives.

It is true that many products are no longer manufactured in the United States, but that alone does not indicate a problem. American manufacturers now operate more efficiently, use fewer natural resources, require less backbreaking and monotonous labor, produce less pollution, and employ more highly educated people than ever. Given how successfully most Americans have adjusted to this changing economic landscape, it is difficult to make a case for going back to the older methods of manufacturing for the sake of creating more (unproductive) jobs. Doing so would amount to paying people to dig and refill holes, but with the added costs of higher consumer prices, increased waste of natural resources, more damage to the environment, and less human capital.

Moreover, it is condescending to insist that "lower-skilled" or "less-educated" American workers should be consigned to any career or lifestyle, even when ignoring the harmful incentives that current government programs provide for people to remain outside the full-time workforce. It is also dangerous to give such power over others to any one group of individuals.

From a macro level, it is true that some American communities—the Rust Belt states in the Midwest, for example—can no longer rely on the same types of manufacturing jobs that were prevalent before the 1970s. It does not follow, however, that the federal government should restrict trade, immigration, or automation to "fix" this situation, even ignoring the fact that many Americans do not want such manufacturing jobs in the first place. In fact, evidence suggests that isolationist policies contributed to Rust Belt–like conditions, and that increased trade, immigration, and automation have benefited millions of people, including many of those living in or near those communities.

Regardless of the politics, the evidence simply does not connect widespread economic difficulties to "trade with China" or competition with "cheap labor." The evidence also fails to support the widely repeated claim that the typical American worker's real wages have not budged in decades. Although there is no single "right" way to measure income growth for the past few decades, the reality is that most of the measures show the typical worker is much better off. Essentially, out of every 10 possible ways to measure income growth from the 1970s to 2019, 9 confirm that income has grown steadily and healthily. Virtually any way we look at it, the average worker is better off now than in the 1970s—much better off, in fact.

Yet according to the naysayers, the only Americans who have done well in the past few decades are the ones that were already well-off. Supposedly, most of the current generation of workers will do worse than their parents, a rarity in American history. As with the typical worker example, there are multiple ways to evaluate such claims, and most of them show that these apparently disturbing trends are simply wrong.

Americans have produced broad-based prosperity during the past few decades, and the middle class is shrinking only in the sense that middle-income earners have been earning too much money to remain in the middle class. Just as important, workers at the lowest end of the income distribution have consistently realized some of the largest—in many instances, *the* largest—income growth figures among all workers during the past several decades.

Still, many critics claim that in the US economy, only low-paying "low-quality" service jobs have replaced all the higher-paying "good" manufacturing jobs that disappeared. Again, the overall evidence shows that both compensation and job quality have improved. Furthermore, the idea that "manufacturing jobs" are high paying while "service jobs" are low paying is simplistic. Only some types of manufacturing jobs—those that require high levels of education and experience—are responsible for the higher average wages found in some parts of the industrial sector, and only some types of service jobs—those that require the lowest levels of education and experience—are responsible for the lower averages in service industries.

At best, the dismal image of middle-aged men who, after being shut out of their factory jobs, have been forced to work in fast-food restaurants for low wages is an exaggeration. It simply is not the case that most, or even a substantial portion, of American workers have been forced to support their families with low-paying jobs in the hospitality industry. Moreover, the trend toward a service-based economy is not a recent phenomenon. It dates to at least the mid-19th century, and it is exactly what should be expected as a society grows wealthier. Overall, the evidence simply does not support the critics' dismal claims.

It is also clear that many Americans still struggle to earn higher income and improve their living standards. However, imposing more government-imposed barriers will only make it more difficult for citizens to improve their living standards. The best way to help people move up the economic ladder is to enact policies that maximize individuals' economic freedom and, therefore, their opportunities. There are countless ways—economists and pro-free-market think tanks have proposed hundreds during the past several decades—in which policymakers can remove the many government-created barriers that harm people's incentives to improve their lives and make positive contributions to society. Doing so does not require Americans to abandon people who need and desire help.

Yet many of the ideas that recent US policy critics prefer would further restrict economic freedom by expanding the worst features of the American economy. For instance, many of these critics promote industrial policy, an idea that relies on more government planning, higher taxes, higher tariffs, and more widespread subsidies. Supposedly, industrial policy will provide more manufacturing jobs while increasing exports and reducing imports, resulting in a labor market that more closely resembles that of the 1950s and 1960s.

Leaving aside the discriminatory policies that produced this supposed heyday of American manufacturing (many jobs were unavailable to blacks and women before the late 1960s), producing more of everything that citizens need while exporting the surplus is both harmful and incoherent as a national policy.[1] It ignores both the benefits of labor-saving productivity and the fact that all nations cannot consistently increase only their exports. One nation's exports are another's imports, so widespread export-promoting and import-substituting policies cannot be sustained.

Critics insist that their industrial policy prescriptions would be better for the typical worker, less-educated workers, and anyone unable to obtain the skills needed to compete in the current job market. But such policies would promote a culture of dependency because they would make it easier for people to remain in the less-educated and lower-skilled categories and thus leave them unprepared to deal with future changes and challenges. Besides, such policies show little faith in the average Americans' ability to better themselves and ignore all the evidence that suggests they can improve their living standards when given the opportunity.

The truth is that industrial policy will lead to a government-planned economy, which—as history has shown repeatedly—is doomed to fail because it seeks to impose the will of a few on everyone else. It rejects the benefits of economic freedom and the free-enterprise system. Industrial policy does not merely redirect the market economy, it takes it over, even if in small steps. Government coercion to achieve the preferred economic outcomes of those in power has demonstrably and repeatedly failed to lift the common people's fortunes. Industrial policy is not a recipe for improving people's lives; it is a way to impoverish them.

If critics want to help people improve their lives, they should work toward lifting the many government policies that have contributed to economic problems and created unequal opportunities for so many people. They should promote pro-growth policies not because higher growth guarantees anyone anything, or because a rising tide lifts all boats (though it clearly does), but because economic growth represents millions of people making decisions and taking actions that improve their living standards. Economic freedom is the sturdiest ladder out of poverty. Extensive government involvement in the market, whether under the name of industrial policy or central planning, destroys the ladder.

Appendixes

APPENDIX A: TRADE RESEARCH OVERVIEW

Other research examines how trade might indirectly cause labor market difficulties. For instance, a 2018 survey of the economics literature reports: "No study captures all aspects of globalization and its effects on manufacturing employment, and the limitations of any single study need to be recognized. Collectively, however, a growing body of research points to sizable adverse effects, operating through various mechanisms."[1] Yet of the seven papers summarized by the review, only two estimated the effect of trade on employment.

The first paper in the survey is the 2013 *American Economic Review* study by Autor, Dorn, and Hanson discussed in chapter 3. The second is a 2016 *American Economic Review* study that examines the relationship between US manufacturing employment and the elimination of *potential* tariff increases (potential tariff increases refer to the possibility that tariffs would increase on Chinese imports unless the existing preferred (lower) rates were renewed each year).[2] The 2016 paper is much narrower in scope. The authors try to quantify "the transition from annual to permanent normal trade relations via the 'NTR [normal trade relations] gap,' defined as the difference between the non-NTR rates to which tariffs would have risen if annual renewal had failed . . . and the

NTR tariff rates that were locked in by PNTR [permanent normal trade relations]."[3] The paper reports a great deal of variation in this NTR gap across industries and estimates that "moving an industry from an NTR gap at the twenty-fifth percentile of the observed distribution to the seventy-fifth percentile increases the implied relative loss of employment by 0.08 log points [roughly 8 percentage points]."[4]

It is very difficult—if not impossible—to generalize this result to explain the overall effects of trade on employment, and the authors report other findings that demonstrate the complex relationship between trade and employment. For instance, they find that shifting to permanent normal trade relations with China increased (a) Chinese exports to the United States and (b) the number of American and Chinese firms engaged in related party trade (defined as trade by American companies with their subsidiaries abroad and trade by American subsidiaries of foreign companies with their parent companies).[5] The authors point out that both these outcomes are "consistent with within-firm relocation of US production to China," but that "some [US] plants were able to adapt to the change in US policy rather than die."[6] Regardless, there is no inherent reason to value increased job opportunities in exporting industries over those related to imports, and the results show a reallocation of production toward less labor-intensive plants, a change that is consistent with taking advantage of higher productivity.[7]

Two of the remaining papers in the 2018 survey demonstrate various "adverse effects" of Chinese imports on US companies' investments, patents, sales, and research and development, while another two examine the relationship between offshoring and employment. The seventh paper in the survey studies the connection between exchange-rate appreciation and manufacturing employment.[8] Broadly, these studies reveal how difficult it is to quantify the effect of trade policies on labor markets without accounting for increased trade's offsetting positive economic effects.

A 2017 paper, for instance, finds that a reduction in "tariff uncertainty" for US firms dealing with China is associated with a "relative decline in investment," but that "plants with the highest levels of initial skill intensity exhibit a positive relationship between exposure to the trade liberalization and relative investment."[9] In other words, this evidence indicates that increased trade leads to further increases in productivity, at least for some firms. These benefits can occur even if trade causes firms to shift industries, reorienting their operations from manufacturing to services (consistent with the findings of George Mason University economist Zhi Wang and his coauthors, as discussed in chapter 4). In fact, the service component of manufacturing companies throughout the developed world has been growing for decades for companies as diverse as Apple, Xerox, Medtronic, and Rolls-Royce.[10]

APPENDIX B: PANEL DATA RESEARCH OVERVIEW

1992 US Treasury report. This study uses a 10-year panel of tax return data that followed income tax filers from 1979 to 1988.[11] The study reports that 86 percent of the taxpayers in the lowest income quintile in 1979 had moved to a higher quintile by the end of the 10-year period, with 15 percent making it to the highest quintile and 25 percent to the second-highest quintile.[12] Of those in the highest quintile in 1979, 65 percent remained in the highest quintile by 1988.[13] To make their research more comparable with other work, the authors ran additional analysis after restricting their sample to tax filers with family members between ages 25 and 54. Using this restricted sample, the results showed that 47 percent of those in the lowest quintile had moved to a higher quintile by 1988, and that only 50 percent of those in the highest quintile in 1979 remained in the highest quintile by the end of the 10-year period.[14]

Urban Institute papers. Researchers at the Urban Institute published several income mobility studies in the 1990s. One paper, authored by Isabel Sawhill and Mark Condon, used the Panel Study of Income

Dynamics (PSID), a longitudinal panel survey of American families, to study income mobility for people who were ages 25 to 54 in two 10-year periods: 1967–1976 and 1977–1986. The authors report that, in both periods, "slightly over 60 percent of individuals were in a different family income quintile a decade later (60.5 percent for 1967–1976, and 60.7 percent for 1977–1986)."[15] Among individuals who began either period in the lowest quintile, 44 percent had moved into a higher quintile by 1976, and 47 percent had moved up by 1986,[16] results that are consistent with those in the 1992 Treasury report. The Urban Institute study reviews the income mobility literature and finds, "There is little evidence that this mobility has changed substantially over time."[17] The study concludes:

> It is clear that there is substantial mobility—both short-term and long-term—over an average life cycle in the United States. The studies reviewed above suggest that approximately one-quarter to one-third of the population moves into a new income quintile in any given year. Given a longer time horizon, an even greater percentage of individuals switch income quintiles—perhaps slightly less than one-half over a five-year period, and about 60 percent over a ten-year period.[18]

Federal Reserve Bank of Boston paper. This 2002 study uses PSID data and, consistent with earlier research, reports that income mobility was "more or less constant from the 1970s to the 1980s."[19] The study reports a decrease in mobility of four percentage points in the 1990s. The authors study mobility for "working-age households," and report that mobility "decreased slightly in the 1990s" for this group.[20] Specifically, the paper reports that 51 percent of workers in the lowest income quintile in 1969 had moved into a higher quintile by 1979, whereas 47 percent of those in the lowest quintile in 1988 had moved into a higher quintile by 1998.[21]

Andrew Young School of Policy Studies research paper. This 2006 study uses a 17-year panel of income tax returns for prime-working-age

Americans, defined as those at least 30 years old in 1979 and no older than 61 by 1995. The authors report that 54 percent of the taxpayers in the lowest quintile in 1979 had moved into a higher quintile by 1995, and approximately 47 percent of those in the highest quintile in 1979 had moved into a lower quintile by 1995.[22] Among those in the lowest quintile in 1979, approximately 4 percent moved into the highest quintile by 1995, and almost 30 percent moved into the second-highest quintile. As for those in the highest quintile in 1979, approximately 7.5 percent moved to the bottom, and 19 percent moved to the fourth quintile.[23] The paper also shows that 70 percent of those in the top 1 percent in 1979 had moved into a lower quintile by 1995, whereas 76 percent in the top 5 percent in 1979 had moved down by 1995.[24] These findings contradict the notion that the same few Americans regularly bring home the largest share of income in the economy.[25]

2007 US Treasury report: Mobility from 1987 to 1996. This paper uses a 10-year panel to study income mobility from 1987 to 1996 and excludes taxpayers under age 25 in the panel's initial year.[26] The authors report that of all tax filers 25 and older in 1987, only 11 percent were in the lowest quintile by 1996, underscoring the fact that younger people are most likely to enter the workforce earning below-average income.[27] The paper also reports that more than 61 percent of those in the lowest quintile in 1987 had moved into a higher quintile by 1996, with 28 percent moving into the second quintile and 7 percent moving into the highest group.[28] Almost one-third of those in the top quintile in 1987 had dropped to a lower quintile by 1996, and more than half (54 percent) of those in the top 1 percent in 1996 were people who had not been in the top 1 percent a decade earlier.[29] Separately, the study reports that almost 55 percent of taxpayers saw real income increases of at least 5 percent between 1987 and 1996, and that median income increased by more than 11 percent.[30] Furthermore, the data show that among all the groups, those in the lowest quintile in 1987 realized the largest income growth. Median income increased by more than 80 percent for the lowest-income group by 1996, 22 percent for the second quintile, 9 percent for the third quintile, and 2 percent for the fourth quintile.

The highest quintile showed a decline of almost 2 percent in median income from 1987 to 1996, whereas the top 1 percent showed a decline of almost 24 percent from 1987 to 1996.[31]

2007 US Treasury report: Mobility from 1996 to 2005. A subsequent Treasury report picks up where the previous study left off and uses a 10-year panel to study income mobility from 1996 to 2005.[32] The study, whose findings are consistent with those of previous research, argues that the degree of mobility among income groups was unchanged from the prior decade. The paper reports that approximately half the taxpayers in the lowest quintile in 1996 had moved into a higher quintile by 2005, and less than half of those in the top 1 percent in 1996 remained in that group by 2005.[33] The results also show that real median incomes for all taxpayers increased by 24 percent over the 10-year period, and that real incomes increased for almost 70 percent of taxpayers from 1996 to 2005.[34] Similar to the preceding Treasury report, which studied the prior 10-year period, median incomes of those starting out in the lowest income quintile increased more than it did for those in the higher groups. Specifically, median income for those in the lowest quintile in 1996 had increased by 90 percent by 2005, and real incomes doubled for more than 49 percent of the group. In contrast, the real median income for those in the top 1 percent in 1996 *decreased* 25 percent by 2005.[35]

Washington Center for Equitable Growth working paper. This 2016 study uses a tax return panel that examines taxpayer income from 1999 to 2011. The authors find, "Almost half of all working adults in the United States experience a change in earnings of at least 25 percent over a two-year period, which is in line with findings by the Congressional Budget Office (2008) using Social Security Administration and Survey of Income and Program Participation (SIPP) data."[36] The authors also report, "Approximately two-fifths of families that maintain the same number of workers still experience upward or downward swings in income of at least 25 percent over two years." The paper attempts to explain these income changes and reports that marriage affects mobility. Specifically, the paper reports: "Marriage improves the earnings trajectory of male workers more than female workers. Marriage is associated with large median gains in male earnings (11 percent), but approximately no change in female earnings (1 percent)."[37]

Public Library of Science paper on poverty. This 2015 study uses the PSID to examine mobility with regard to how likely working-age people ages 25 to 60 were to experience poverty (defined as falling into either the bottom quintile or the 10th percentile of income) from 1968 to 2011. The authors report that by age 30, 41.6 percent of the population had experienced at least one year in the bottom 20 percent, and almost 23 percent had experienced at least one year in the bottom 10 percent.[38] Each of these figures increases with age: by age 60, almost 62 percent of Americans reported having spent at least one year in the bottom 20 percent, and approximately 42 percent reported income that falls in the lowest 10 percent of the distribution. Naturally, these figures mean that, by age 60, approximately 60 percent of working-age Americans have never had income low enough to be in the bottom 10 percent. The paper also shows that only 45 percent of prime-working-age Americans experience at least two years in the bottom 20 percent, only 35 percent experience three or more years, and only about 12 percent encounter 10 or more years in the bottom 20 percent.[39] The results also show that 80 percent of working-age Americans never spend more than two consecutive years in the bottom 10 percent, and more than 60 percent never spend more than two consecutive years in the lowest 20 percent of the distribution.[40] Staying in either category for 10 or more years is practically unheard of in the United States—almost 95 percent never spend 10 or more consecutive years in the bottom 20 percent and nearly 99 percent never spend 10 or more consecutive years in the bottom 10 percent.[41] These figures are inconsistent with the notion that the same people, year after year, populate the lowest quintile in the US income distribution.

Public Library of Science paper on affluence. This 2015 study uses the PSID to examine mobility in relation to how likely working-age people (ages 25 to 60) were to experience a stint of relative affluence from 1968 to 2011 (defined as having sufficient income to fall into the

80th percentile, the 90th percentile, 95th percentile, or 99th percentile). The authors report that by age 60, (a) approximately 70 percent of the population spent at least one year in the top income quintile, (b) approximately 53 percent spent at least one year in the top 10 percent, (c) more than 36 percent had income that qualified at least once for the top 5 percent, and (d) more than 11 percent reached the top 1 percent at least once.[42] The paper also shows that reaching these high-earner categories is far from a guarantee of remaining there. For instance, only 2 percent of the population remains in the top 1 percent of the income distribution for more than 5 years, and only 1 percent does so for more than 10 years.[43] Attaining 10 consecutive years at the very top (1 percent) of the income scale is very rare, with only 0.6 percent of the population achieving that.[44] The authors also show that the people most likely to hit a year of "relative affluence"—defined as the top 20 percent, 10 percent, 5 percent, or 1 percent—are those in their prime earning ages of 45 to 54.[45] Thus, as with similar studies, this report suggests that a great deal of both upward and downward mobility occurs in the United States. The results contradict the notion that the same people, year after year, populate the very highest income group in the US income distribution.

ACKNOWLEDGMENTS

I would like to thank Whitney Michel for reading so many drafts, Gabriella Beaumont-Smith for reading even more drafts and for providing helpful suggestions and encouragement, as well as Jack Spencer. I would also like to thank Jerome Famularo for an enormous amount of incredible research assistance, as well as Drew Gonshorowski for his invaluable research assistance. I'd also like to thank my editor, Ivan Osorio, as well as Nick Anthony (especially for helping with one-fifth of the title), Ryan Bourne, Colin Grabow, Jennifer Huddleston, Jai Kedia, Dominik Lett, Adam Michel, Alex Nowrasteh, Ann Rulon, Jennifer Schulp, George Selgin, and Simone Shenny.

Chapter 1

1. For more on how the human condition has improved, and why it has improved, worldwide, see the general description at HumanProgress.org, available at https://www.humanprogress.org/about/.

2. Joseph E. Stiglitz, "Progressive Capitalism Is Not an Oxymoron," *New York Times*, April 19, 2019; David Leonhardt, "O.K., but What's Your Plan?," *New York Times*, June 11, 2019.

3. Samuel Hammond, "Op-Ed: Marco Rubio Wants a National Innovation Strategy," Niskanen Center, February 15, 2019. The "Made in China 2025" plan, released in 2015, had the goal of rapidly expanding 10 high-tech manufacturing industries, including electric cars, next-generation information technology, and advanced robotics. The stated goal was for China to achieve, by 2025, "70 percent self-sufficiency in high-tech industries." James McBride and Andrew Chatzky, "Is 'Made in China 2025' a Threat to Global Trade?," Council on Foreign Relations, New York, May 13, 2019.

4. Subcommittee on Economic Policy of the Senate Committee on Banking, Housing, and Urban Affairs, Hearing on "Economic Mobility: Is the American Dream in Crisis?," 116th Cong., 1st sess., July 17, 2019.

5. These phrases are from the written testimonies of Ponnuru and Levin, both scholars with the American Enterprise Institute. See Subcommittee on Economic Policy.

6. This phrase is taken from the written testimony of Oren Cass before the Subcommittee on Economic Policy.

7. Oren Cass, *The Once and Future Worker: A Vision for the Renewal of Work in America* (New York: Encounter Books, 2018), p. 1.

8. Cass, *The Once and Future Worker*, p. 2.

9. Subcommittee on Economic Policy.

10. Samantha Smith, "Most Think the 'American Dream' Is within Reach for Them," Pew Research Center, Washington, October 31, 2017.

11. In the same survey, 77 percent of US adults say that "freedom of choice in how to live" is essential to their view of the American dream, and only 11 percent report that becoming wealthy is essential. Smith, "Most Think 'American Dream' Is within Reach."

12. Jeff Greenfield, "Trump Is Pat Buchanan with Better Timing," *Politico*, September–October 2016.

13. John McMickle, "Trump Win Provides Moment of Clarity on Income Equality," *The Hill*, November 21, 2016.

14. Theodore Roosevelt campaigned on a promise to "promote prosperity" and to see to it "that prosperity is passed around." *The Farmer and the Businessman*, recorded August 1912, available from the Theodore Roosevelt Association. In 1934, President Franklin D. Roosevelt chastised Congress for having "done little to prevent an unjust concentration of wealth and economic power." Paul Winfree, *A History (and Future) of the Budget Process in the United States: Budget by Fire* (Cham, Switzerland: Palgrave Macmillan, 2019), p. 126. In the late 1930s, FDR expressed concern over workers who had been "displaced by machines" and called for income redistribution through federal farm programs because the agriculture industry was not "receiving the proper share of the national income." Winfree, *Budget by Fire*, p. 121. In 1964, President Lyndon B. Johnson launched the federal War on Poverty and stressed, "The Great Society rests on abundance and liberty for all." Johnson, "Remarks at the University of Michigan," May 22, 1964.

15. Stephen A. Smith, ed., *Preface to the Presidency: Selected Speeches of Bill Clinton 1974–1992* (Fayetteville: University of Arkansas Press, 2016), p. 80.

16. In 1984, Democratic presidential candidate Walter Mondale derided President Ronald Reagan's trade policies as having turned "our industrial Midwest into a rust bowl," a term that eventually morphed into "Rust Belt." Anne Trubek, "Our Collective Ignorance about the Rust Belt Is Getting Dangerous," *Time*, April 3, 2018.

17. By the 1990s, this low-cost foreign labor/cheap import story was so pervasive that many economists—generally the biggest supporters of free trade—began arguing against it. Paul Krugman and Robert Lawrence, "Trade, Jobs, and Wages," National Bureau of Economic Research Working Paper no. 4478, September 1993, p. 1. Also see George Will, "Buchanan's Nonsense," *Washington Post*, November 5, 1995. For an anecdote of two lower-middle-income Buchanan supporters who feared that the American dream had "passed them by," see Jane Gross, "'Average' Family Struggles on Edge of Financial Collapse," *Los Angeles Times*, March 30, 1996.

18. Robert Samuelson, "We've Become Addicted to the Income Stagnation Story. It's Probably Not True," *Washington Post*, December 9, 2018. Also see Michael Strain, "The Story of Stagnating Wages Was Mostly Wrong: The Measures Can Be Misleading," Bloomberg, May 15, 2019.

19. For a review of income inequality during the 20th century, see Robert D. Plotnick et al., "The Twentieth Century Record of Inequality and Poverty in the United States," Institute for Research on Poverty Discussion Paper no. 1166-98, July 1998. For studies that examine US inequality in earlier periods, see Lee Soltow, "Wealth Inequality in the United States in 1798 and 1860," *Review of Economics and Statistics* 66, no. 3 (1984): 444–51; and Joshua L. Rosenbloom and Gregory W. Stutes, "Reexamining the Distribution of Wealth in 1870," National Bureau of Economic Research Working Paper no. 11482, July 2005.

20. Isabel V. Sawhill, "Capitalism and the Future of Democracy," Brookings Institution, Washington, July 2019, pp. 15–16.

21. An extensive reference list is included in Douglas Irwin, "The Rise and Fall of Import Substitution," National Bureau of Economic Research Working Paper no. 27919, October 2020. Also see William Easterly, "In Search of Reforms for Growth: New Stylized Facts on Policy and Growth Outcomes," National Bureau of Economic Research Working Paper no. 26318, September 2019; and Pedro Cezar Dutra Fonseca and Ivan Colangelo Salomão, "Furtado Vs. Prebisch: A Latin American Controversy," *Investigación Económica* 77, no. 306 (2018): 74–93.

Chapter 2

1. Marco Rubio, "Industrial Policy, Right and Wrong," *National Affairs*, Spring 2024.

2. Adam Posen, "The Price of Nostalgia: America's Self-Defeating Economic Retreat," *Foreign Affairs*, May–June 2021.

3. Posen, "The Price of Nostalgia."

4. Scott Lincicome and Huan Zhu, "Questioning Industrial Policy," white paper, Cato Institute, Washington, September 28, 2021.

5. Chris Edwards, "Entrepreneurs and Regulations: Removing State and Local Barriers to New Businesses," Cato Institute Policy Analysis no. 916, May 5, 2021; Paul C. Light, "The True Size of Government Is Nearing a Record High," Brookings Institution, Washington, October 7, 2020.

6. The total was 170,325 in the 1960s, then increased more than fourfold in the 1970s. Clyde Wayne Crews Jr., *Ten Thousand Commandments: An Annual Snapshot of the Federal Regulatory State* (Washington: Competitive Enterprise Institute, 2023), p. 35, Figure 11.

7. Kofi Ampaabeng et al., "RegAuthorities: The Regulations Authorities Dataset," working paper, Mercatus Center at George Mason University, Arlington, VA, July 2022, p. 3. The *Code of Federal Regulations* is the codification of the general and permanent rules published in the *Federal Register*.

8. Nicole V. Crain and W. Mark Crain, *The Cost of Federal Regulation to the US Economy, Manufacturing and Small Business* (Washington: National Association of Manufacturers, 2023), p. 4.

9. "All Employees, Total Nonfarm and All Employees, Manufacturing," retrieved from the Federal Reserve Bank of St. Louis Economic Data, October 3, 2019.

10. Isabel V. Sawhill, "Capitalism and the Future of Democracy," Brookings Institution, Washington, July 2019, p. 15.

11. Oren Cass, "The Working Hypothesis," *The American Interest*, October 15, 2018. Cass even blames this consumer-centered approach for helping "bring about a dramatic expansion of the welfare state." Oren Cass, "Economic Piety Is a Crisis for Workers: Government Policy Should Emphasize Production, Not Consumption," *The Atlantic*, November 27, 2018.

12. Peter Navarro and Wilbur Ross, "Scoring the Trump Economic Plan: Trade, Regulatory, & Energy Policy Impacts," September 29, 2016, p. 3.

13. Navarro and Ross, "Scoring the Trump Economic Plan," p. 19.

14. Elizabeth Warren, "A Plan for Economic Patriotism," *Medium*, June 4, 2019.

15. Lael Brainard, "Is the Middle Class within Reach for Middle-Income Families?" (speech, Federal Reserve System Community Development Research Conference, Washington, May 10, 2019).

16. Sawhill, "Capitalism and the Future of Democracy," pp. 15–16.

17. Oren Cass, "America Should Adopt an Industrial Policy" (remarks, National Conservatism Conference, Washington, July 14, 2019).

18. Cass, "America Should Adopt an Industrial Policy."

19. Cass, "America Should Adopt an Industrial Policy."

20. Cass, "America Should Adopt an Industrial Policy."

21. Oren Cass, "What If We Paid Employers to Train Workers?," Manhattan Institute, New York, July 17, 2019; Oren Cass, "The Workforce-Training Grant: A New Bridge from High School to Career," Manhattan Institute, New York, July 16, 2019.

22. Warren, "A Plan for Economic Patriotism"; Pat Buchanan, "Pat Buchanan: Did Tariffs Make America Great?," AP News, August 12, 2018.

23. Warren, "A Plan for Economic Patriotism."

24. Rubio, "Industrial Policy, Right and Wrong."

25. Cass, "America Should Adopt an Industrial Policy."

26. Cass, "America Should Adopt an Industrial Policy."

27. Categorizing energy production and resource extraction as part of manufacturing is strange because those industries open access to using raw materials. Similarly, the utility and construction industries are generally viewed differently from those that produce physical goods for sale to consumers. Regardless, as described later in this chapter, including the utility and construction industries as part of the manufacturing sector inflates the average wages for manufacturing, relative to the average if the utility and construction industries were not included.

28. Formal industrial policy does not require the same type of government control over industry that a socialist system does. In Japan, for instance, the Ministry of International Trade and Industry (MITI) was able to delay Sony's entrance into the consumer electronics industry, but not to prevent it. Similarly, MITI was unsuccessful at persuading Japanese automobile manufacturers to merge into one company. David R. Henderson, "Japan and the Myth of MITI," Library of Economics and Liberty, 2002.

29. Laura LaHaye, "Mercantilism," Library of Economics and Liberty, 2019; Lawrence W. Reed, "Pelatiah Webster: America's Adam Smith and a Forgotten Founder," Foundation for Economic Education, Atlanta, July 21, 2019.

30. Douglas Irwin, "Historical Aspects of US Trade Policy," NBER Reporter, Summer 2006.

31. A 1983 New York Times article proclaimed: "Now, a new prescription—industrial policy—is sweeping intellectual and political circles. It is an idea that has been spurred by the success of the Japanese economy, and by the crucial role played by Japanese industrial policy and its centerpiece, the Ministry of International Trade and Industry." Karen Arenson, "Debate Grows over Adoption of National Industrial Policy," New York Times, June 19, 1983.

32. Robert Reich, "Why the U.S. Needs an Industrial Policy," Harvard Business Review, January 1982.

33. Reich, "Why the U.S. Needs an Industrial Policy."

34. Laura D'Andrea Tyson chaired President Clinton's Council of Economic Advisers. Robert Reich served as secretary of labor. Mitch Pearlstein, "Czary Knights for American Manufacturing?," Center of the American Experiment, Minnetonka, MN, June 18, 2019. The original source, cited by Pearlstein, is Ian Maitland, "Who Won the Industrial Policy Debate?," Center of the American Experiment, November 1994.

35. Lester C. Thurow, "Review: Free Market Fallacies—*Who's Bashing Whom? Trade Conflict in High-Technology Industries*, by Laura D'Andrea Tyson," *Foreign Policy* (Autumn, 1993): 187–91; James Risen, "Manufacturing Matters: The Myth of the Post-Industrial Economy, by Stephen S. Cohen and John Zysman," review, *Los Angeles Times*, July 26, 1987.

36. A related version of the spillover-effect argument is that the manufacturing sector is particularly important because a disproportionately large share of R&D occurs in manufacturing firms. There is evidence, however, that R&D is heavily concentrated in only a few manufacturing industries, such as pharmaceuticals and medical devices, computers and electronics, and aerospace (with the highest relative importance in pharmaceuticals and medical devices, two of the fastest-growing US manufacturing industries). Sree Ramaswamy et al., *Making It in America: Revitalizing U.S. Manufacturing* (New York: McKinsey Global Institute 2017), Exhibit E1.

37. Risen, "Manufacturing Matters."

38. Risen, "Manufacturing Matters."

39. "Largest Semiconductor Companies," CompaniesMarketCap, February 2024.

40. Richard B. McKenzie, "Industrial Policy: A Summary of Bills before Congress," Heritage Foundation Backgrounder no. 275, July 12, 1983, p. 2.

41. McKenzie, "Industrial Policy," p. 18.

42. McKenzie, "Industrial Policy," p. 18.

43. Cass, "America Should Adopt an Industrial Policy." Additionally, Cass writes, "Also probative, we should admit, is China."

44. The growth and transformation of the South Korean economy is a testament to the effect that opening markets can have. Even the *chaebols*—the large South Korean conglomerates controlled by a few wealthy families and individuals—changed the way they operated as they faced increased competition. Jung Ku-Hyun, "The Changing Face of South Korea's Business Sector amid Global Competition," in *How South Korea Is Honing a Competitive Edge*, ed. Chung Min Lee (Washington: Carnegie Endowment for International Peace, 2022); "In Brief: S. Korean Unveils Plan for Imports," *Los Angeles Times*, January 30, 1989.

45. Arvind Panagariya, "Debunking Protectionist Myths," Cato Economic Development Bulletin no. 31, July 18, 2019; Arvind Panagariya, *India: The Emerging Giant* (New York: Oxford University Press, 2008).

46. Marc Levinson, "U.S. Manufacturing in International Perspective," Congressional Research Service Report no. R42135, February 21, 2018, pp. 9–10.

47. Levinson, "U.S. Manufacturing in International Perspective," p. 10.

48. Levinson, "U.S. Manufacturing in International Perspective," p. 10.

49. Rolf Wank, "Non-Regular Employment in Germany and in Japan," Center for Asian Legal Exchange Discussion Paper no. 10, June, 2014, pp. 10–11. As of September 2019, approximately 17 percent of the US workforce reported working part time. See Bureau of Labor Statistics, Household Data, table A-9, October 4, 2019. The 2019 US figure is not grossly out of line with historical data. In 1968, less than 14 percent of Americans worked part time, and the figure peaked at 20 percent in 2010. Jill Mislinski, "The Ratio of Part-Time Employed: September 2019," Advisor Perspectives, October 7, 2019.

50. Wank, "Non-Regular Employment in Germany and Japan," p. 11.

51. Andrew Gordon, "New and Enduring Dual Structures of Employment in Japan: The Rise of Non-Regular Labor, 1980s–2010s," *Social Science Japan Journal* 20, no. 1 (2017): 9.

52. Gordon, "Dual Structures of Employment in Japan," p. 9. According to World Bank data, the Japanese population increased 7.5 percent from 1982 to 2014. World Bank, "Population Total—Japan," 2024.

53. Hartmut Seifert, "Atypical Employment in Japan and Germany," Japan Institute for Labour Policy and Training, Nerima, May 2010, p. 3.

54. In some respects, both countries underwent similar labor union reforms. See Karen Shire and Danielle Dorice Van Jaarsveld, "The Temporary Staffing Industry in Protected Employment Economies: Germany, Japan and the Netherlands," *SSRN Electronic Journal*, January 2008.

55. Werner Eichhorst and Verena Tobsch, "Not So Standard Anymore? Employment Duality in Germany," Institute for the Study of Labor Discussion Paper no. 8155, April 2014, p. 23; "The Hartz Employment Reforms in Germany," Centre for Public Impact, Australia, September 2, 2019.

56. Eichhorst and Tobsch, "Not So Standard Anymore?," p. 23.

57. Eichhorst and Tobsch, "Not So Standard Anymore?," p. 4.

58. Eichhorst and Tobsch, "Not So Standard Anymore?," p. 23.

59. Eichhorst and Tobsch, "Not So Standard Anymore?," p. 4.

60. Eichhorst and Tobsch, "Not So Standard Anymore?," p. 9.

61. Eichhorst and Tobsch, "Not So Standard Anymore?," pp. 13–14.

62. This discussion also overlooks the cost of expanding to a European-style social welfare/workforce system. Currently, European workers earning $40,000 per year pay $6,000 more in taxes than their American counterparts. See Adam Michel, "Big Government Requires High Taxes on the Middle Class," Heritage Foundation Issue Brief no. 5007, November 3, 2019.

63. OECD, "More Than 3 Million German Emigrants in OECD Countries," January 6, 2015. As a percentage, this figure (more than 4 percent of the German population) is so large that it is not even comparable to that of China or India, and it is more than double the rate of emigration for the United States, the lowest rated of the OECD countries (in absolute terms).

64. OECD, "More Than 3 Million German Emigrants." The OECD reports that the number of college-educated (tertiary) German emigrants rose by 40 percent over the previous decade mainly because of an increase in college-educated females leaving the country.

65. OECD, "More Than 3 Million German Emigrants."

66. The shift to a larger share of employment occurring in the service sector is a long-term trend in most developed nations, with the share rising to nearly 75 percent in several OECD countries during the 1990s. "The Characteristics and Quality of Service Sector Jobs," in *OECD Employment Outlook* (Paris: OECD, 2001), p. 89. More recent data show these trends exist in 21 OECD countries. See OECD Employment Outlook, "How Technology and Globalisation Are Transforming the Labour Market," 2017, Figure 3.8.

67. Colin Grabow, "The Reality of American 'Deindustrialization,'" Cato Institute, Washington, October 24, 2023.

68. Mark Riddix, "U.S. Needs to Return to Its Manufacturing Base," *Seeking Alpha*, February 8, 2009.

69. These data, "Manufacturing Sector: Real Output," are available from the Federal Reserve Bank of St. Louis Economic Data, at https://fred.stlouisfed.org /series/OUTMS. For perspective, the value of manufacturing output increased by 33 percent from 1991 to 2000; by 16 percent from 2001 to 2007, before the Great Recession; and by 16 percent from 2009 to 2014 after the recession. As a share of GDP, the real value of manufacturing output varied little between 1947 and 2019, ranging between 11.17 percent and 13.62 percent. For data through 2015, see YiLi Chien and Paul Morris, "Is U.S. Manufacturing Really Declining?," Federal Reserve Bank of St. Louis, April 11, 2017.

70. Robert Reich, "America's Problem Isn't Free Trade—It's the Demise of an Entire Economic System," *Salon*, March 17, 2016; Cass, "America Should Adopt an Industrial Policy"; David Langdon and Rebecca Lehrman, "The Benefits of Manufacturing Jobs," Economics and Statistics Administration Issue Brief no. 01-12, May 2012.

71. Reich, "America's Problem Isn't Free Trade."

72. Though not *steadily* decreasing, the overall declining trend actually started in 1920. Stanley Lebergott, "Labor Force and Employment, 1800–1960," in *Output, Employment, and Productivity in the United States after 1800*, ed. Dorothy S. Brady (Cambridge, MA: National Bureau of Economic Research, 1966), pp. 117–204. Separately, the same decreasing trend is seen in all G7 countries starting in 1970. Ryan Bourne, "Do Oren Cass's Justifications for Industrial Policy Stack Up?," Cato Institute, Washington, August 15, 2019.

73. Louis D. Johnston, "History Lessons: Understanding the Decline in Manufacturing," *MinnPost*, February 22, 2012; Thomas Weiss and Susan Carter, "Services and Utilities," in *Historical Statistics of the United States*, Millennial Edition Online, ed. Susan B. Carter et al. (New York: Cambridge University Press, 2006).

74. Johnston, "Understanding the Decline in Manufacturing."

75. Evidence suggests that, internationally, economies shift away from manufacturing and into services as people's living standards rise. For a summary, see "People Want to Spend More on Services as They Get Rich," *The Week*, March 23, 2021. Also see Diego Comin, Danial Lashkari, and Martí Mestieri, "Structural Change with Long-Run Income and Price Effects," *Econometrica* 89, no. 1 (2021): 311–74; Gale Pooley and Marian L. Tupy, "How Dematerialization Is Changing the World: A Response to Giorgos Kallis," Cato Unbound, April 27, 2021; and

Andrew McAfee, *More from Less: The Surprising Story of How We Learned to Prosper Using Fewer Resources—and What Happens Next?* (New York: Scribner, 2019).

76. Marc Levinson, "Job Creation in the Manufacturing Revival," Congressional Research Service Report no. R41898, July 19, 2019.

77. Levinson, "Job Creation in the Manufacturing Revival," p. 8.

78. Bureau of Labor Statistics, Establishment Data, table B-8, October 4, 2019. "Manufacturing earnings" refers to combined durable and nondurable goods manufacturing.

79. Levinson, "Job Creation in the Manufacturing Revival," p. 7. The 2023 data are available at Bureau of Labor Statistics, Current Population Survey, table 18b.

80. Levinson, "Job Creation in the Manufacturing Revival," p. 15.

81. For several examples, see Alana Semuels, "America Is Still Making Things," *The Atlantic*, January 6, 2017.

82. Robert Z. Lawrence, "Recent Manufacturing Employment Growth: The Exception That Proves the Rule," National Bureau of Economic Research Working Paper no. 24151, December 2017, p. 3.

83. Levinson, "Job Creation in the Manufacturing Revival," pp. 5–6 (emphasis added).

84. All these figures are from industries in the "51-0000 Production Occupations" classification of the Bureau of Labor Statistics' May 2018 Occupation Profiles. Bureau of Labor Statistics, Occupational Employment Statistics, March 29, 2019.

85. The annual mean wage for Rhode Island was $37,620, and $28,680 for California. The annual mean wage in the *textile furnishing mills* industry was $33,720, and $26,570 in the *knitting mills* industry. See Bureau of Labor Statistics, Occupational Employment and Wages, May 2018, *51-6061 Textile Bleaching and Dyeing Machine Operators and Tenders*, March 29, 2019.

86. Levinson, "Job Creation in the Manufacturing Revival," p. 5.

87. Other industries within the manufacturing sector display the same types of job diversity. Levinson, "Job Creation in the Manufacturing Revival," p. 5.

88. Charlotte Oslund, "Which Industries Need Workers? Exploring Differences in Labor Market Activity," *Monthly Labor Review*, BLS, January 2016.

89. Oslund, "Which Industries Need Workers?," p. 17.

90. Oslund, "Which Industries Need Workers?," p. 13.

91. Edward Lazear and Kristin McCue, "What Causes Labor Turnover to Vary?," National Bureau of Economic Research Working Paper no. 24873, December 2018, p. 4.

92. Perhaps owing to the translation from German to English, the age range for "young people" is unclear. For 2018, the government reports that "the calculated proportion is 54.5 percent of young people (resident population) who begin dual vocational training at some point in their lives," and includes various descriptive statistics for people ages 16 to 24. Federal Institute for Vocational Education and Training, *Data Report 2020*. For 2017, the government reports, "In 2017 the calculated share of the resident population starting an apprenticeship in the dual system was 52.9 percent." German population statistics appear to indicate that the correct denominator is a subgroup of younger German workers rather

than the whole population. Apprenticeship Toolbox, *Apprenticeship System in Germany*, October 4, 2019. In a 2022 report, the government attributes the long-term decline to, among other factors, (a) the "declining numbers of school leavers," (b) "a trend towards higher school qualifications," (c) an "increased willingness to study," and (d) continuing "difficulties in matching training supply and demand." The 2022 report also attributes a temporary rise between 2015 and 2016 to an increased number of refugees. Federal Institute for Vocational Education and Training, *Data Report 2022*.

93. Apprenticeship Toolbox.

94. Dietmar Harhoff and Thomas Kane, "Is the German Apprenticeship System a Panacea for the US Labour Market?," *Journal of Population Economics* 10, no. 2 (1997): 172. Although it appears that little empirical work on this issue has been done recently, researchers at the Richmond Federal Reserve provided an overview in 2014. Nika Lazaryan, Urvi Neelakantan, and David Price, "The Prevalence of Apprenticeships in Germany and the United States," Federal Reserve Bank of Richmond Economic Brief no. 14-08, August 2014.

95. The departure rate was 50 percent for large industrial firms. Harhoff and Kane, "Is the German Apprenticeship System a Panacea?," pp. 172–73.

96. Harhoff and Kane, "Is the German Apprenticeship System a Panacea?," p. 187. Both groups earn between 40 and 50 percent less than their respective college graduate populations.

97. Rainer Winkelmann, "Employment Prospects and Skill Acquisition of Apprenticeship-Trained Workers in Germany," *Industrial and Labor Relations Review* 49, no. 4 (1996): 658.

98. Winkelmann, "Employment Prospects and Skill Acquisition," p. 658.

99. Winkelmann, "Employment Prospects and Skill Acquisition," p. 671.

100. Eric Hanushek et al., "General Education, Vocational Education, and Labor-Market Outcomes over the Lifecycle," *Journal of Human Resources* 52, no. 1 (2017): 83–84.

101. Giorgio Brunello, "The Effect of Economic Downturns on Apprenticeships and Initial Workplace Training: A Review of the Evidence," OECD, Paris, June 2009, p. 4.

102. American colonists provided long-term indentures for many poor children, a system that developed into formal apprenticeships that, in turn, fell out of favor as the K–12 public education system developed. John Murray and Ruth Herndon, "Markets for Children in Early America: A Political Economy of Pauper Apprenticeship," *Journal of Economic History* 62, no. 2 (2002): 356–82; Mark R. Snyder, "The Education of Indentured Servants in Colonial America," *Journal of Technology Studies* 33, no. 2 (2007): 65–72. Of course, several trades, such as electrical and plumbing, still require formal apprentice training to obtain a license. See Vista College, "9 Big Differences between Electrical, Plumbing, and HVAC Career Paths," January 2, 2019.

103. *Apprenticeship Training in the 1970s: Report of a Conference*, Manpower Administration Research Monograph no. 37, 1974.

104. Benjamin Collins, "Registered Apprenticeship: Federal Role and Recent Federal Efforts," Congressional Research Service Report no. R45171, September 25, 2019.

105. Jeffrey Zients and Thomas Perez, "ApprenticeshipUSA Is Upskilling America," White House, October 21, 2016.

106. See The German Way & More, "Education," 2019. Homeschooling is forbidden in the German system.

107. Hiroshi Ono, "Who Goes to College? Features of Institutional Tracking in Japanese Higher Education," *American Journal of Education* 109, no. 2 (2001): 161–95.

108. Cass, *The Once and Future Worker*, p. 102.

109. Cass, *The Once and Future Worker*, p. 103.

110. There is surely much room to improve the government-monopoly public education system in the United States, but the nation has a long and controversial history with efforts to differentiate students on the basis of academic potential. Indeed, the term "tracking" was long ago misappropriated by those who opposed efforts to differentiate students based on academic ability. For a description of the effort to eradicate programs for gifted students from US public schools in the name of equity, see Cheri Yecke, *The War against Excellence: The Rising Tide of Mediocrity in America's Middle Schools* (Westport, CT: Praeger, 2003). For a different perspective, see George Ansalone, "Tracking: A Return to Jim Crow," *Race, Gender & Class* 13, no. 1–2 (2006): 144–53.

111. *County of Butler, et al., v. Thomas W. Wolf, et al.*, Civil Action no. 2:20-cv-677, Hon. William S. Stickman IV, US District Court for the Western District of Pennsylvania, Filed September 14, 2020, pp. 51–52.

112. "Are Too Many Students Going to College?," *Chronicle Review*, November 8, 2009.

113. The 1965 Higher Education Act authorizes many federal programs that support individuals pursuing a postsecondary education as well as the institutions providing such education, including all major federal student financial aid programs. Kyle Shohfi and Rita Zota, "The Higher Education Act (HEA): A Primer," Congressional Research Service, Washington, April 10, 2023.

114. Mary Clare Amselem, "The Johnson Era: Federal Involvement in Higher Education," in *The Not-So-Great Society*, ed. Lindsey Burke and Jonathan Butcher (Washington: Heritage Foundation, 2019), pp. 113–24.

115. Neal McCluskey, "Is College Worth It? How the War on Poverty Relates to the 'Sheepskin Effect' and Upward Mobility in America," in Burke and Butcher, *The Not-So-Great Society*, pp. 133–40; Erin Valdez, "No, You Don't 'Have to Go to College to Become a Welder,'" *National Review*, December 2, 2019; Walter E. Williams, "Fraud in Higher Education," *Daily Signal*, December 4, 2019.

116. Cass, "What If We Paid Employers to Train Workers?"

117. In general, the results of federal job training programs have been poor. David B. Muhlhausen, "Federal Job Training Fails Again," Heritage Foundation Backgrounder no. 3198, March 10, 2017; David B. Muhlhausen, *Do Federal Social Programs Work?* (Santa Barbara, CA: Praeger, 2013), pp. 212–303.

118. House Committee on Ways and Means, "Summary of Welfare Reforms Made by Public Law 104-193, the Personal Responsibility and Work Opportunity Reconciliation Act and Associated Legislation," 104th Cong., 2nd sess., November 6, 1996, table 1; and US Government Accountability Office, "Multiple Employment

and Training Programs: Providing Information on Colocating Services and Consolidating Administrative Structures Could Promote Efficiencies," GAO-11-92, January 2011.

119. The Wagner-Peyser Act of 1933 established a national system of public employment offices known as the Employment Service. US Department of Labor, Wagner-Peyser Act of June 6, 1933, November 10, 2010.

120. David Bradley, "The Workforce Investment Act and the One-Stop Delivery System," Congressional Research Service Report no. R41135, June 14, 2013, p. 2. According to a 1967 Department of Labor report, between 1962 and 1966, "training opportunities under institutional, on-the-job, and combination programs were authorized for over 835,000 persons at a cost of over $1 billion," and training occurred "in all the major occupational groups and in more than 1300 different occupations." Manpower Administration, *The Manpower Development and Training Act: A Review of Training Activities* (Washington: US Department of Health, Education and Welfare, 1967); John F. Kennedy, "Special Message to the Congress: The Manpower Report of the President," March 11, 1963.

121. Bradley, "Workforce Investment Act," p. 3.

122. Bradley, "Workforce Investment Act," p. 3. According to the Center for the Study of Federalism (citing multiple government reports), under the Comprehensive Employment and Training Act of 1973, the Department of Labor "spending for employment and training during the Carter years totaled $34 billion, more than 2.5 times the amount during 1973–76, with about 4 million eligible individuals receiving training or public service jobs each year." Center for the Study of Federalism, *Comprehensive Employment and Training Act*, 2006.

123. Bradley, "Workforce Investment Act," p. 3; Robert Guttman, "Job Training Partnership Act: New Help for the Unemployed," *Monthly Labor Review*, BLS, March 1983.

124. US Government Accountability Office, "Multiple Employment and Training Programs: Providing Information on Colocating Services and Consolidating Administrative Structures Could Promote Efficiencies," GAO-11-92, January 2011, p. 3; US Government Accountability Office, "Multiple Employment Training Programs Overlapping Programs Can Add Unnecessary Administrative Costs," GAO-94-80, January 1994.

125. H.R. 1385, Workforce Investment Partnership Act of 1998, 105th Cong., 2nd sess., 1997–1998.

126. Bradley, "Workforce Investment Act." Many other federal programs are not listed in this summary. For instance, the Economic Opportunity Act of 1964 created the Job Corps, a program that still exists today and has always provided job training for disadvantaged youths.

127. It is difficult to precisely measure the amount of federal money flowing to such programs because some colleges that receive funds are highly specialized (such as game developer DigiPen Institute of Technology and the Refrigeration School), but others are four-year degree-granting institutions. Adam Andrzejewski and Thomas W. Smith, *Open the Books Oversight Report* (Washington: US Department of Education, April 2019). It is also difficult to gauge the precise

amount that states spend—though many spend millions per year—on vocational training, frequently referred to as "career and technical education." Advance CTE and the Association for Career and Technical Education, *State Policies Impacting CTE: 2018 Year In Review* (Alexandria, VA: Association for Career and Technical Education, 2019).

128. Bradley, "Workforce Investment Act," pp. 40–42.

129. Molly Forman and Ann Lordeman, "The Job Training Partnership Act: Training Programs at a Glance," Congressional Research Service Report for Congress no. 94-807 EPW, February 19, 1998; Robert Guttman, "Job Training Partnership Act: New Help for The Unemployed," *Monthly Labor Review*, BLS, March 1983. Page 3 of Guttman notes: "In its brief history, from 1973 to 1982, CETA [Comprehensive Employment and Training Act] was amended eight times and proliferated 12 separate programmatic titles, parts, and subparts. The instability of program design resulting from the constant legislative changes was exacerbated by even more severe funding instabilities. In 8 fiscal years, there were 26 separate appropriations for the program."

130. Author's calculations based on the original statutes that created the programs, agency budget justifications and operating plans, and multiple reports by the Congressional Research Service and the US Government Accountability Office. Any missing appropriations between renewal dates are assumed to have increased by 2 percent over the previous year; holding these values constant does not materially change the total. All amounts are adjusted to 2013 dollars with the personal consumption expenditure. Clarence C. Crawford, associate director of education and employment issues, Health, Education, and Human Services Division, US Government Accountability Office, Testimony on "Multiple Employment Training Programs" before the House Subcommittee on Postsecondary Education, Training and Lifelong Learning of the Committee on Economic and Educational Opportunities, 104th Cong., 1st sess., February 6, 1995; (author's name redacted), "The Workforce Investment Act and the One-Stop Delivery System," Congressional Research Service Report no. R41135, January 2015; Karen Spar, "Job Training Programs: Reauthorization and Funding Issues," Congressional Research Service Issue Brief no. IB82005, January 3, 1983; Forman and Lordeman, "The Job Training Partnership Act."

131. Technically, the DOL's Employment and Training Administration (ETA) funded the organization. R. Thayne Robson, ed., *Employment and Training R&D: Lessons Learned and Future Directions* (Kalamazoo, MI: Upjohn Institute for Employment Research, 1984), pp. vii–viii. In fiscal year 2019, the ETA's budget was $36.9 billion, down from $143 billion in 2012. See US Department of Labor, Employment and Training Administration website, updated August 12, 2019.

132. Zients and Perez, "ApprenticeshipUSA Is Upskilling America"; Naomi Jagoda, "Obama Administration Awards $50M in Apprenticeship Grants," *The Hill*, October 21, 2016.

133. US Department of Labor, Apprenticeship Grant Opportunities website.

134. D. Wilson and D. Mark Wilson, "Time to End the Troubled School-to-Work Program," Heritage Foundation, Washington, September 22, 1999. All 50 states received School-to-Work implementation grants. In 1999, Congress

appropriated $503 million for the program, and as of 1999, a total of $2 billion had been appropriated.

135. Bradley, "Workforce Investment Act and the One-Stop Delivery System."

136. Marcus Penny, "The Perkins Act Has Finally Been Reauthorized," *Innovation and Policy Blog*, Education Evolving, August 1, 2018.

137. Individual annual totals available (from 1997 through 2010) at US Department of Education, Vocational Education—Basic Grants to States, January 31, 2012.

138. States allocate federal CTE funding to their own districts based on various criteria, including education funding calculations, historical practices, governance, and state-level priorities. State of CTE, "Secondary CTE Funding Basics," 2024.

139. Author's calculations using US Department of Education, *Career and Technical Education State Grants*, July 2019, p. 20.

140. Jolanta Juszkiewicz, "Trends in Community College Enrollment and Completion Data, Issue 5," American Association of Community Colleges, Washington, May 2019, p. 5; National Center for Education Statistics, "Total Fall Enrollment in Degree-Granting Postsecondary Institutions, by Attendance Status, Sex of Student, and Control of Institution: Selected Years, 1947 through 2023," table 303.10; National Center for Education Statistics, "Number and Percentage Distribution of Students Enrolled at Title IV Institutions, by Control of Institution, Student Level, Level of Institution, Enrollment Status, and Other Selected Characteristics: United States, Fall 2018," table 01 (school year 2018–19).

141. For comparison, 10.8 million students were enrolled in (all) four-year institutions as of 2017. For both two-year and four-year enrollment figures, see US Department of Education, National Center for Education Statistics, "Undergraduate Enrollment," May 2019.

142. US Department of Education, National Center for Education Statistics, "Fast Facts, Financial Aid."

143. US Department of Education, National Center for Education Statistics, "Trends in Pell Grant Receipt and the Characteristics of Pell Grant Recipients: Selected Years, 1999–2000 to 2011–12," September 2015, p. 21, table 1.4.

144. US Department of Education, National Center for Education Statistics, "Trends in Pell Grant Receipt and the Characteristics of Pell Grant Recipients: Selected Years, 2003–04 to 2015–16," September 2019, p. 19, table 1.4.

145. Tad DeHaven, "Corporate Welfare in the Federal Budget," Cato Institute Policy Analysis no. 703, July 25, 2012.

146. Chris Edwards, "Independence in 1776; Dependence in 2023," *Cato at Liberty* (blog), July 3, 2023. Data drawn from SAM.gov, July 2023.

147. Jacob Kastrenakes, "Amazon Cancels HQ2 in New York after Backlash," *The Verge*, February 14, 2019.

148. David R. Henderson, "Rent Seeking," Library of Economics and Liberty, n.d.

149. Cass, for instance, argues: "Whether we do nothing . . . whether we do what I might propose, we are going to have that set of problems [including cronyism and failed projects funded by taxpayers]. And it seems to me that's almost a

baseline that we need to work within." Cass, "America Should Adopt an Industrial Policy."

150. Cronyism diminishes opportunities for people because it boosts profits for the well-connected at the expense of others. Policies like tariffs create opportunities for the well-connected to gain at the expense of others. Virtually all tariffs are implemented with certain exemptions and exceptions because companies petition the government. At best, these exemptions give certain companies a small advantage over their competitors who fail to win exemptions; at worst, they harm American consumers and workers through higher prices, fewer goods and services, and fewer jobs.

151. This same problem applies to industrial policy under various names, including mercantilism, corporate welfare, crony capitalism, state capitalism, venture socialism, political capitalism, and political entrepreneurship. See David Burton, "Comparing Free Enterprise and Socialism," Heritage Foundation, Special Report No. 213, April 30, 2019, pp. 2–3.

152. Robert Anderton, Benedetta Di Lupidio, and Barbara Jarmulska, "Product Market Regulation, Business Churning and Productivity: Evidence from the European Union Countries," European Central Bank Working Paper no. 2332, November 2019. Research also shows that a larger volume of nonproductive government spending, and the associated taxation, decrease economic growth. Robert J. Barro, *Determinants of Economic Growth: A Cross-Country Empirical Study* (Cambridge, MA: MIT Press, 1997), p. 26.

Chapter 3

1. Christopher Klein, "The Original Luddites Raged against the Machine of the Industrial Revolution," *History*, January 4, 2019.

2. In 1961, labor secretary Arthur Goldberg created a group to explore this issue because of concerns that automation had contributed to recent job losses. "Business: The Automation Jobless," *Time*, February 24, 1961.

3. National Commission on Technology, Automation and Economic Progress, *Technology and the American Economy*, Vol. 1 (Washington: Government Printing Office, 1966), p. xi.

4. Steve Ditlea, "Steve Jobs, the Man Who Changed Business Forever," *Inc.*, October 1981.

5. Ditlea, "Steve Jobs."

6. For a formal theoretical treatment of the complementary and substitutable nature of capital and labor (the scale effects and the substitution effects), see Sonia Jaffe et al., *Chicago Price Theory* (Princeton: NJ: Princeton University Press, 2019), pp. 126–34.

7. For a historical perspective, see Joel Mokyr, Chris Vickers, and Nicolas L. Ziebarth, "The History of Technological Anxiety and the Future of Economic Growth: Is This Time Different?," *Journal of Economic Perspectives* 29, no. 3 (2015): 31–50.

8. David H. Autor, "Why Are There Still So Many Jobs? The History and Future of Workplace Automation," *Journal of Economic Perspectives* 29, no. 3 (2015): 5.

9. Michael Corkery and David Gelles, "Robots Welcome to Take Over, as Pandemic Accelerates Automation," *New York Times*, April 10, 2020; Richard Morrison,

"Robots Are Here to Make Your Job Safer and Cleaner," *Open Market Blog*, April 10, 2020.

10. Claire Miller, "The Long-Term Jobs Killer Is Not China. It's Automation," *New York Times*, December 21, 2016. The article quotes Harvard economist Lawrence Katz: "Over the long haul, clearly automation's been much more important—it's not even close."

11. In the 1940s, author Henry Hazlitt wrote of the belief that automation causes unemployment, "Destroyed a thousand times, it has risen a thousand times out of its own ashes as hard and vigorous as ever." Henry Hazlitt, *Economics in One Lesson*, 2nd ed. (New York: Crown Publishing, 1979), p. 49. Hazlitt also cites a syndicated column by Eleanor Roosevelt from 1945, in which she proclaims, "We have reached a point today where labor-saving devices are good only when they do not throw the worker out of his job" (see p. 54).

12. Paul Krugman and Robert Lawrence, "Trade, Jobs, and Wages," National Bureau of Economic Research Working Paper no. 4478, September 1993, p. 3.

13. David H. Autor, David Dorn, and Gordon H. Hanson, "The China Shock: Learning from Labor-Market Adjustment to Large Changes in Trade," *Annual Review of Economics* 8, no. 1 (2016): 206; Claudia Goldin and Lawrence Katz, *The Race between Education and Technology* (Cambridge, MA: Belknap Press of Harvard University Press, 2009). Goldin and Katz argue that, for most of the 20th century, jobs created by new technologies were "skill-biased" in that they required new skills, but that skill development did not keep pace with technological change. They reject the idea that changes in the demand for skills have resulted in higher income inequality (p. 101) and also rule out immigration as a source of higher earnings differentials (p. 309). Additionally, evidence shows that higher productivity growth has led to more jobs in US manufacturing, even as manufacturing employment declined. William Nordhaus, "The Sources of the Productivity Rebound and the Manufacturing Employment Puzzle," National Bureau of Economic Research Working Paper no. 11354, May 2005.

14. Autor, Dorn, and Hanson, "The China Shock," pp. 208–9; Susan Houseman, "Understanding the Decline of U.S. Manufacturing Employment," Upjohn Institute Working Paper no. 18-287, January 2018 (revised June 2018).

15. John Keilman, "America Is Back in the Factory Business," *Wall Street Journal*, April 8, 2023.

16. Bureau of Labor Statistics, *Employment Situation Summary*, November 1, 2019.

17. Gross job gains and losses for various years are available from Bureau of Labor Statistics, *Business Employment Dynamics*; figures from 1994, as reported here, are available from the BLS at https://data.bls.gov/cgi-bin/dsrv?bd.

18. Gil Press, "Is AI Going to Be a Jobs Killer? New Reports about the Future of Work," *Forbes*, July 15, 2019; Ben Casselman and Adam Satariano, "Amazon's Latest Experiment: Retraining Its Work Force," *New York Times*, July 11, 2019; Jennifer Huddleston, "What Might Good AI Policy Look Like? Four Principles for a Light Touch Approach to Artificial Intelligence," *Cato at Liberty* (blog), November 9, 2023; "How Businesses Are Actually Using Generative AI," *The Economist*, February 29, 2024.

19. Erik Brynjolfsson, Danielle Li, and Lindsey Raymond, "Generative AI at Work," National Bureau of Economic Research Working Paper no. 31161, revised November 2023.

20. Shakked Noy and Whitney Zhang, "Experimental Evidence on the Productivity Effects of Generative Artificial Intelligence," working paper, March 1, 2023.

21. Sida Peng et al., "The Impact of AI on Developer Productivity: Evidence from GitHub Copilot," arXiv, February 13, 2023; Jakob Nielsen, "AI Improves Employee Productivity by 66%," Nielsen Norman Group, Fremont, CA, July 16, 2023; McKinsey Digital, "The Economic Potential of Generative AI: The Next Productivity Frontier," June 14, 2023.

22. Carl Benedikt Frey and Michael Osborne, "The Future of Employment: How Susceptible Are Jobs to Computerisation?," working paper, September 17, 2013, p. 38. The paper was republished in 2017 in the *Journal of Technological Forecasting and Social Change* 114, no. 1 (2017): 254–80.

23. Frey and Osborne, "The Future of Employment," pp. 36, 42.

24. As noted in Michael Coelli and Jeff Borland, "Behind the Headline Number: Why Not to Rely on Frey and Osborne's Predictions of Potential Job Loss from Automation," Melbourne Institute Working Paper no. 10/19, October 2019, p. 4. A 2017 McKinsey study uses a similarly subjective method to estimate that "about half of all the *activities* people are paid to do in the world's workforce could potentially be automated by adapting currently demonstrated technologies" (emphasis added). The McKinsey study does not estimate how many jobs could be automated. McKinsey & Company, "A Future That Works: Automation, Employment, and Productivity," January 2017, Executive Summary.

25. Coelli and Borland, "Behind the Headline Number," p. 3.

26. Coelli and Borland, "Behind the Headline Number," p. 20.

27. Melanie Arntz, Terry Gregory, Ulrich Zierahn, "Revisiting the Risk of Automation," *Economics Letters* 159 (2017): 157–60.

28. Daron Acemoglu and Pascual Restrepo, "Robots and Jobs: Evidence from US Labor Markets," National Bureau of Economic Research Working Paper no. 23285, March 2017, p. 4. The authors note that their estimates imply that the addition of one more robot reduces employment in a commuting zone (a geographic area designed to fully capture a location's economy) by 6.2 workers. These results are difficult to generalize to the overall economy, where total nonfarm employment increased 25 percent (to 137.5 million jobs) from 1993 to 2007, partly because industrial robots are not in widespread use and are heavily concentrated in the automotive (39 percent) and electronics (19 percent) industries; see p. 2.

29. Georg Graetz and Guy Michaels, "Robots at Work," *Review of Economics and Statistics* 100, no. 5 (2018): 753–68. Graetz and Michaels report that increased industrial robot use added about 0.36 percentage points to annual labor productivity growth. Although the results suggest that low-skilled laborers' relative share of hours decreased, they do not show that their wage *levels* declined. The fact that the *share* decreased only suggests that there will likely be a larger wage (and investment) effect in the long run because diminishing returns to investments

in new machines set in rather slowly. A 2014 *American Economic Review* paper suggests that automation had virtually no effect on manufacturing employment from 1980 to 2009 except in the *computer and electronic product manufacturing* industry. The authors report, "There is some differential productivity growth in IT-intensive industries in the late 1990s, but this effect is very small (on the order of a few percentage points at its peak) and subsides after 2001. By 2009, there is no net relative productivity gain in IT-intensive industries over the full sample period." Daron Acemoglu et al., "Return of the Solow Paradox? IT, Productivity, and Employment in US Manufacturing," *American Economic Review, Papers & Proceedings* 104, no. 5 (2014): 396. For a discussion of how long time lags can explain why some recent technological advances have not yet resulted in measurable productivity increases, see Erik Brynjolfsson, Daniel Rock, and Chad Syverson, "Artificial Intelligence and the Modern Productivity Paradox: A Clash of Expectations and Statistics," National Bureau of Economic Research Working Paper no. 24001, November 2017.

30. Seiko Kitahara and Toshiaki Shinozaki, "Do Digital Technologies Complement or Substitute for Human Labor?," Economic and Social Research Institute Discussion Paper Series no. 351, September 2019, pp. 16–17.

31. As of 2016, the United States, with only 8.6 percent of its population employed in manufacturing, used just 189 industrial robots per 10,000 manufacturing workers, whereas Japanese, German, and South Korean manufacturers used 303, 309, and 631 robots per 10,000 workers, respectively, while 16.9 percent, 19 percent, and 16.9 percent of their countries' populations, respectively, were employed in manufacturing. Riley Ohlson, "John Oliver's Segment on Jobs and Automation Doesn't Quite Get It Right," Alliance for American Manufacturing, Washington, March 7, 2019. For the United States, 8.6 percent refers to the ratio of total manufacturing employees to total nonfarm employees.

32. For a brief discussion, see Autor, "The History and Future of Workplace Automation."

33. Autor, "The History and Future of Workplace Automation," p. 6.

34. Daron Acemoglu and Pascual Restrepo, "Automation and New Tasks: How Technology Displaces and Reinstates Labor," *Journal of Economic Perspectives* 33, no. 2 (2019): 3–30.

35. Jon Greenberg, "What's the Manufacturing Job Killer, Automation or Trade?," *Politifact*, October 16, 2019, quoting Dartmouth's Teresa Fort. For recent evidence of this sort of effect, where productivity is endogenously enhanced by trade, see Wen-Tai Hsu, Raymond Riezman, and Ping Wang, "Innovation, Growth, and Dynamic Gains from Trade," National Bureau of Economic Research Working Paper no. 26470, November 2019.

36. Economist William Nordhaus has estimated that 98 percent of the economic gains from innovation and entrepreneurship are received by persons other than the innovator. William D. Nordhaus, "Schumpeterian Profits in the American Economy: Theory and Measurement," National Bureau of Economic Research Working Paper no. 10433, April 2004.

37. These figures refer to the Bureau of Labor Statistics' series *All Employees, Thousands, Finance and Insurance, Seasonally Adjusted, (CES5552000001),* available from the Federal Reserve Bank of St. Louis Economic Data.

38. These employment data are for the occupation codes 13-2051 (*financial analysts*) and 13-2052 (*personal financial advisors*), both taken from the BLS Occupational Employment Statistics Surveys in 2000 and 2018, respectively. The data are available from the BLS at https://www.bls.gov/oes/tables.htm.

39. James Bessen, "Toil and Technology," *Finance & Development* 52, no. 1 (2015): 16–19.

40. Bessen, "Toil and Technology," p. 17.

41. Research suggests that ATMs improved the quality of banking services among many dimensions, including, but not limited to, reduced waiting times in lines to withdraw or deposit cash. See, for example, Bernardo Bátiz-Lazo, "A Brief History of the ATM," *The Atlantic*, March 26, 2015.

42. Bessen, "Toil and Technology," p. 17.

43. These figures refer to the official employment–population ratio, which reports the percentage of the civilian noninstitutional population that is employed. The numbers do not reflect a percentage of the overall population.

44. Each of these figures is available from the Federal Reserve Bank of St. Louis Economic Data https://fred.stlouisfed.org/ using the following series: Population, Total for United States (POPTOTUSA647NWDB); Employment-Population Ratio (EMRATIO); All Employees, Total Nonfarm (PAYEMS); and, All Employees, Manufacturing (MANEMP).

45. Oren Cass, "The Terminator Myth: It's Not Robots That Hurt Workers," *e21* commentary, Manhattan Institute, New York, June 27, 2019.

46. Cass, "The Terminator Myth."

47. Tori Smith and Gabriella Beaumont-Smith, "11 Common Questions about U.S. Trade with China," Heritage Foundation, Washington, April 30, 2019, Chart 1. The author's own calculations, using multiple metrics released by the BLS and Bureau of Economic Analysis, also support this finding.

48. Donald Schneider, "Pay, Productivity, and the Labor Share," *Medium*, July 11, 2023.

49. Figure 3.3 is based on authors' calculations using "Gross Output by Industry: US Bureau of Economic Analysis (BEA)." Bureau of Labor Statistics, All Employees, Manufacturing [MANEMP], retrieved from the Federal Reserve Bank of St. Louis Economic Data, April 5, 2024. Bureau of Economic Analysis, Personal Consumption Expenditures Excluding Food and Energy (Chain-Type Price Index) [PCEPILFE], retrieved from the Federal Reserve Bank of St. Louis Economic Data, March 29, 2024.

50. American Institute of Steel Construction, "Structural Steel: An Industry Overview," white paper, August 2018, p. 3.

51. In 1950, global crude steel production was less than 200 million metric tons. Throughout the 1950s, the United States produced under half the world's annual steel consumption. Worldsteel.org, *World Steel in Figures*, 2007; Lloyd Kenward, "The Decline of the US Steel Industry," International Monetary Fund, Washington, December 1987; Chris Isadore, "When American Steel Was King," *CNN Money*, March 9, 2018. The author's estimate assumes 398,829 workers were employed in steel production in 1980. It assumes an eight-hour day for 251 workdays per year, resulting in 2,008 hours per year and 800,848,632 work-hours per

year. The hypothetical total steel production is 1.3 billion tons, compared with global steel production of 2.1 billion tons. For the 1980 steel production employment figure, see David Tarr, "The Steel Crisis in the United States and the European Community: Causes and Adjustments," in *Issues in US-EC Trade Relations*, ed. Robert E. Baldwin, Carl B. Hamilton, and André Sapir (Chicago: University of Chicago Press, 1988), pp. 173–200. For global steel production, see US Department of Commerce, International Trade Administration, Global Steel Report 2019.

Chapter 4

1. Thomas Holmes and James A. Schmitz, "Competition and Productivity: A Review of Evidence," Federal Reserve Bank of Minneapolis, Research Department Staff Report no. 439, February 2010; Competition and Markets Authority, *Productivity and Competition: A Summary of the Evidence* (London: Competition and Markets Authority, 2015).

2. It stands to reason that increased trade, because it leads to lower consumer prices, would most benefit the lowest-income Americans, who spend a greater share of their household budgets on necessities like housing, food, and clothing. The flip side of the finding, from this chapter, is that tariffs and trade barriers harm the lowest-income Americans the most. For evidence that supports this position, see Xavier Jaravel and Erick Sager, "What Are the Price Effects of Trade? Evidence from the U.S. and Implications for Quantitative Trade Models," Federal Reserve Board of Governors, Washington, September 2019; and Daniel Carroll and Sewon Hur, "On the Heterogeneous Welfare Gains and Losses from Trade," Federal Reserve Bank of Cleveland Working Paper no. 19-06R2, September 2019.

3. Adam Smith, "On the Unreasonableness of Those Extraordinary Restraints upon Other Principles," in *An Inquiry into the Nature and Causes of the Wealth of Nations*, ed. Edwin Cannan (London: W. Strahan and T. Cadell, 1776; New York: Random House, 1994), bk 4, chap. 3, pt 2, p. 527.

4. US International Trade Commission, "Harmonized Tariff Schedule of the United States (2016) Supplement 1, Update 1," Publication no. 4635, August 2016; "Big Government Policies That Hurt the Poor and How to Address Them," Daren Bakst and Patrick Tyrell, eds., Heritage Foundation Special Report no. 176, April 5, 2017, pp. 7–11; Gabriella Beaumont-Smith, "Trade in Real Life: Sorry Charlie (and Senator Warner) for Terrible Tuna Tariffs," *Cato at Liberty* (blog), June 12, 2023. For the origin of the US tariff schedule's detailed classifications, see Miguel Acosta and Lydia Cox, "The Regressive Nature of the U.S. Tariff Code: Origins and Implications," conditionally accepted, *Quarterly Journal of Economics*, February 2024.

5. Bakst and Tyrell, "Big Government Policies That Hurt the Poor," p. 11.

6. Dan Griswold, "Why Are Pickups So Expensive? Blame the Chicken Tax," Cato Institute, Washington, March 13, 2022; "The Chicken War: A Battle Guide," *New York Times*, January 10, 1964.

7. International Trade Commission, "Harmonized Tariff Schedule."

8. International Trade Commission, "Harmonized Tariff Schedule." These figures have been similar for several years. For an example using 2015 data, see Bakst and Tyrell, eds., "Big Government Policies That Hurt the Poor."

9. Adam Smith wrote, "Nothing, however, can be more absurd than this whole doctrine of the balance of trade, upon which, not only these restraints, but almost all of the other regulations of commerce are founded." Smith, *Wealth of Nations*, p. 521.

10. Economists use the term "comparative advantage" to explain why people should either trade for a product that someone else makes or make it on their own. Essentially, people who can spend their time more productively doing something else should trade instead of making the item on their own (as their making it themselves has a higher opportunity cost). *Comparative Advantage and the Benefits of Trade*, Library of Economics and Liberty, n.d.

11. Smith, *Wealth of Nations*, pp. 485–86.

12. Critics have long held that a misplaced emphasis on the benefit for consumers from trade ignores the workers, but this critique ignores that there is no reason to produce anything—that is, to work—other than to consume. Consumption and production are inseparable and, therefore, workers and consumers are not at odds. This analysis also abstracts from the fact that all imported products are not perfect substitutes for domestically produced goods. As such, imports can add to consumer welfare by increasing product variety. Robert Feenstra, "Restoring the Product Variety and Pro-Competitive Gains from Trade with Heterogeneous Firms and Bounded Productivity," *Journal of International Economics* 110 (2018): 16–27; Treb Allen and Costas Arkolakis, "Lecture 1: The Armington Model," Northwestern ECON 460 (Graduate International Trade), Spring 2014.

13. Will Kimball and Susan Balding, "The Trade Deficit Is Responsible for Manufacturing Job Loss," Economic Policy Institute, Washington, August 19, 2015; Glenn Kessler, "Are Jobs Lost Due to 'Bad Trade Policy' or Automation?," *Washington Post*, October 17, 2019.

14. The same holds for the opposite situation, known as a trade surplus, whereby the flow of the amount of money coming into the United States from selling exports exceeds the amount leaving the United States to buy imports. Norbert Michel, "Trade and Investment Are Not a Balancing Act," Cato Institute Policy Analysis no. 964, November 9, 2023.

15. Daniel B. Klein and Donald J. Boudreaux, "The 'Trade Deficit': Defective Language, Deficient Thinking," Library of Economics and Liberty, June 5, 2017.

16. Technically, the trade balance is part of the current account balance. Nonetheless, the two are frequently used interchangeably. Greg Mankiw, "The Current Account vs the Trade Deficit," *Greg Mankiw's Blog*, July 1, 2006; Tori Smith and Gabriella Beaumont-Smith, "11 Common Questions about U.S. Trade with China," Heritage Foundation, Washington, April 30, 2019; Federal Reserve Bank of New York, "Balance of Payments."

17. For more on how this misunderstanding regarding trade deficits is based on how GDP is calculated, see Daniel Griswold, "The Trade-Balance Creed: Debunking the Belief That Imports and Trade Deficits Are a 'Drag on Growth,'" Cato Institute Policy Analysis no. 45, April 11, 2011.

18. For example, on an annual basis, the United States ran a trade surplus only twice from 1790 to 1819, 11 times from 1820 to 1860, twice from 1861 to 1875, and zero times from 1971 to 2019. David Burton, "Regulation of International Investment: Focus on China," Heritage Foundation Backgrounder no. 3517, August 10, 2020; Douglass C. North, "The United States Balance of Payments, 1790–1860," in *The Conference on Research in Income and Wealth, Trends in the American Economy in the Nineteenth Century* (Princeton, NJ: Princeton University Press, 1960), pp. 573–628 (especially tables B-1 and B-5); Matthew Simon, "The United States Balance of Payments, 1861–1900," in *Trends in the American Economy in the Nineteenth Century*, pp. 629–715 (especially table 27).

19. Donald J. Boudreaux, "If Trade Surpluses Are So Great, the 1930s Should Have Been a Booming Decade," *Café Hayek* (blog), December 21, 2006.

20. Richard Cooper, "The Balance of Payments in Review," *Journal of Political Economy* 74, no. 4 (1966): 383.

21. Robert Z. Lawrence, "Recent Manufacturing Employment Growth: The Exception That Proves the Rule," National Bureau of Economic Research Working Paper no. 24151, December 2017, p. 9.

22. Lawrence, "Recent Manufacturing Employment Growth," p. 9.

23. Adam Posen, "Despite Germany's Trade Surplus, Manufacturing Employment Share of Total Employment Has Fallen in Its Industrial Hub at a Similar Rate as in Ohio," Peterson Institute for International Economics, Washington, October 6, 2021.

24. Author's calculations using the following: World Bank, "Net Trade in Goods and Services (BoP, current US$)," 2000–2019, and International Labour Organization, "SDG Indicator 9.2.2—Manufacturing Employment as a Proportion of Total Employment (%)—Annual," 2000–2019. The countries included are Japan, Germany, Russia, Switzerland, Canada, the United Kingdom, India, Brazil, and Pakistan. From 1994 to 2019, some of the countries consistently ran a surplus, some typically showed a deficit, and others varied.

25. Lawrence, "Recent Manufacturing Employment Growth," p. 6.

26. The import and export data are almost perfectly correlated (the correlation coefficient is 99 percent). Author's calculations using "International Trade in Goods and Services," retrieved from Bureau of Economic Analysis, March 28, 2024, and Bureau of Economic Analysis, "Gross Domestic Product (GDP)," retrieved from the Federal Reserve Bank of St. Louis Economic Data, March 28, 2024; J. Bradford Jensen, "Importers Are Exporters: Tariffs Would Hurt Our Most Competitive Firms," Peterson Institute for International Economics, Washington, December 7, 2016.

27. Author's calculations, Bureau of Economic Analysis.

28. Author's calculations, Bureau of Economic Analysis.

29. In fact, it can precisely forecast with only a linear projection of manufacturing employment data from 1960 to 1980. Lawrence, "Recent Manufacturing Employment Growth," p. 6. Lawrence uses the share of manufacturing employment in total nonfarm employment.

30. Lawrence, "Recent Manufacturing Employment Growth," p. 6.

31. Author's calculations using Bureau of Labor Statistics (BLS) data series *Civilian Labor Force Participation Rate: Men, Percent, Annual, Seasonally Adjusted*

(*LNS11300001*), available from the Federal Reserve Bank of St. Louis Economic Data. The projection for 2018 is 68.4 percent versus the actual labor force participation of 69.1 percent. Thus, the projection is 0.7 percentage points too low, indicating that a change pushed the 2018 labor force participation rate slightly above its trend. Using labor force participation data for white males age 20 and older produces nearly the same results. Additionally, the same findings hold when looking at 1960 to 1980, the dates used in Lawrence, "Recent Manufacturing Employment Growth," in 2017. This alternative linear trend projects that labor force participation for males would be 68.6 percent in 2010, 2.6 percentage points lower than the actual figure realized in 2010 (71.2 percent). Finally, using the (alternative) dates 1948 through 1980 to project the economy's share of manufacturing employment for 2018 essentially replicates Lawrence's original results.

32. See, for example, the poll results in *Fast-Track Authority*, Initiative on Global Markets, University of Chicago Booth School of Business, November 11, 2014; N. Gregory Mankiw, "Economists Actually Agree on This: The Wisdom of Free Trade," *New York Times*, April 24, 2015; and Cletus C. Coughlin, "The Controversy over Free Trade: The Gap between Economists and the General Public," *Federal Reserve Bank of St. Louis Review*, January–February 2002, pp. 1–22.

33. BLS, "Worker Displacement: 2015–17," news release, August 28, 2018, p. 1. The BLS defines "displaced workers" as "persons 20 years of age and over who lost or left jobs because their plant or company closed or moved, there was insufficient work for them to do, or their position or shift was abolished."

34. The BLS reports that all displaced workers for this period (with no job tenure restrictions) totaled 6.8 million, and that 68 percent were reemployed as of January 2018. BLS, "Worker Displacement: 2015–17," p. 3.

35. BLS, "Worker Displacement, 2001–03," news release, July 30, 2004, p. 1. This figure represents an increase from the 1999 to 2001 figure of 4 million displaced workers, likely due to the 2001 recession. The total displaced worker population (without tenure restrictions) for 2001 to 2003 was 11.4 million, and 66.5 percent were reemployed by 2004 (see table 8 of the technical note at the end of the news release).

36. Jennifer Gardner, "Worker Displacement: A Decade of Change," *Monthly Labor Review*, BLS, April 1995, pp. 45, 48. The total displacement figure for this period (without tenure restrictions) was 5.5 million displaced workers.

37. Gardner, "Worker Displacement: A Decade of Change," p. 45.

38. Gardner, "Worker Displacement: A Decade of Change," p. 50.

39. BLS, "Worker Displacement, 2001–03," p.1; and "Worker Displacement: 2015–17," p. 1.

40. Gardner, "Worker Displacement: A Decade of Change," pp. 45–46.

41. BLS, "Worker Displacement, 2001–03," p. 2.

42. BLS, "Worker Displacement: 2015–17," p. 2. Not all BLS reports adhere to the same definition of "long-tenured displacements," but the trend away from disproportionately higher displacements in manufacturing holds across the past few decades. Also see Michael Podgursky, "The Industrial Structure of Job Displacement, 1979–89," *Monthly Labor Review*, BLS, September 1992.

43. BLS, "Incidence of Displaced Workers Becoming Reemployed in the Same Industry," *Economics Daily*, October 12, 1999; BLS, "Displaced Workers Reemployed in the Same Industry, 2000," *Economics Daily*, July 24, 2001.

44. James Borbely, "Characteristics of Displaced Workers 2007–2009: A Visual Essay," *Monthly Labor Review*, BLS, September 2011, p. 13.

45. BLS, "Worker Displacement: 2015–17," table 1.

46. Lori Kletzer, "Job Displacement, 1979–1986: How Blacks Fared Relative to Whites," *Monthly Labor Review*, BLS, July 1991.

47. A University of Houston study suggests that the shift away from working in the hospitality industry will be a long-term change that the overall labor market absorbs. Bryan Luhn, "Anger over COVID-19 Layoffs Keeping Hospitality Workers from Returning to Jobs," University of Houston, December 21, 2022. A similar employment shift occurred in the health care industry. Karen Shen, Julia Eddelbuettel, and Matthew Eisenberg, "Job Flows into and out of Health Care before and after the COVID-19 Pandemic," *JAMA* Health Forum, January 26, 2024.

48. For a broad discussion, see Scott Kennedy and Ilaria Mazzocco, "The China Shock: Reevaluating the Debate," Big Data China, Center for Strategic and International Studies, Washington, October 14, 2022, last modified March 17, 2023.

49. Wayne M. Morrison, "China-U.S. Trade Issues," Congressional Research Service Report no. RL33536, July 30, 2018, p. 11.

50. David H. Autor, David Dorn, and Gordon H. Hanson, "The China Syndrome: Local Labor Market Effects of Import Competition in the United States," *American Economic Review* 103, no. 6 (2013): p. 2140.

51. David H. Autor, David Dorn, and Gordon Hanson, "The China Shock: Learning from Labor-Market Adjustment to Large Changes in Trade," *Annual Review of Economics* 8, no. 1 (2016): 227. Using alternative methods, the authors estimate that the lost employment figure could be as high as 2.4 million (p. 228). This alternative estimate does not change the analysis in the main text. Scott Lincicome, "Testing the 'China Shock': Was Normalizing Trade with China a Mistake?," Cato Institute Policy Analysis no. 895, July 8, 2020.

52. Autor, Dorn, and Hanson, "The China Shock," p. 215, figure 5. In a 2021 paper, the authors argue that the shock plateaued in 2010, and that increased trade with China explains 59.3 percent of the overall reduction in the manufacturing employment share between 2001 and 2019. David H. Autor, David Dorn, and Gordon H. Hanson, "On the Persistence of the China Shock," *Brookings Papers on Economic Activity*, Fall 2021, abstract and p. 401.

53. For additional research that reports increased trade leads to job losses in a similar range to that of Autor, Dorn, and Hanson, see Daron Acemoglu et al., "Import Competition and the Great US Employment Sag of the 2000s," *Journal of Labor Economics* 34, no. S1 (part 2, 2016): S141–S198; Michael Hicks and Srikant Devaraj, "The Myth and Reality of Manufacturing in America," Ball State University Center for Business and Economic Research, Muncie, IN, April 2017.

54. In addition to the research described in the main text, other studies support the proposition that increased trade with China was not the main cause of

the decrease in US manufacturing employment and that domestic shocks better explain changes in local employment and wages. Jonathan Rothwell, "Cutting the Losses: Reassessing the Costs of Import Competition to Workers and Communities," Brookings Institution, Washington, October 19, 2017; Lorenzo Caliendo and Fernando Parro, "Lessons from US–China Trade Relations," *Annual Review of Economics* 15 (2023). Another paper reports that increased trade with China "over 1995–2011 created net demand for about 1.7 million jobs." Robert C. Feenstra and Akira Sasahara, "The 'China Shock,' Exports and U.S. Employment: A Global Input–Output Analysis," *Review of International Economics* 26, no. 5 (2018): 1053–83.

55. The authors report that the positive effects "led to overall improved labor market conditions." Nicholas Bloom et al., "The Impact of Chinese Trade on U.S. Employment: The Good, the Bad, and the Apocryphal," Society for Economic Dynamics 2019 Meeting Paper no. 1433, p. 3.

56. Wang et al., "Re-Examining the Effects of Trading with China on Local Labor Markets: A Supply Chain Perspective," National Bureau of Economic Research Working Paper no. 24886, August 2018. Unlike many earlier research papers, the authors distinguish between the production of intermediate goods and final goods.

57. Wang et al., "Re-Examining the Effects of Trading with China," p. 2.

58. The real value of Chinese imports refers to the value of US imports from China as reported on the United Nations Comtrade Database, adjusted for inflation with the personal consumption expenditure price index. The same increase is found using, instead, "US Imports of Goods by Customs Basis from China" from the Federal Reserve Bank of St. Louis Economic Data. Additionally, the share of total US import volume from Chinese imports rose consistently between 2010 and 2019, from 28.87 percent in 2010 to 34.84 percent in 2019. Import volume data are available from the US International Trade Commission's DataWeb portal at https://dataweb.usitc.gov/.

59. In fact, several research papers report that the Trump administration tariffs were an economic failure. For instance, Federal Reserve researchers who studied the 2018–2019 tariff increase report "relative reductions in manufacturing employment and relative increases in producer prices" and suggest that increasing input costs and retaliatory tariffs contributed to the decline in manufacturing employment. Aaron Flaaen and Justin Pierce, "Disentangling the Effects of the 2018–2019 Tariffs on a Globally Connected U.S. Manufacturing Sector," Finance and Economics Discussion Series no. 2019-086, Board of Governors of the Federal Reserve System, Washington, 2019, p. 3. Separately, in a new research paper, the same authors of the original China Shock paper report, "The net effect of import tariffs, retaliatory tariffs, and farm subsidies on employment in locations exposed to the trade war was at best a wash, and it may have been mildly negative." David Autor et al., "Help for the Heartland? The Employment and Electoral Effects of the Trump Tariffs in the United States," National Bureau of Economic Research Working Paper no. 32082, January 2024. Also see Mary Amiti, Stephen Redding, and David Weinstein, "The Impact of the 2018 Tariffs on Prices and Welfare," *Journal of Economic Perspectives* 33, no. 4 (2019): 187–210; Mary Amiti, Stephen Redding, and David Weinstein, "Who's Paying for the US

Tariffs? A Longer-Term Perspective," *American Economic Association Papers and Proceedings* 110 (2020): 541–46; and David Johanson et al., "Economic Impact of Section 232 and 301 Tariffs on U.S. Industries," US International Trade Commission Publication no. 5405, May 2023.

60. Autor, Dorn, and Hanson, "The China Syndrome," p. 2148.

61. Public Citizen, "NAFTA at 20: One Million Lost U.S. Jobs, Higher Income Inequality, Doubled Agriculture Trade Deficit with Mexico and Canada, Displacement and Instability in Mexico, and Corporate Attacks on Environmental Laws," news release, December 28, 2013.

62. An Economic Policy Institute report gives a much larger number, but it states, "Growing trade deficits and the *collapse of manufacturing output following the Great Recession* are directly responsible for the loss of 5 million U.S. manufacturing jobs that occurred between 2000 and 2014" (emphasis added). Kimball and Balding, "The Trade Deficit Is Responsible for Manufacturing Job Loss." Although this estimate is not directly comparable with those in other studies, even this higher figure represents only about 2.5 percent of annual turnover.

63. Sherry Stephenson, "The Linkage between Services and Manufacturing in the U.S. Economy," Washington International Trade Association, Washington, May 23, 2017. Stephenson provides references to multiple studies, including a 2013 study by the US International Trade Commission titled *Recent Trends in U.S. Services Trade 2013 Report: Services Contribution to Manufacturing*, which notes, "Services can include a wide variety of activities, such as trade, transportation, information, education, health, and financial and professional services," as well as to a 2017 OECD report that states, "Across countries, between 25% and 60% of employment in manufacturing firms is found in service support functions such as R&D, engineering, transport, logistics, distribution, marketing, sales, after-sale services, IT [information technology], management and back-office support." US International Trade Commission, "Services' Contribution to Manufacturing," in *The Economic Effects of Significant U.S. Import Restraints* (Washington: US International Trade Commission, 2013); Sébastien Miroudot and Charles Cadesti, "Services in Global Value: From Inputs to Value-Creating Activities," Organisation for Economic Co-operation and Development Trade Policy Paper no. 197, March 15, 2017.

64. Apple is perhaps the best-known company that fits this category. For two studies that report evidence for these types of effects, see Andrew Bernard, Valerie Smeets, and Frederic Warzynski, "Rethinking Deindustrialization," National Bureau of Economic Research Working Paper no. 22114, March 2016; and Andrew Bernard and Teresa Fort, "Factoryless Goods Producers in the US," National Bureau of Economic Research Working Paper no. 19396, August 2013.

65. For a comprehensive review of why "both the seen and unseen economic benefits that free trade has delivered to countless individuals, businesses, and communities in America are undeniable and irreplaceable," and why "the lone alternative to free trade, protectionism, has repeatedly proved to impose high costs for minimal benefits," see Scott Lincicome, "The (Updated) Case for Free Trade," Cato Institute Policy Analysis no. 925, April 19, 2022.

66. For evidence and a wider discussion of how a lack of competitive pressure in both product and labor markets contributed to the US Rust Belt's decline, see

Lee E. Ohanian, "Competition and the Decline of the Rust Belt," Federal Reserve Bank of Minneapolis, economic policy paper, December 20, 2014.

Chapter 5

1. Christopher Klein, "When America Despised the Irish: The 19th Century's Refugee Crisis," History.com, March 14, 2019.

2. In the same poll, 28 percent of respondents reported that immigrants made "Job opportunities for you/your family" worse. See all results at https://news.gallup.com/poll/1660/immigration.aspx. In 2015, Donald Trump exemplified this attitude, saying of immigrants, "They're taking our jobs, they're taking our manufacturing jobs, they're taking our money, they're killing us." Josh Boak, "AP Fact Check: Trump Plays on Immigration Myths," *PBS NewsHour*, February 8, 2019.

3. Salena Zito and Brad Todd, *The Great Revolt: Inside the Populist Coalition Reshaping American Politics* (New York: Crown Forum, 2018), p. 44.

4. Bob Davis and John Harwood, "Kerry Targets Job Outsourcing with Corporate-Tax Overhaul," *Wall Street Journal*, March 26, 2004; N. Gregory Mankiw and Phillip Swagel, "The Politics and Economics of Offshore Outsourcing," National Bureau of Economic Research Working Paper no. 12398, July 2006.

5. A relatively small quantity of research on the labor market effects of offshoring exists compared with the effects of immigration, partly due to a lack of high-quality offshoring data. Timothy Sturgeon, "Why We Can't Measure the Economic Effects of Services Offshoring: The Data Gaps and How to Fill Them," Massachusetts Institute of Technology Industrial Performance Center, Cambridge, September 10, 2006. For estimates of the (relatively small) size of offshoring in the information technology sector, see Robert Bednarzik, "Restructuring Information Technology: Is Offshoring a Concern?," *Monthly Labor Review*, BLS, August 2005.

6. The previous high mark for the foreign-born share was at 14.7 percent in 1910. Audrey Singer, "Contemporary Immigrant Gateways in Historical Perspective," *Dædalus* 142, no. 3 (2013): 79; Migration Policy Institute, "U.S. Immigrant Population and Share over Time, 1850–Present," 1999; Statista, "Percentage of Foreign-Born Population in the United States in 2019, by State," 2023.

7. These figures are the author's calculations using 2019 data from the OECD's International Migration Database, available at https://stats.oecd.org/.

8. These figures represent the annual number of H (temporary workers and trainees) and L (intracompany transfers) visas issued—including immediate family members of H and L visa holders, most of whom are not eligible to work, as reported by the Department of State (from various reports available at https://travel.state.gov/content/travel/en/legal/visa-law0/visa-statistics/nonimmigrant-visa-statistics.html)—as well as the annual number of legal permanent resident permits (green cards) issued as reported by the Department of Homeland Security, from 1998 to 2018 (from Yearbook of Immigration Statistics 2018).

9. This analysis ignores several other temporary visa categories, such as J-1 exchange visas, because they make up a relatively small portion of temporary visas. David Bier, "Facts about the Summer Work and Travel Program," *Cato at Liberty* (blog), May 27, 2020.

10. These figures represent the annual number of H-2A and H-2B visas issued as reported by the Department of State, relative to the number of people (25 years and older) without a high school diploma as reported by the Census Bureau, from 2006 to 2019. The number of people in this low-education category has been consistently falling for decades, and it was 21 percent lower in 2019 than in 2006. Using statistics of the lower-educated labor force and using the "18 and older" age cutoff for those without a high school diploma produces nearly identical results. The high school completion rate for 18- to 24-year-olds not enrolled in high school has been rising steadily since the 1970s for all ethnic groups. As of 2017, the completion rate was 88 percent for Hispanics, and it exceeded 94 percent for whites, blacks, and Asians. National Center for Education Statistics, "High School Completion Rate of 18- to 24-Year-Olds Not Enrolled In High School (Status Completion Rate), by Sex and Race/Ethnicity: 1972 through 2017," November 2018, table 219.65.

11. Julian Simon, *The Economic Consequences of Immigration* (Cambridge, MA: Basil Blackwell, 1989), p. 174.

12. James Bacchus, "The Globalization of Ideas Enriches the World," Cato Institute, Washington, March 19, 2024.

13. For international evidence that immigration boosts exports through this productivity channel, see Dany Bahar and Hillel Rapoport, "Migration, Knowledge Diffusion and the Comparative Advantage of Nations," working paper, 2019. Using international data that cover 1990 to 2000, the authors estimate that an increase of only 65,000 migrants is associated with a 15 percent increase in the probability that a country will add a new product to its overall export basket.

14. Gianmarco Ottaviano, Giovanni Peri, and Greg Wright, "Immigration, Offshoring and American Jobs," National Bureau of Economic Research Working Paper no. 16439, October 2010, pp. 2–3. As with trade and automation, complex interactions can also magnify the effects immigration and offshoring have on labor markets. Lower immigration costs can, for example, lead to the substitution of immigrants for offshore workers.

15. Bureau of Labor Statistics, All Employees, Manufacturing [MANEMP], retrieved from the Federal Reserve Bank of St. Louis Economic Data, November 20, 2019.

16. Ottaviano, Peri, and Wright, "Immigration, Offshoring and American Jobs," p. 15.

17. Ottaviano, Peri, and Wright, "Immigration, Offshoring and American Jobs," pp. 15–16.

18. Ottaviano, Peri, and Wright, "Immigration, Offshoring and American Jobs," p. 4.

19. Ottaviano, Peri, and Wright, "Immigration, Offshoring and American Jobs," p. 4.

20. William Olney, "Offshoring, Immigration, and the Native Wage Distribution," *Canadian Journal of Economics* 45, no. 3 (2012): 832. Olney separately analyzes workers' wages at various skill levels, as well as various wage deciles and reports (on p. 832) that the wage decile analysis provides even stronger support for the productivity effect.

21. Olney, "Offshoring, Immigration, and the Native Wage Distribution," p. 832.

22. Olney, "Offshoring, Immigration, and the Native Wage Distribution," p. 848.

23. George J. Borjas, "Yes, Immigration Hurts American Workers," *Politico*, September–October 2016 (emphasis added). The result discussed in the *Politico* article is from George J. Borjas, "The Labor Demand Curve Is Downward Sloping: Reexamining the Impact of Immigration on the Labor Market," *Quarterly Journal of Economics* 118, no. 4 (2003).

24. David Card and Giovanni Peri, "Immigration Economics by George J. Borjas: A Review Essay," *Journal of Economic Literature* 54, no. 4 (2016): 1344–45.

25. Alan de Brauw and Joseph R. D. Russell, "Revisiting the Labor Demand Curve: The Wage Effects of Immigration and Women's Entry into the US Labor Force, 1960–2010," International Food Policy Research Institute Discussion Paper no. 01402, December 2014, pp. 14–15.

26. Simonetta Longhi, Peter Nijkamp, and Jacques Poot, "The Fallacy of 'Job Robbing': A Meta-Analysis of Estimates of the Effect of Immigration on Employment," *Journal of Migration and Refugee Issues* 1, no. 4 (2006): 131–52; Liesbet Okkerse, "How to Measure Labour Market Effects of Immigration: A Review," *Journal of Economic Surveys* 22, no. 1 (2008): 1–30; Simonetta Longhi, Peter Nijkamp, and Jacques Poot, "Meta-Analysis of Empirical Evidence on the Labour Market Impact of Immigration," Institute for the Study of Labor Discussion Paper no. 3418, March 2008, pp. 1–38; Simonetta Longhi, Peter Nijkamp, Jacques Poot, "Joint Impacts of Immigration on Wages and Employment: Review and Meta-Analysis," *Journal of Geographical Systems* 12, no. 4 (2010): 355–87.

27. Longhi, Nijkamp, and Poot, "Joint Impacts of Immigration," p. 357.

28. Longhi, Nijkamp, and Poot, "Joint Impacts of Immigration," p. 357.

29. Longhi, Nijkamp, and Poot, "Meta-Analysis of the Impact of Immigration," p. 22.

30. Rachel Friedberg and Jennifer Hunt, "The Impact of Immigrants on Host Country Wages, Employment and Growth," *Journal of Economic Perspectives* 9, no. 2 (1995): 42 (emphasis added).

31. Friedberg and Hunt, "Impact of Immigrants on Host Country Wages," p. 42.

32. Francine Blau and Christopher Mackie, eds., *The Economic and Fiscal Consequences of Immigration* (Washington: National Academies Press, 2016), p. 204 (emphasis added).

33. Blau and Mackie, *Economic and Fiscal Consequences of Immigration*, p. 183.

34. Two such examples are Joseph G. Altonji and David Card, "The Effects of Immigration on the Labor Market Outcomes of Less-Skilled Natives," in *Immigration, Trade and the Labor Market*, ed. John M. Abowd and Richard B. Freeman (Chicago: University of Chicago Press, 1991), pp. 201–34; and Patricia Cortés, "The Effect of Low-Skilled Immigration on US Prices: Evidence from CPI Data," *Journal of Political Economy* 116, no. 3 (2008): 381–422.

35. Joan Monras, "Immigration and Wage Dynamics: Evidence from the Mexican Peso Crisis," Institute for the Study of Labor Discussion Paper no. 8924, March 30, 2015, p. 3.

36. A third event occurred in the 1930s, when the federal government approved repatriating approximately 400,000 Mexicans and Mexican Americans to boost native employment and wages. Because the effort occurred during the Great Depression, it is not discussed here. For more on this event, and its failure to boost native wages or employment, see Jongkwan Lee, Giovanni Peri, and Vasil Yasenov, "The Labor Market Effects of Mexican Repatriations: Longitudinal Evidence from the 1930s," Institute of Labor Economics Discussion Paper no. 12689, October 2019, p. 2.

37. David Card, "The Impact of the Mariel Boatlift on the Miami Labor Market," *Industrial and Labor Relations Review* 43, no. 2 (1990): 246.

38. Card chose these cities "because they had relatively large populations of blacks and Hispanics and because they exhibited a pattern of economic growth similar to that in Miami over the late 1970s and early 1980s." Card, "Impact of the Mariel Boatlift," p. 249.

39. Card, "Impact of the Mariel Boatlift," p. 251.

40. Card, "Impact of the Mariel Boatlift," pp. 249–50.

41. Card, "Impact of the Mariel Boatlift," p. 256. See also Michael Clemens and Jennifer Hunt, "The Labor Market Effects of Refugee Waves: Reconciling Conflicting Results," National Bureau of Economic Research Working Paper no. 23433, May 2017 (revised July 2017), pp. 1–57.

42. Clemens and Hunt, "Labor Market Effects of Refugee Waves." The paper concludes, "For the Mariel Boatlift, all important discrepancies between the original analysis and reanalyses can be explained by the sensitivity of the [newer] results to the selection of small subsamples, often without a clear theoretical basis" (see p. 29). For a less technical read, see Michael Clemens, "There's No Evidence That Immigrants Hurt Any American Workers: The Debate over the Mariel Boatlift, a Crucial Immigration Case Study, Explained," *Vox*, August 3, 2017.

43. Michael A. Clemens, Ethan G. Lewis, and Hannah M. Postel, "Immigration Restrictions as Active Labor Market Policy: Evidence from the Mexican Bracero Exclusion," *American Economic Review* 108, no. 6 (2018): 1468–87.

44. Clemens, Lewis, and Postel, "Immigration Restrictions as Active Labor Market Policy," p. 1470.

45. George J. Borjas and Lawrence F. Katz, "The Evolution of the Mexican-Born Workforce in the United States," National Bureau of Economic Research Working Paper no. 11281, p. 3. In the United States, labor unions opposed the program in the interest of keeping out lower-priced foreign labor. In Mexico, opposition to the program came from the Catholic Church. As David Fitzgerald of the Migration Policy Institute explains, "The Church feared that migration caused the breakup of families, religious conversions, and the introduction of dangerous foreign ideas." Susan Ferriss and Ricardo Sandoval, *The Fight in the Fields: Cesar Chavez and the Farmworkers Movement* (Boston: Mariner Books, 1998); David Fitzgerald, "Uncovering the Emigration Policies of the Catholic Church in Mexico," Migration Policy Institute, Washington, May 21, 2009. In 1965, the federal government recruited 20,000 high school students to replace the migrant workers, an experiment that did not end well. Gustavo Arellano, "When the U.S. Government Tried to Replace Migrant Farmworkers with High Schoolers," NPR, August 23, 2018.

46. Clemens, Lewis, and Postel, "Immigration Restrictions as Active Labor Market Policy," p. 1471.

47. Clemens and coauthors identify two additional academic studies that evaluate the effects of the exclusion but note that both are hampered by either data or specification problems. For instance, one study does not have state-level bracero counts, and the second study does not control for the nationwide increase in farm wages across the period. Clemens, Lewis, and Postel, "Immigration Restrictions as Active Labor Market Policy," p. 1471.

48. Though not a clean natural experiment, evidence shows that the country-of-origin quotas implemented in the 1920s—which gradually reduced the annual number of immigrants coming into the United States from countries outside the Western Hemisphere—had the opposite of the predicted effect on wages. In urban areas, most affected by the reduced supply of immigrant labor, wages went down. Ran Abramitzky et al., "The Effects of Immigration on the Economy: Lessons from the 1920s Border Closure," National Bureau of Economic Research Working Paper no. 26536, December 2019.

49. Michael Clemens, "Economics and Emigration: Trillion-Dollar Bills on the Sidewalk?," *Journal of Economic Perspectives* 25, no. 3 (2011): 85.

50. Gihoon Hong and John McLaren, "Are Immigrants a Shot in the Arm for the Local Economy?," National Bureau of Economic Research Working Paper no. 21123, April 2015.

51. Hong and McLaren, "Are Immigrants a Shot in the Arm?," p. 37. The authors note that their estimates vary widely with their different estimation methods, but that the "results consistently indicate a strong positive effect of immigrants on employment" (p. 37).

52. Hong and McLaren, "Are Immigrants a Shot in the Arm?," p. 46. The authors estimate that for every 1,000 new immigrants, 360 workers move into the area within five years. A 2023 study finds that an influx of immigrant physicians—at state and local levels across the United States through a special visa waiver program—does not crowd out domestically trained doctors. Breno Braga, Gaurav Khanna, and Sarah Turner, "Migration Policy and the Supply of Foreign Physicians: Evidence from the Conrad 30 Waiver Program," National Bureau of Economic Research Working Paper no. 32005, December 2023.

53. For examples, see Florence Jaumotte, Ksenia Koloskova, and Sweta Chaman Saxena, "Impact of Immigration on Income Levels in Advanced Economies," International Monetary Fund Spillover Note no. 2016.008, October 24, 2016; Francesc Ortega and Giovanni Peri, "The Causes and Effects of International Migrations: Evidence from OECD Countries 1980–2005," National Bureau of Economic Research Working Paper no. 14833, April 2009; Alberto Alesina, Johann Harnoss, and Hillel Rapoport, "Birthplace Diversity and Economic Prosperity," National Bureau of Economic Research Working Paper no. 18699, January 2013, p. 37; Mariya Aleksynska and Ahmed Tritah, "The Heterogeneity of Immigrants, Host Countries' Income and Productivity: A Channel Accounting Approach," *Economic Inquiry* 53, no. 1 (2015): 150–72; and Peter Dungan, Tony Fang, and Morely Gunderson, "Macroeconomic Impacts of Canadian Immigration," Institute of Labor Economics Discussion Paper no. 6743, July 2012, abstract.

54. Patrick J. Carr, Daniel T. Lichter, and Maria J. Kefalas, "Can Immigration Save Small-Town America? Hispanic Boomtowns and the Uneasy Path to Renewal," *Annals of the American Academy of Political and Social Science* 641 (2012): 42.

55. Carr, Lichter, and Kefalas, "Can Immigration Save Small-Town America?," p. 45.

56. Carr, Lichter, and Kefalas, "Can Immigration Save Small-Town America?," p. 45. The paper also discusses similar cases in rural Minnesota and Pennsylvania, where immigration has saved schools from being shuttered because of previously low enrollment (see pp. 48–53).

57. Erie's total population is almost 100,000. Miriam Jordan, "The Town That Can't Do without Refugees," *Wall Street Journal*, February 28, 2017. Jordan identifies 15 other small US cities that received relatively large shares of refugees from 2012 to 2016.

58. For evidence that lower-skilled immigration complements existing higher-skilled workers by allowing more of the latter to enter the labor force, see Patricia Cortés and José Tessada, "Low-Skilled Immigration and the Labor Supply of Highly Skilled Women," *American Economic Journal: Applied Economics* 3, no. 3 (2011): 88–123. For evidence that immigration leads to productivity gains that "come from specialization, competition, and the choice of appropriate techniques in traditional sectors," see Giovanni Peri, "The Effect of Immigration on Productivity: Evidence from U.S. States," *Review of Economics and Statistics* 94, no. 1 (2012): 348. For evidence that lower-skilled immigrants boost overall productivity through improving specialization, see Giovanni Peri and Chad Sparber, "Task Specialization, Immigration, and Wages," *American Economic Journal, Applied Economics* 1, no. 3 (2009): 135–69; and Mette Foged and Giovanni Peri, "Immigrants and Native Workers: New Analysis on Longitudinal Data," National Bureau of Economic Research Working Paper no. 19315, August 2013, p. 21.

59. Michael Clemens, Claudio Montenegro, and Lant Pritchett, "The Place Premium: Wage Differences for Identical Workers across the US Border," Harvard Kennedy School Faculty Research Working Paper Series no. RWP09-004, 2009.

60. For direct evidence that low-skilled immigrants boost overall productivity, see Peri and Sparber, "Task Specialization, Immigration, and Wages"; and Foged and Peri, "Immigrants and Native Workers."

61. Robert VerBruggen, "Harvard's George J. Borjas," *American Conservative*, January 2, 2017.

62. Catherine Clifford, "Jeff Bezos Says Dad Emigrated from Cuba Alone At 16: 'His Grit, Determination, Optimism Are Inspiring,'" CNBC, May 16, 2019.

63. "Women In Technology: Hedy Lamarr, the Mother of Wi-Fi," Thales, 2024; *Bombshell: The Hedy Lamarr Story*, Netflix documentary, 2017.

64. Kathleen Elkins, "How a Janitor Invented Flamin' Hot Cheetos and Became an Exec at Pepsico," CNBC, March 27, 2018. Controversy has surrounded Montañez's version of events regarding the launch of the product, but Frito-Lay's 2021 statement says that there is "no reason to doubt" his stories about new product development for Cheetos. Dom DiFurio, "Frito-Lay Defends Richard Montañez's Legacy after Flamin' Hot Cheetos Dustup," *Dallas Morning News*, May 24, 2021. The story also inspired the movie *Flamin' Hot* about Montañez's life.

65. Ray Kroc, Biography, April 16, 2021.

66. Robert McFadden, "Evelyn Berezin, 93, Dies; Built the First True Word Processor," *New York Times,* December 10, 2018.

67. Jerry Yang, 2024, *Forbes* Profile.

68. Steve Chen, Immigrant Learning Center, July 2022.

69. "Daughter of Latvian Refugees Receives Top Technological Award at White House," *Baltic Course*, October 14, 2009.

70. Dr. David D. Ho: A First Responder in the HIV/AIDS Epidemic, *Himmelfarb Library News*, George Washington University, May 24, 2021.

71. For evidence of the latter proposition, see Robert Shimer, "The Impact of Young Workers on the Aggregate Labor Market," *Quarterly Journal of Economics* 116, no. 3 (2001): 969–1007. This empirical research shows that an unusually large, anticipated labor shock lowers the unemployment rate, and increases both labor participation and wages. It also suggests that an influx of immigrant labor might cement a region's dominance in a particular industry.

Chapter 6

1. *The World's Largest Economies*, WorldData.info, 2021. The United States' GDP is more than $5 trillion larger than the world's second-largest economy, China. It is more than four times the size of Japan, the world's third-largest economy with a GDP of $4.9 trillion. The United States has by far the largest population of all Organisation for Economic Co-operation and Development (OECD) member countries, exceeding the second-largest, Mexico, by 200 million people. World Bank, Population, Total—OECD Members, 2022.

2. The index measures "the degree to which the policies and institutions of countries are supportive of economic freedom." James Gwartney et al., *Economic Freedom of the World: 2022 Annual Report* (Vancouver: Fraser Institute, 2022). The six countries that rank ahead of the United States, with their respective 2020 populations, are as follows: New Zealand (5.1 million), Singapore (5.7 million), Denmark (5.8 million), Hong Kong (7.5 million people), Switzerland (8.6 million), and Australia (25.7 million). Though the ranking system is not directly comparable with that of the Fraser Institute's *Economic Freedom of the World* index, the United States ranks 17th (identified as "mostly free") in the Heritage Foundation's economic freedom index. Terry Miller, Anthony B. Kim, and James M. Roberts, *2019 Index of Economic Freedom* (Washington: Heritage Foundation, 2019).

3. States and local governments add harmful regulatory and tax restrictions on top of the federal layer. For research on the effects of local regulatory and tax policy on housing costs, see John Quigley and Steven Raphael, "Regulation and the High Cost of Housing in California," *American Economic Review* 95, no. 2 (2005): 323–28. For research on the effects of local licensing laws on employment, see Will Flanders and Collin Roth, *Land of the Free? 50 State Study on How Professional Licensing Laws Lead to Fewer Jobs* (Milwaukee: Wisconsin Institute for Law and Liberty, 2017).

4. Chris Edwards, "Entrepreneurs and Regulations: Removing State and Local Barriers to New Businesses," Cato Institute Policy Analysis no. 916, May 5,

2021 (according to the *Federal Register*, there are currently 438 federal agencies); Paul C. Light, "The True Size of Government Is Nearing a Record High," Brookings Institution, Washington, October 7, 2020.

5. Peter Van Doren and Thomas A. Firey, "Regulation at 40," *Regulation*, Spring 2017.

6. Richard A. Harris and Sidney M. Milkis, *The Politics of Regulatory Change*, 2nd ed. (New York: Oxford University Press, 1996).

7. It is also true that the Carter administration began many broader deregulatory efforts in the 1970s, some of which the Reagan administration continued. See, for example, Andrew Crain, "Ford, Carter, and Deregulation in the 1970s," *Journal on Telecommunications and High Technology Law* 5 (2007): 413–31; and John Brown, "Jimmy Carter, Alfred Kahn, and Airline Deregulation: Anatomy of a Policy Success," *Independent Review* 19, no. 1 (2014): 85–99.

8. In 1987, the Heritage Foundation published *Steering the Elephant*, an "account told by Reagan appointees about what has happened in the first six years of the Reagan Administration," that tells of conservatives' disappointment that the administration's agenda failed to produce the permanent change it had promised. Robert Rector and Michael Sanera, eds., *Steering the Elephant: How Washington Works* (New York: Universe Books, 1987), p. xiii. Contemporaneous accounts demonstrate that conservatives were disappointed even in the early years of the Reagan administration. Phil Gailey, "Heritage Foundation Disappointed by Reagan," *New York Times*, November 22, 1981.

9. Harris and Milkis, *Politics of Regulatory Change*, p. 275.

10. Harris and Milkis, *Politics of Regulatory Change*, p. 5.

11. Harris and Milkis, *Politics of Regulatory Change*, pp. 133–39.

12. Veronique de Rugy and Melinda Warren, "The Incredible Growth of the Regulators' Budget," Mercatus Center Working Paper no. 08-36, September 2008, pp. 3–4; Robert Higgs, "The Growth of Government in the United States," Foundation for Economic Education, Atlanta, August 1, 1990; Robert Higgs, *Crisis and Leviathan: Critical Episodes in the Growth of American Government* (New York: Oxford University Press, 1987); Stephen Moore, "The Growth of Government in America," Foundation for Economic Education, Atlanta, April 1, 1993; Light, "The True Size of Government"; Mark Febrizio and Melinda Warren, *Regulators' Budget: Overall Spending and Staffing Remain Stable: An Analysis of the U.S. Budget for Fiscal Years 1960 to 2021* (St. Louis and Washington: Weidenbaum Center on the Economy, Government, and Public Policy at Washington University and George Washington University, 2020).

13. Harris and Milkis, *Politics of Regulatory Change*, p. 92.

14. Edwards, "Entrepreneurs and Regulations."

15. Clyde Wayne Crews Jr., *Ten Thousand Commandments, An Annual Snapshot of the Federal Regulatory State* (Washington: Competitive Enterprise Institute, 2023), p. 35, figure 11.

16. Edwards, "Entrepreneurs and Regulations"; and Council of Economic Advisers, *Economic Report of the President*" (Washington: White House, 2019), p. 83. Separately, textual analysis of the *Code of Federal Regulations* shows that the use of words such as "shall" and "must" nearly tripled between 1970 and

2016, from 400,000 to 1.1 million. Council of Economic Advisers, *Economic Report of the President* (Washington: White House, 2020), pp. 109–10.

17. Kofi Ampaabeng et al., "RegAuthorities: The Regulations Authorities Dataset," working paper, Mercatus Center at George Mason University, Arlington, VA, July 2022, p. 3.

18. Norbert Michel, "The Myth of Financial Market Deregulation," Heritage Foundation Backgrounder no. 3094, April 26, 2016.

19. Jim Zarroli, "Visiting New York City, Bernie Sanders Attacks Clinton, 'Greed' of Wall Street," NPR, January 6, 2016; James Rickards, "Repeal of Glass-Steagall Caused the Financial Crisis," *U.S. News & World Report*, August 27, 2012; Joseph Stiglitz, "Capitalist Fools," *Vanity Fair*, December 31, 2008.

20. Norbert Michel, "The Glass–Steagall Act: Unraveling the Myth," Heritage Foundation Backgrounder no. 3104, April 28, 2016. Section 101 of the Gramm-Leach-Bliley Act repealed Sections 20 and 32 of the 1933 act but left Sections 16 and 21 intact. For a historical timeline of financial regulation in the United States, see Norbert Michel and Jennifer Schulp, *Financing Opportunity: How Financial Markets Have Fueled American Prosperity for More than Two Centuries* (Washington: Cato Institute, 2024).

21. Nancy Pelosi, "Pelosi Statement on $85 Billion AIG Loan," news release, September 16, 2008.

22. Dodd-Frank Act, History.com, August 21, 2018.

23. Norbert Michel and Tamara Skinner, "The Popular Narrative about Financial Deregulation Is Wrong," *Daily Signal*, July 29, 2016.

24. Michel, "The Myth of Financial Market Deregulation."

25. Money market mutual funds are a prime microcosm—they are highly regulated and, through the past several decades, have become more heavily regulated. For a brief description, see Martha L. Cochran, David F. Freeman, and Helen Mayer Clark, "Money Market Fund Reform: SEC Rulemaking in the FSOC Era," *Columbia Business Law Review* 2015, no. 3 (2016): 861–966; and Hester Peirce and Robert Greene, "Opening the Gate to Money Market Fund Reform," Mercatus Center at George Mason University, Arlington, VA, June 2018, pp. 5–10.

26. Norbert Michel and David Burton, "Financial Institutions: Necessary for Prosperity," Heritage Foundation Backgrounder no. 3108, April 14, 2016; Paul Mahoney, *Wasting a Crisis: Why Securities Regulation Fails* (Chicago: University of Chicago Press, 2015).

27. Norbert Michel, "The Financial Stability Oversight Council: Helping to Enshrine 'Too Big to Fail,'" Heritage Foundation Backgrounder no. 2900, April 1, 2014; Norbert Michel, "Fixing the Regulatory Framework for Derivatives," Heritage Foundation Backgrounder no. 3156, September 14, 2016.

28. Charles A. Calomiris and Stephen Haber, *Fragile by Design: The Political Origins of Banking Crises and Scarce Credit* (Princeton, NJ: Princeton University Press, 2014), pp. 4–7.

29. Michael Bordo, "Some Historical Evidence 1870–1933 on the Impact and International Transmission of Financial Crises," National Bureau of Economic Research Working Paper no. 1606, April 1985.

30. Calomiris and Haber, *Fragile by Design*, pp. 6–7.

31. Charles A. Calomiris, "Banking Crises Yesterday and Today," *Financial History Review* 17, no. 1 (2010): 4.

32. John Ligon and Norbert Michel, "Why Is Federal Housing Policy Fixated on 30-Year Fixed-Rate Mortgages?," Heritage Foundation Backgrounder no. 2917, June 18, 2014, pp. 3–4.

33. For the fiscal year ending December 31, 2020, Fannie Mae reported $4 trillion in total assets, whereas Freddie Mac reported $2.6 trillion. Federal National Mortgage Association, "Annual Report," December 31, 2020, p. 61; Federal Home Loan Mortgage Corporation, "Annual Report," December 31, 2020, p. 34. The 42 percent figure is the author's estimate using the Federal Reserve's (now discontinued) 2019 reported total for mortgage debt outstanding ($15.8 trillion). Board of Governors of the Federal Reserve System, "Mortgage Debt Outstanding, All Holders (Discontinued) [(MDOAH])," retrieved from the Federal Reserve Bank of St. Louis Economic Data, October 15, 2021.

34. US Department of Housing and Urban Development, "FHA Single Family Market Share, 2020 Q1," p. 4.

35. These figures include both single-family and multifamily MBSs. Securities Industry and Financial Markets Association, "US MBS Securities: Issuance, Trading Volume, Outstanding," October 13, 2021; Ginnie Mae, *Insurance Summary*, March 2021. Ginnie Mae primarily securitizes FHA loans. The FHA was created in 1934 mainly as a way to boost construction employment. Marie Justine Fritz, "Federal Housing Administration (FHA)," *Encyclopedia Britannica*, 2024.

36. Board of Governors of the Federal Reserve System, "Assets: Securities Held Outright: Mortgage-Backed Securities: Wednesday Level [WSHOMCB]," retrieved from the Federal Reserve Bank of St. Louis Economic Data, June 26, 2022.

37. US Census Bureau, Homeownership Rate in the United States [RHORUSQ156N], retrieved from the Federal Reserve Bank of St. Louis Economic Data, March 8, 2024.

38. These figures represent the combined ownership rate for people who own their home outright and those who own a mortgage, for both the United States and all OECD member countries, using 2019 data, as reported in the OECD Affordable Housing Database, October 15, 2021, available at https://www .oecd.org/housing/data/affordable-housing-database/.

39. This figure updates the estimate provided in Diane Katz, "The Massive Federal Credit Racket," Heritage Foundation Backgrounder no. 3179, February 14, 2017. It primarily includes obligations related to Fannie Mae and Freddie Mac, Federal Home Loan Banks, federal deposit insurance, and multiple federal credit programs.

40. Tariffs were relatively higher in the late 19th century, before the pervasive use of the income tax to raise government funding. Edward John Ray, "Changing Patterns of Protectionism: The Fall in Tariffs and the Rise in Non-Tariff Barriers Symposium: The Political Economy of International Trade Law and Policy," *Northwestern Journal of International Law & Business* 285, no. 2 (1987–88): 285–327. These nontariff trade barrier figures refer to the ad valorem equivalent. Chris Milner, Zhaohui Niu, and Saileshsingh Gunessee, "Growing Non-Tariff and Overall Protection," Centre for Economic Policy Research, London, June 19, 2018.

41. Holman Jenkins, "Your Pickup Truck Takes You for a Ride," *Wall Street Journal*, March 30, 2018; Colin Grabow, "Rust Buckets: How the Jones Act Undermines U.S. Shipbuilding and National Security," Cato Institute Policy Analysis no. 882, November 12, 2018; Americans import almost all their clothing and footwear, see Bryan Riley, "Back to School Season Highlights Heavy Burden of Tariffs on Families and Students," National Taxpayers Union Foundation, Washington, August 25, 2021; the volume restrictions are known as "tariff rate quotas," see Bryan Riley, "Monstrous Sugar Program Costs Americans Billions," National Taxpayers Union Foundation, Washington, October 27, 2021; and Gabriella Beaumont-Smith, "Trade's Trick or Treat," *Cato at Liberty* (blog), October 31, 2023.

42. David Bier, "Deregulating Legal Immigration: A Blueprint for Agency Action," Cato Institute, Washington, December 18, 2020; David Bier, "H-2B Visas: The Complex Process for Nonagricultural Employers to Hire Guest Workers," Cato Institute Policy Analysis no. 910, February 16, 2021; David Bier, "Why Legal Immigration Is Nearly Impossible," Cato Institute Policy Analysis no. 950, June 13, 2023.

43. Michael Poliakoff and Armand Alacbay, "Middle America Pays the Price for War on Poverty Policies—Including in College," in *The Not-So-Great Society*, ed. Lindsey Burke and Jonathan Butcher (Washington: Heritage Foundation, 2019), pp. 141–49; Michael Cannon, "Yes, Mr. President: A Free Market Can Fix Health Care," Cato Institute Policy Analysis no. 650, October 21, 2009.

44. Nick Loris, "Free Markets Supply Affordable Energy and a Clean Environment," Heritage Foundation Backgrounder no. 2966, October 31, 2014.

45. David R. Burton, "A Guide to Labor and Employment Law Reforms," Heritage Foundation Backgrounder no. 3535, October 9, 2020.

46. From an economic standpoint, what matters most is the overall cost and benefits of these regulations, but they are often difficult to measure. As a result, the quality of regulatory cost–benefit analyses remains controversial, and estimates tend to vary a great deal. Richard D. Morgenstern, "The RFF Regulatory Performance Initiative: What Have We Learned?," discussion paper, Resources for the Future, Washington, October 30, 2015, pp. 15–47; Robert W. Hahn and Paul C. Tetlock, "Has Economic Analysis Improved Regulatory Decisions?," AEI–Brookings Joint Center Working Paper no. 07-08, April 2007; Susan Dudley, "OMB's Reported Benefits of Regulation: Too Good to Be True?," *Regulation*, Summer 2013, pp. 26–30.

47. For example, incumbent railroad firms typically supported regulation. Gabriel Kolko, *Railroads and Regulations, 1877–1916* (Princeton, NJ: Princeton University Press, 2016). For more modern examples, see Timothy Carney, "Dodd-Frank Helps JP Morgan," *Washington Examiner*, February 14, 2013. More formally, the idea that regulators and the industries they regulate will end up in partnership, rather than remain adversarial, has been in the economics literature for years. For the seminal work on this theory of regulatory capture, see George Stigler, "The Economic Theory of Regulation," *Bell Journal of Economics and Management Science* 2, no. 1 (1971): 3–21.

48. Peter T. Calcagno and Russell S. Sobel, "Regulatory Costs on Entrepreneurship and Establishment Employment Size," *Small Business Economics* 41, no. 1 (2013): 541–59; Roy Rothwell, "The Impact of Regulation on Innovation: Some U.S. Data," *Technological Forecasting and Social Change* 17, no. 1 (1980): 7–34; Jonathan Munemo, "The Effect of Regulation-Driven Trade Barriers and Governance Quality on Export Entrepreneurship," *Regulation and Governance* 16, no. 4 (2022): 1119–40; and Dongmin Kong and Ni Qin, "Does Environmental Regulation Shape Entrepreneurship?," *Environmental and Resource Economics* 80 (2021): 169–96.

49. The rate of entrepreneurship refers to the entry rate for new firms. US Census Bureau, "Legacy BDS Establishment Characteristics Tables 1977–2014"; US Census Bureau, "2016 Firm and Estab Release Tables." The Census Bureau also released the "2021 Business Dynamics Statistics Data Tables," and the number of establishments "born" is included in the tables under the title "Business Dynamics Statistics: Establishment Age by Establishment Size: 1978–2021." David Burton, senior fellow in economic policy, Thomas A. Roe Institute, "Building an Opportunity Economy: The State of Small Business and Entrepreneurship," Testimony before the House Committee on Small Business, 114th Cong., 1st sess., March 4, 2015; Ryan Decker et al., "The Role of Entrepreneurship in US Job Creation and Economic Dynamism," *Journal of Economic Perspectives* 28, no. 3 (2014): 3–24; Salim Furth, "Research Review: Who Creates Jobs? Start-Up Firms and New Businesses," Heritage Foundation Issue Brief no. 3891, April 4, 2013.

50. Burton, "Building an Opportunity Economy"; Ian Hathaway and Robert Litan, "The Other Aging of America: The Increasing Dominance of Older Firms," Brookings Institution, Washington, July 2014.

51. Burton, "Building an Opportunity Economy," pp. 6–7.

52. Regulatory cost estimates can vary a great deal. For instance, the regulatory burden for new major rules, as estimated by the government agencies responsible for those regulations, was $70 billion during the George W. Bush administration and $100 billion for the Obama administration. James Gattuso and Diane Katz, "Red Tape Rising 2016: Obama Regs Top $100 Billion Annually," Heritage Foundation Backgrounder no. 3127, May 23, 2016; James Gattuso, Stephen Keen, and Diane Katz, "Red Tape Rising: Obama's Torrent of New Regulation," Heritage Foundation Backgrounder no. 2482, October 26, 2010. One study estimates that the cumulative regulatory costs from 1980 to 2012 were much larger, having shrunk the overall size of the economy by an estimated 25 percent, a figure that represents lost income of $13,000 per person. Bentley Coffey, Patrick A. McLaughlin, and Pietro Peretto, "The Cumulative Cost of Regulations," Mercatus Center at George Mason University, Arlington, VA, April 2016.

53. Ariel J. Binder and John Bound, "The Declining Labor Market Prospects of Less-Educated Men," *Journal of Economic Perspectives* 33, no. 2 (2019): 164.

54. Donald Parsons, "The Decline in Male Labor Force Participation," *Journal of Political Economy* 88, no. 1 (1980): 117–34.

55. Mary Daly, Brian Lucking, and Jonathan Schwabish, "The Future of Social Security Disability Insurance," Federal Reserve Bank of San Francisco Economic Letter, June 24, 2013.

56. Nicholas Kristof, "Profiting from a Child's Illiteracy," *New York Times*, December 7, 2012.

57. Kevin Williamson, *Big White Ghetto: Dead Broke, Stone-Cold Stupid, and High on Rage in the Dank Woolly Wilds of the "Real America,"* (Washington: Regnery, 2020), p. 12.

58. For more research on the relationship between disability insurance and labor force participation, see Kathleen Mullen and Stefan Staubli, "Disability Benefit Generosity and Labor Force Withdrawal," National Bureau of Economic Research Working Paper no. 22419, July 2016; Courtney Coile, "Disability Insurance Incentives and the Retirement Decision: Evidence from the U.S.," National Bureau of Economic Research Working Paper no. 20916, January 2015, revised in February 2015; Jonathan Gruber and Jeffrey Kubik, "Disability Insurance Rejection Rates and the Labor Supply of Older Workers," *Journal of Public Economics* 64, no. 1 (1997): 1–23; and David Autor and Mark Duggan, "The Rise in the Disability Rolls and the Decline in Unemployment," *Quarterly Journal of Economics* 118, no. 1 (2003): 157–205.

59. Nicole Maestas, Kathleen Mullen, and Alexander Strand, "The Effect of Economic Conditions on the Disability Insurance Program: Evidence from the Great Recession," National Bureau of Economic Research Working Paper no. 25338, December 2018; James Sherk, "Not Looking for Work: Why Labor Force Participation Has Fallen during the Recovery," Heritage Foundation Backgrounder no. 2722, August 30, 2012, revised and updated September 4, 2014.

60. Alan Krueger and Bruce Meyer, "Labor Supply Effects of Social Insurance," in *Handbook of Public Economics*, vol. 4, ed. Alan J. Auerbach and Martin Feldstein (Amsterdam and New York: Elsevier, 2002), pp. 2327–92.

61. Casey Mulligan, *The Redistribution Recession* (New York: Oxford University Press, 2012), p. 99. Mulligan provides a list of research papers.

62. Mulligan, *The Redistribution Recession*, pp. 41–96, 109. Casey Mulligan, "Do Welfare Policies Matter for Labor Market Aggregates? Quantifying Safety Net Work Incentives since 2007," National Bureau of Economic Research Working Paper no. 18088, May 2012.

63. See, for example, Oren Cass, "The Case for the Wage Subsidy," *National Review*, November 16, 2016.

64. The EITC has long been criticized for many problems, including "fraud and erroneous payments due to false reports of earnings and false residence claims, benefits intended for working parents going to nonparents, very high multi-tier benefits, and discrimination against married couples." Robert Rector and Jamie Hall, "Reforming the Earned Income Tax Credit and Additional Child Tax Credit to End Waste, Fraud, and Abuse and Strengthen Marriage," Heritage Foundation Backgrounder no. 3162, November 16, 2016.

65. Austin Nichols and Jesse Rothstein, "The Earned Income Tax Credit (EITC)," National Bureau of Economic Research Working Paper no. 21211, May 2015, p. 19.

66. Nichols and Rothstein, "The Earned Income Tax Credit," pp. 40–46.

67. Henrik Kleven, "The EITC and the Extensive Margin: A Reappraisal," National Bureau of Economic Research Working Paper no. 26405, October 2019, revised March 2023.

68. The findings from these experiments showed no statistically significant increase on employment among the eligible group in Atlanta, a 1.8 percentage

point increase in employment among the eligible population in New York City, and no earnings increase in either city. Robert Rector, Jamie Hall, and Noah Patterson, "The Earned Income Tax Credit for Childless Workers Largely Fails to Increase Employment or Earnings: Better Alternatives Needed," Heritage Foundation Backgrounder no. 3558, December 3, 2020. Other evidence indicates that, owing to faulty program design, the EITC is more likely to be used by people who are unemployed rather than by regular workers. Casey Mulligan, "Earned-Income Ironies," *New York Times*, February 6, 2013.

69. Jesse Rothstein, "Is the EITC as Good as an NIT? Conditional Cash Transfers and Tax Incidence," *American Economic Journal: Economic Policy* 2, no. 1 (2010): 177–208; Andrew Leigh, "Who Benefits from the Earned Income Tax Credit? Incidence among Recipients, Coworkers and Firms," *B.E. Journal of Economic Analysis & Policy Advances* 10, no. 1 (2010): article 45. For similar findings in the United Kingdom, see Ghazala Azmat, "Incidence, Salience and Spillovers: The Direct and Indirect Effects of Tax Credits on Wages," London School of Economics, Center for Economic Performance Discussion Paper no. 724, June 2015.

70. Rothstein, "Is the EITC as Good as an NIT?," p. 179.

71. Leigh, "Who Benefits from the Earned Income Tax Credit?," p. 35. Some evidence even suggests that wage subsidy programs (including the EITC) could produce disincentives to work by decreasing the income of workers ineligible for the subsidy. Nichols and Rothstein, "The Earned Income Tax Credit," p. 49.

72. David Altig et al., "Marginal Net Taxation of Americans' Labor Supply," National Bureau of Economic Research Working Paper no. 27164, May 2020, p. 2.

73. Altig et al., "Marginal Net Taxation," pp. 12, 19.

74. For example, at income levels of $4,900 and $23,500, a recipient loses eligibility for Temporary Assistance for Needy Families (TANF) and SNAP, respectively. However, the benefits from TANF and SNAP do not phase out completely before reaching these income thresholds, so the loss of eligibility causes a large jump in the recipient's marginal tax rate. Congressional Budget Office, "Illustrative Examples of Effective Marginal Tax Rates Faced by Married and Single Taxpayers: Supplemental Material for Effective Marginal Tax Rates for Low- and Moderate-Income Workers," November 2012, p. 3. For more research on these labor disincentives, see Robert Moffitt, "The US Safety Net and Work Incentives: Is There a Problem? What Should Be Done?," in *The US Labor Market Questions and Challenges for Public Policy*, ed. Michael R. Strain (Washington: American Enterprise Institute, 2016), pp. 122–37; Robert Moffitt, "Welfare Programs and Labor Supply," National Bureau of Economic Research Working Paper no. 9168, September 2002, pp. 32–41; and Jennifer Romich, Jennifer Simmelink, and Stephen Holt, "When Working Harder Does Not Pay: Low-Income Working Families, Tax Liabilities, and Benefit Reductions," *Families in Society* 88, no. 3 (2007): 418–26.

75. Congressional Budget Office, "The Distribution of Household Income, 2016," July 9, 2019. An earlier CBO report states: "In 2015, average household income before accounting for means-tested transfers and federal taxes was $20,000 for the lowest quintile and $292,000 for the highest quintile. After transfers and taxes, those averages were $33,000 and $215,000." Congressional Budget Office, "The Distribution of Household Income, 2015," November 2018.

76. Gary D. Alexander, secretary of public welfare, Commonwealth of Pennsylvania, "Welfare's Failure and the Solution" (American Enterprise Institute presentation, July 2012). For a similar story regarding a single mother in the Boston area, see Megan McArdle, "The Truth about Taxes: The Poor Pay the Highest Marginal Rates in the Country," *The Atlantic*, December 17, 2011.

77. And though it may not be so obvious, only a wealthy society could support so many people who actively choose not to work, a choice that many Americans have made in the past several decades.

78. Scott Winship, "Understanding the Data: The American Working-Class and the Economy," *National Review*, December 3, 2018; Regis Barnichon and Andrew Figura, "Declining Desire to Work and Downward Trends in Unemployment and Participation," National Bureau of Economic Research Working Paper no. 21252, June 2015.

79. Howard Husock, "How Housing Assistance Leads to Long-Term Dependence—and How to Fix It," Heritage Foundation Index of Culture and Opportunity, July 20, 2017.

80. Husock, "How Housing Assistance Leads to Long-Term Dependence."

81. John L. Ligon and Norbert J. Michel, "GSE Reform: The Economic Effects of Eliminating a Government Guarantee in Housing Finance," Heritage Foundation Backgrounder no. 2877, February 7, 2014.

82. Evidence also shows that state and local zoning and land-use regulations restrict the supply of housing, thus contributing to this price appreciation, especially in highly regulated coastal cities. Vanessa Brown Calder, "Zoning, Land-Use Planning, and Housing Affordability," Cato Institute Policy Analysis no. 823, October 18, 2017; Edward L. Glaeser, Joseph Gyourko, and Raven Saks, "Why Is Manhattan So Expensive? Regulation and the Rise in House Prices," National Bureau of Economic Research Working Paper no. 10124, November 2003.

83. Edward Pinto, Norbert Michel, and Tobias Peter, Public Comment on Qualified Mortgage Definition under the Truth in Lending Act (Regulation Z), Consumer Financial Protection Bureau, September 16, 2019, pp. 7–20.

84. The resulting financial regulatory framework that was spawned by this arrangement was ostensibly necessary to protect taxpayers, but it has not done so. Instead, it has imposed high costs on banks, which pass at least a portion of those costs on to employees (through lower wages) and on to consumers (through higher prices and fewer services). Charles Calomiris, "Restoring the Rule of Law in Financial Regulation," *Cato Journal* 38, no. 3 (2018): 701.

85. James Whitford, "Crowding Out Compassion," Heritage Foundation Index of Culture and Opportunity, July 20, 2017. Whitford's organization works with local churches to help people escape poverty and homelessness.

86. Whitford, "Crowding Out Compassion." Whitford's organizations provide outreach services aimed at helping the poor.

87. Jon D. Ponder, "Restoring Hope for Ex-Prisoners: The Key to Reducing Crime," Heritage Foundation Index of Culture and Opportunity, July 20, 2017.

88. Whitford, "Crowding Out Compassion."

89. For broader examples of welfare state policies that crowd out privately provided social services, see David Beito, *From Mutual Aid to the Welfare State:*

Fraternal Societies and Social Services, 1890–1967 (Chapel Hill: University of North Carolina Press, 2000).

90. Gwartney et al., *Economic Freedom of the World*, p. viii.

91. Gwartney et al., *Economic Freedom of the World*, p. viii.

92. Miller, Kim, and Roberts, *2019 Index of Economic Freedom*, p. 2.

Chapter 7

1. For example, a book review of J. D. Vance's popular book, *Hillbilly Elegy*, proclaims, "Wall Street, wage stagnation, foreign competition and the closing of mines and mills have gutted Appalachia and the Rust Belt." Jeffrey Fleishman, "Review: J. D. Vance's 'Hillbilly Elegy' Provides a Window into the Pain and Anger of Trump's America," *Los Angeles Times*, October 7, 2016.

2. For example, former Mitt Romney adviser Oren Cass insists, "The question is: given all our challenges, the hollowing out of industry, stalled productivity growth, aggressive strategies pursued by other countries, is trying to adopt some form of industrial policy preferable to doing nothing?" Arthur Bloom, "Seven Questions for Oren Cass on the New Conservatism," *American Conservative*, May 4, 2020.

3. Salena Zito and Brad Todd, *The Great Revolt: Inside the Populist Coalition Reshaping American Politics* (New York: Crown Forum, 2018), p. 20.

4. Zito and Todd, *Inside the Populist Coalition Reshaping American Politics*, p. 223. Tedrow also believed: "The economic problems of this country were not Obama's creation, but he did nothing to apply the brakes. In fact, if anything he put the gas pedal on them. The regulations that hurt farming and . . . energy impacted the small towns . . . more so than they were already hurting; it was like shoveling salt on big wounds" (p. 226).

5. Philip Bump, "In 2016, Trump Won Voters Who Disliked Both Candidates. In 2020, Biden Has That (Dubious) Advantage," *Washington Post*, April 8, 2020.

6. Jim Hinckley, *Ghost Towns of Route 66* (Beverly, MA: Quarto Publishing Group, 2020); Publications International Ltd., *Ghost Towns* (Morton Grove, IL: Publications International Ltd., 2021).

7. Kevin Williamson, *Big White Ghetto: Dead Broke, Stone-Cold Stupid, and High on Rage in the Dank Woolly Wilds of the "Real America"* (Washington: Regnery Publishing, 2020), p. 18.

8. This passage was written by historian George Slocum in 1908. Williamson, *Big White Ghetto: Dead Broke, Stone-Cold Stupid, and High on Rage in the Dank Woolly Wilds of the "Real America*,*" p. 18.

9. Ben Cosgrove, "War on Poverty: Portraits from an Appalachian Battleground, 1964," *Life*, 2022.

10. Cosgrove, "War on Poverty."

11. Cosgrove, "War on Poverty."

12. Pam Fessler, "In Appalachia, Poverty Is in the Eye of the Beholder," *Weekend Edition Saturday*, NPR, January 18, 2014; and Appalachian Regional Development Act, S. 3, 89th Cong. (1965). Separately, Johnson signed into law the Manpower Act (February 1, 1965) to expand federal jobs training programs, and the Elementary and Secondary Education Act (March 28, 1965) to provide federal funds to local school districts.

13. Appalachian Regional Development Act.

14. According to Section 202 of the act, the federal government was authorized to make "grants for the planning, construction, equipment, and operation of multi-county demonstration health, nutrition, and child care projects, including hospitals, regional health diagnostic and treatment centers and other facilities and services." Appalachian Regional Development Act of 1965 (40 U.S.C. App. 402).

15. Congress amended the act in 1967, 1969, 1971, 1975, 1998, and multiple times in the 2000s.

16. David Tarr, "The Steel Crisis in the United States and the European Community: Causes and Adjustments," in *Issues in US-EC Trade Relations*, ed. Robert E. Baldwin, Carl B. Hamilton, and André Sapir (Chicago: University of Chicago Press, 1988), p. 175; Douglas Irwin, "How Did the United States Become a Net Exporter of Manufactured Goods?," National Bureau of Economic Research Working Paper no. 7638, April 2000.

17. Oren Cass, *The Once and Future Worker: A Vision for the Renewal of Work in America* (New York: Encounter Books, 2018), p. 1.

18. This group, *all production and nonsupervisory employees*, has accounted for approximately 70 percent of annual nonfarm employment since 1964. Author's calculation based on "Production and Nonsupervisory Employees: Total Private, Thousands of Persons, Monthly, Seasonally Adjusted" and "All Employees: Total Nonfarm Payrolls, Thousands of Persons, Monthly, Seasonally Adjusted," both available from the Federal Reserve Bank of St. Louis Economic Data.

19. Although the federal government still uses the CPI to adjust Social Security benefits for inflation, the Federal Reserve and the Congressional Budget Office rely on the PCE to make inflation adjustments. James Bullard, "President's Message: CPI vs. PCE Inflation: Choosing a Standard Measure," Federal Reserve Bank of St. Louis, July 2013; Congressional Budget Office, "The Distribution of Household Income and Federal Taxes, 2008 and 2009," July 10, 2012, p. 13.

20. Even if the PCE were restricted to include the same goods and services used to construct the CPI, the PCE would still report slower inflation growth relative to the CPI. Salim Furth, "Measuring Inflation Accurately," Heritage Foundation Backgrounder no. 3213, June 23, 2017. Bureau of Labor Statistics, "Consumer Price Index: First Quarter 2011," *Focus on Prices and Spending* 2, no. 3, May 2011; Clinton P. McCully, Brian C. Moyer, and Kenneth J. Stewart, "Comparing the Consumer Price Index and the Personal Consumption Expenditures Price Index," *Survey of Current Business*, November 2007.

21. The Bureau of Labor Statistics does report median wages for all workers, but that series does not directly compare with Cass's statement because it begins in 1979 rather than 1975. The BLS also reports median and average wages for many different subcategories of workers, all of which begin at different points in time. Notably, in 2005, the BLS announced it would phase out the series for production/nonsupervisory workers' income and hours worked because those series' "limited scope makes them of limited value in analyzing economic trends." Nonetheless, the BLS has not phased out these series. US Department of Labor, Submission for OMB Review: Comment Request, 70 Fed. Reg., 20177, April 18, 2005.

22. Figure 7.1 plots the growth rate in real income—average hourly earnings of production and nonsupervisory employees—with the rate calculated using every year from 1964 to 2000, respectively, as the starting point, and 2015 as the ending year. It shows the analysis using both the consumer price index (CPI) and personal consumption expenditure (PCE) indexes to convert nominal wages to real. The income series is available from Federal Reserve Bank of St. Louis, FRED Economic Data, "Average Hourly Earnings of Production and Nonsupervisory Employees, Total Private (AHETPI)."

23. James Sherk, "A Good Job Is Not So Hard to Find," Heritage Foundation Center For Data Analysis Report 08-04, June 17, 2008, p. 9. The average increase of the five percentiles was 4 percent; the increases for the 10th and 25th percentiles were 1.5 percent and 2.4 percent, respectively. These figures refer to the mean wage and salary income within each percentile, for all US-born workers, between the ages of 25 and 65, who annually worked at least 1,250 hours. This research was conducted in 2008, and the dates were chosen to study two 10-year increments (ending in 2000) and to exclude recessionary effects from the Great Recession, which began in 2007. The data are from the 1 percent samples of the 1980, 1990, and 2000 Censuses and the 2000 and 2006 American Community Surveys; all income figures are adjusted for inflation based on the PCE.

24. Statisticians use the term "distribution" to describe an ordered list of numbers. An income distribution, therefore, refers to a list of incomes, from lowest to highest. The term does not mean that income was literally distributed to anyone, and it says nothing about how people may have earned their income.

25. The first decile's growth figure is 26.44 percent, and the sixth decile's is 12.47 percent. The decile growth figures are the author's calculations using 2019 Current Population Survey Data. BLS, Current Population Survey, 2019 March Supplement. All income figures are adjusted for inflation using the PCE.

26. Although it is a simple statistic, it is also the case that the cumulative growth for the lowest and highest deciles are highly correlated (the correlation coefficient is 92 percent), suggesting that both low-income and high-income individuals tend to do well (or poorly) at the same time.

27. They also report that real hourly earnings for the typical male high school dropout (ages 25–54) decreased approximately 17 percent (from roughly $17 to $14) from 1973 to 2015. Ariel J. Binder and John Bound, "The Declining Labor Market Prospects of Less-Educated Men," *Journal of Economic Perspectives* 33, no. 2 (2019): 163–67. The authors use the March Supplement to the Current Population Survey to provide estimates for hourly earnings, calculated as three-year moving geometric averages adjusted for inflation with the PCE.

28. Binder and Bound, "Declining Labor Market Prospects of Less-Educated Men," p. 166.

29. James Sherk, "Productivity and Compensation: Growing Together," Heritage Foundation Backgrounder no. 2825, July 17, 2013; BLS, "Employer Costs for Employee Compensation—December 2019," news release, March 19, 2020. In the national income accounts, using different definitions of income, the figure is 23 percent. Bureau of Economic Analysis, "Gross Domestic Product, Fourth Quarter and Year 2019 (Second Estimate)," news release, February 27, 2020, p. 13.

30. BLS, "Technical Information about the BLS Major Sector Productivity and Costs Measures," Major Sector Productivity and Costs, March 11, 2008, p. 5. This compensation measure consists of "wages and salaries, supplements (like shift differentials, all kinds of paid leave, bonus and incentive payments, and employee discounts), and employer contributions to employee-benefit plans (like medical and life insurance, workmen's compensation, and unemployment insurance)." BLS, "What Is Included in Compensation?," Labor Productivity and Costs, August 6, 2012. According to the BLS, one caveat for these data is: "The measures of compensation published with the major sector productivity measures and most of the nonmanufacturing industry labor productivity measures include an imputation of the earnings of the self-employed. This is because the output of proprietorships is included in the output measures for these sectors and industries."

31. Jay Shambaugh and Ryan Nunn, "Why Wages Aren't Growing in America," *Harvard Business Review*, October 24, 2017. The article argues, "The wage stagnation of the past 40 years is also linked to some developments that may have suppressed productivity growth, which has slowed since 1973." Separately, a 2017 National Bureau of Economic Research paper provides evidence that productivity growth and compensation growth are strongly linked and that they have *not* statistically diverged since the 1970s. Anna M. Stansbury and Lawrence H. Summers, "Productivity and Pay: Is the Link Broken?," National Bureau of Economic Research Working Paper no. 24165, December 2017. Michael Strain, "The Link between Wages and Productivity Is Strong," in *Expanding Economic Opportunity for More Americans*, ed. Melissa S. Kearney and Amy Ganz (Washington: Aspen Institute, 2019), pp. 168–79.

32. Alternate dates around 1957, such as 1955–1974 or 1959–1974, produce similar results in that total compensation from 1975 to 2015 did not appreciably decline. These estimates refer to the end-of-year index values for the BLS's real hourly compensation series (series ID PRS84006153).

33. Eleanor Krause and Isabel V. Sawhill, "Seven Reasons to Worry about the American Middle Class," Brookings Institution, Washington, June 5, 2018.

34. Author's calculations using the US Census income and household size data in table a-2 and table hh-4. From 1967 to 2019, the entire series of US household median income, per-person median household income increased by almost 88 percent, whereas the unadjusted data show that median household income increased by 43 percent.

35. Author's calculations using the US Census income and household size data. Krause and Sawhill's Brookings article reports the growth rate in the non-size-adjusted figure, as reported by the Census with a CPI adjustment, from 1967 to 2015. Adjusting this (non-size-adjusted) figure for inflation with the PCE instead of the CPI shows that real growth from 1967 to 2015 was 62 percent (rather than 27 percent with the CPI).

36. US Census Bureau, *Total Households*, available from the Federal Reserve Bank of St. Louis Economic Data, November 10, 2023.

37. US Census Bureau, *Income and Poverty in the United States: 2017*, September 12, 2018. The income data in the Census Bureau's report are from its Annual Social and Economic Supplements of the Current Population Survey; the Census Bureau adjusts income figures for inflation using the CPI.

38. Alana Semuels, "New Census Data Shows More Americans Emerging from Poverty," *The Atlantic*, September 12, 2017.

39. Mark J. Perry, "Three Charts Based on Today's Census Report Show That the US Middle-Class Is Shrinking . . . Because They're Moving Up," American Enterprise Institute, Washington, September 10, 2019; and Perry, "Three Charts Based on Today's Census Report."

40. Perry, "Three Charts Based on Today's Census Report."

41. Semuels, "New Census Data Shows More Americans Emerging from Poverty."

42. As a strict accounting exercise, the official Census data exaggerate differences between low-income and high-income households because, among other things, it publishes income before taxes and transfers, meaning that it does not include income from means-tested welfare programs, such as the Supplemental Nutrition Assistance Program or Temporary Assistance for Needy Families. For more on inequality issues, see Phil Gramm, Robert Ekelund, and John Early, *The Myth of American Inequality: How Government Biases Policy Debate* (Lanham, MD: Rowman & Littlefield, 2022).

43. For an older report that examines some of these issues, see Robert Rector and Rea Hederman, *Income Inequality: How Census Data Misrepresent Income Distribution* (Washington: Heritage Foundation, 1999).

44. Unless otherwise noted, the figures in this section are the author's calculations using 2019 Current Population Survey Data. BLS, Current Population Survey 2019 March Supplement. With respect to the author's calculations, unless otherwise noted, income figures are adjusted for inflation using the PCE.

45. "Prime working age" is defined as 35 to 64.

46. Of the households in the top quintile, 81.4 percent contain at least one adult of prime working age.

47. Arthur M. Okun, *Equality and Efficiency: The Big Tradeoff* (Washington: Brookings Institution Press, 1975).

48. The authors—economists Dan Andrews, Christopher Jencks, and Andrew Leigh—report that "a one percentage point rise in the top decile's income share is associated with a statistically significant 0.12 point rise in GDP growth during the following year." Dan Andrews, Christopher Jencks, and Andrew Leigh, "Do Rising Top Incomes Lift All Boats?," *B.E. Journal of Economic Analysis & Policy* 11, no. 1 (2011): article 6.

49. Lane Kenworthy, "Has Rising Inequality Reduced Middle-Class Income Growth?," in *Income Inequality: Economic Disparities and the Middle Class in Affluent Countries*, ed. Janet C. Gornick and Markus Jäntti (Stanford, CA: Stanford University Press, 2013), p. 107. Robert Barro, "Inequality, Growth, and Investment," National Bureau of Economic Research Working Paper no. 7038, March 1999; Vincent Geloso, "Actually, the Gilded Age Was Awesome for Equality," American Institute for Economic Research, Great Barrington, MA, October 25, 2019.

50. Alan Reynolds, "The Misuse of Top 1 Percent Income Shares as a Measure of Inequality," Cato Institute Working Paper no. 9, October 4, 2012, pp. 18–20.

51. For this analysis, we track the most comprehensive government data available. Most official US government surveys do not follow the same individuals

through time. Instead, those survey questions are sent to new groups of workers each year (or quarter, month, or week, depending on the survey), providing what is called "cross-section data." All the income measures discussed in the previous chapters—median wages for all employees, average hourly earnings for all private employees, average hourly earnings for all production and nonsupervisory employees, and median household income—come from surveys that produce cross-section data. These surveys effectively take a snapshot of what is going on each week, month, quarter, or year, though not necessarily of the same group of people.

52. Scott Winship, "Economic Mobility in America, a Primer," Archbridge Institute, Washington, March 20, 2017.

53. For more on income mobility in the United States, see Winship, "Economic Mobility in America"; and Scott Winship, "Economic Mobility in America, A State-of-the-Art Primer, Part 2: The United States in Comparative Perspective," Archbridge Institute, Washington, December 2018.

54. For a full review of the many claims, see Scott Winship, "Overstating the Costs of Inequality," *National Affairs*, Spring 2013.

55. The notion that income inequality is economically harmful appears to be rooted in the Progressive Era view that tagged the early American industrial entrepreneurs with the label "robber barons." The truth, though, is that the most successful of those entrepreneurs, such as Cornelius Vanderbilt and John D. Rockefeller, made so much money because they helped millions of people gain affordable access to products that they would not have otherwise had at all. Burton Folsom Jr., "How the Myth of the 'Robber Barons' Began—and Why It Persists," Foundation for Economic Education, Atlanta, September 21, 2018.

56. Winship, "Overstating the Costs of Inequality"; Paolo Brunori, Francisco Ferreira, and Vito Peragine, "Inequality of Opportunity, Income Inequality and Economic Mobility: Some International Comparisons," Institute for the Study of Labor Discussion Paper no. 7155, January 2013, p. 3; Scott Winship and Donald Schneider, "The Collapse of the Great Gatsby Curve," Manhattan Institute, New York, February 3, 2014; Jim Manzi, "The Great Gatsby, Moby Dick, and Omitted Variable Bias," *National Review*, February 7, 2012; Winship, "Economic Mobility in America, A State-of-the-Art Primer."

57. Daniel Alpert and Michael Stumo, "America's Workers Continue to Struggle Despite 'Strong' Jobs Reports," *The Hill*, November 16, 2019.

58. "Bernie Sanders on the Minimum Wage," FeelTheBern.org, 2019. Also see David Cooper, "The Minimum Wage Used to Be Enough to Keep Workers out of Poverty—It's Not Anymore," Economic Policy Institute, Washington, December 4, 2013. For the Bloomberg article, which admits that the United States is not turning into "a nation of temps, burger flippers and retail sales associates," see Mark Whitehouse, "A Nation of Temps and Burger Flippers?," Bloomberg, May 2, 2014.

59. This figure is for workers 16 and older. Bureau of Labor Statistics, Occupational Employment Statistics, "May 2019 National Occupational Employment and Wage Estimates United States"; BLS, "Characteristics of Minimum Wage Workers, 2019," BLS Reports, April 2020. The 10th percentile hourly wage was $9.61 in 2019, 33 percent higher than the minimum wage.

60. BLS, "Characteristics of Minimum Wage Workers, 2019."

61. BLS, "Characteristics of Minimum Wage Workers, 2019," table 10. The percentage of the labor force averaged 1.7 percent for the past two decades. The US government first established a federal minimum wage with the Fair Labor Standards Act of 1938. Jonathan Grossman, "Fair Labor Standards Act of 1938: Maximum Struggle for a Minimum Wage," US Department of Labor, June 1978.

62. BLS, "Characteristics of Minimum Wage Workers, 2019." This high percentage is not a recent occurrence; see Sherk, "A Good Job Is Not So Hard to Find," p. 9.

63. BLS, "Characteristics of Minimum Wage Workers, 2019," table 1; and BLS, "Characteristics of Minimum Wage Workers, 2019," table 8.

64. These figures are reported in "Poverty and Use of Selected Federal Social Safety Net Programs Persist among Working Families," US Government Accountability Office, GAO-17-677, September 2017, p. 47. Also see Sherk, "A Good Job Is Not So Hard to Find," p. 9.

65. BLS, "Characteristics of Minimum Wage Workers, 2019."

66. The median-age worker in the manufacturing industry is 44.1, and the median-age worker in leisure and hospitality is 31.9. BLS, "Household Data Annual Averages," table 18b.

67. Joseph Sabia and Richard Burkhauser, "Minimum Wages and Poverty: Will the Obama Proposal Help the Working Poor?," Employment Policies Institute, Washington, September 2008; James Sherk, "Raising the Minimum Wage Will Not Reduce Poverty," Heritage Foundation Backgrounder no. 1994, January 8, 2007.

68. For recent evidence, see Ekaterina Jardim et al., "Minimum Wage Increases, Wages, and Low-Wage Employment: Evidence from Seattle," National Bureau of Economic Research Working Paper no. 23532, May 2018.

69. Thomas Sowell, *Basic Economics: A Common Sense Guide to the Economy*, 3rd ed. (Cambridge, MA: Basic Books, 2007), p. 219. Sowell argues that a minimum-wage law "makes it cheaper to discriminate against minority workers than it would be in a free market" (p. 220).

70. David Neumark and William L. Wascher, *Minimum Wages* (Cambridge, MA: MIT Press, 2008); Richard Ippolito, "The Impact of the Minimum Wage if Workers Can Adjust Effort," *Journal of Law and Economics* 46, no. 1 (2003): 207–27; Harry Holzer, Lawrence Katz, and Alan Krueger, "Job Queues and Wages," *Quarterly Journal of Economics* 106, no. 3 (1991): 739–68.

71. For additional resources, see David R. Burton, "A Guide to Labor and Employment Law Reforms," Heritage Foundation Backgrounder no. 3535, October 9, 2020, pp. 6–7.

72. Neumark and Wascher, *Minimum Wages*, pp. 189, 201.

73. Donald J. Boudreaux, "The Myth of American Middle-Class Stagnation," American Institute for Economic Research, Great Barrington, MA, July 29, 2019.

74. Bruce Meyer and James Sullivan, "Annual Report on U.S. Consumption Poverty: 2017," American Enterprise Institute, Washington, November 1, 2018.

75. Meyer and Sullivan, "Annual Report on U.S. Consumption Poverty: 2017," pp. 3–4. The authors report that a narrower consumption measure displays

the same downward trend as the broader measure, with the only difference being an upturn after the Great Recession.

76. Bruce Meyer and James Sullivan, "The Material Well-Being of the Poor and the Middle Class Since 1980," American Enterprise Institute Working Paper no. 2011-04, October 25, 2011, pp. 3–4. The findings also suggest that the median income "rose by more than 50 percent in real terms between 1980 and 2009."

77. Author's calculations using the following BLS data: "All Employees, Service-Providing, Thousands of Persons, Annual, Seasonally Adjusted (SRVPRD)"; "All Employees, Goods-Producing, Thousands of Persons, Annual, Seasonally Adjusted (USGOOD)"; and "All Employees, Total Nonfarm, Thousands of Persons, Annual, Seasonally Adjusted (PAYEMS)." Each series is available from the Federal Reserve Bank of St. Louis Economic Data, https://fred.stlouisfed.org.

78. See, for example, Richard M. Reinsch II, "Can American Capitalism Survive?," National Affairs, Spring 2020; and Nicholas Eberstadt, "The Future of the Work Ethic," Claremont Review of Books, Fall 2019.

79. Chuck Almdale, "Opinion: A 'Golden Age'? Factory Work in the 60s Was Tedious, Dangerous and Soul-Crushing," letter to the editor, Los Angeles Times, June 19, 2017.

80. BLS, "Table B-8. Average Hourly and Weekly Earnings of Production and Nonsupervisory Employees on Private Nonfarm Payrolls by Industry Sector, Seasonally Adjusted," October 4, 2019; Colin Grabow, "The Reality of American 'Deindustrialization,'" Cato Institute, Washington, October 24, 2023.

81. BLS, Table B-8.

82. Total nonfarm employment increased from 109.5 million to 151 million from 1990 to 2019. All these employment figures refer to annual BLS data for the following series: "All Employees, Total Nonfarm (PAYEMS)"; "All Employees, Retail Trade (USTRADE)"; and "All Employees, Leisure and Hospitality (USLAH)." Each is available from the Federal Reserve Bank of St. Louis Economic Data.

83. Author calculations using 2019 Current Population Survey Data; the statistics for full-time workers include those who annually worked at least 1,250 hours. Although the average age for all full-time workers in the service sector (34.1) is several years lower, it is very similar for those in sales (37.2) and production (37.6). Thus, many of the lower-wage service jobs must be going to younger people.

84. The data show that 50.3 percent of full-time service-sector workers in the first income decile, and 47.4 percent of full-time sales-sector workers in the first decile, are single with no children. Similarly, 78.9 percent of full-time *retail trade* workers in the first decile, and 66.4 percent of full-time *leisure and hospitality* workers in the first decile, are single with no children. Finally, 26.4 percent of full-time *retail trade* workers in the first decile, and 46 percent of full-time *leisure and hospitality* workers in the first decile, are between 16 and 25 years old. Though more technical, the evidence also shows that the dispersion in the 2019 distributions for all full-time workers in the manufacturing and service sectors exhibits very similar patterns. That is, the distributions exhibit a similar proportion of jobs with wages well below the average, near the average, and above the average. In the higher deciles, where full-time workers earn $1,200 per week or more, the distributions are almost identical. Author's calculations using 2019 Current Population Survey Data;

the statistics are for all workers who annually worked at least 1,250 hours. In 1998, the BLS reported a very similar finding for the distributions of wages among service and manufacturing workers, so the 2019 data do not appear to be anomalous. Joseph Meisenheimer II, "The Services Industry in the 'Good' versus 'Bad' Jobs Debate," *Monthly Labor Review*, BLS, 1998, p. 28.

85. This percentage appears to reflect a rising trend. Meisenheimer, "The Services Industry in the 'Good' Versus 'Bad' Jobs Debate," p. 31.

86. Brahima Coulibaly, "Changes in Job Quality and Trends in Labor Hours," Federal Reserve Board of Governors International Finance Discussion Paper no. 882, October 2006, p. 15. Using data from the University of Michigan's Health and Retirement Study, the author reports that people tend to work more in these types of jobs based on their less demanding physical nature. Coulibaly, "Changes in Job Quality," p. 25, table VII.

87. US Department of Labor, "Timeline of OSHA's 40 Year History," n.d. The total number of workplace fatalities was 5,333 in 2019, and the total number of fatalities in private industry was 4,907 in 2019. See US Department of Labor, "National Census of Fatal Occupational Injuries," table A-1. The total number of fatalities in private industry was 5,497 in 1992 and 4,978 in 2002. BLS, "Fatal Occupational Injuries by Selected Characteristics: State of Incident, Employee Status, Sex, Age, Race, Event or Exposure, Source, Secondary Source, Nature, Part of Body, Worker Activity, Location, Occupation, and Industry, 1992–2002 (revised final counts)," p. 24.

88. US Department of Labor, "Timeline of OSHA's 40 Year History"; and US Department of Labor, "Employer-Reported Workplace Injuries and Illnesses—2019 November 4, 2020, table 1.

89. BLS, Census of Fatal Occupational Injuries Charts, 1992–2006, p. 2; Bureau of Labor Statistics, Graphics for Economic News Release, "Rate of Fatal Work Injuries per 100,000 Full-Time Equivalent Workers by Age Group." The fatalities are reported from 1992 because, according to the Department of Labor, accurate statistics on fatalities were not kept in the 1970s. US Department of Labor, "Timeline of OSHA's 40 Year History."

90. Boudreaux, "The Myth of American Middle-Class Stagnation."

91. Michael Cox and Richard Alm, *Myths of Rich and Poor: Why We're Better Off Than We Think* (New York: Basic Books), 1999.

92. Donald J. Boudreaux, "Myths of Rich and Poor: Why We're Better Off Than We Think by W. Michael Cox and Richard Alm: Cox and Alm Blow the Myth of '73 to Smithereens," book review, Foundation for Economic Education, Atlanta, January 1, 2000.

93. Simon Project, HumanProgress.org; Marian L. Tupy and Gale L. Pooley, *Superabundance: The Story of Population Growth, Innovation, and Human Flourishing on an Infinitely Bountiful Planet* (Washington: Cato Institute, 2022).

Chapter 8

1. Historically, one main reason that blacks' economic opportunities have been reduced, even during the first few decades of the post–World War II era, was pro-union legislation that required prevailing/minimum wages. See Walter

Williams, *Race and Economics* (Stanford, CA: Hoover Institution Press, 2011), pp. 83–109.

Appendixes

1. Susan N. Houseman, "Understanding the Decline of U.S. Manufacturing Employment," Upjohn Institute Working Paper no. 18-287, June 7, 2018, p. 21.

2. Before permanent normal trade relations (PNTR) status, China did receive the low tariff rates typically reserved for World Trade Organization members, but they had to be renewed annually. Thus, PNTR status eliminated this renewal process, removing the uncertainty that the tariffs might not be renewed. But it did not lower tariffs. Justin Pierce and Peter Schott, "The Surprisingly Swift Decline of US Manufacturing Employment," *American Economic Review* 106, no. 7 (2016): 1632–62.

3. Pierce and Schott, "Decline of US Manufacturing Employment," p. 1633.

4. Pierce and Schott, "Decline of US Manufacturing Employment," pp. 1633–34.

5. Pierce and Schott, "Decline of US Manufacturing Employment," p. 1634.

6. Pierce and Schott, "Decline of US Manufacturing Employment," p. 1634.

7. Generalizing these results is even more complicated than it may seem because the United States also maintains significant tariffs and tariff-rate quotas on imports, as well as nontariff barriers to trade, including nearly 200 special duties, such as antidumping and anti-(foreign)-subsidy measures. Scott Lincicome, "Testing the 'China Shock': Was Normalizing Trade with China a Mistake?," Cato Institute Policy Analysis no. 895, July 8, 2020.

8. Houseman, "Understanding the Decline of U.S. Manufacturing Employment," pp. 21–23.

9. Justin Pierce and Peter Schott, "Investment Responses to Trade Liberalization: Evidence from U.S. Industries and Plants," National Bureau of Economic Research Working Paper no. 24071, November 2017, p. 2.

10. Sherry Stephenson, "The Linkage between Services and Manufacturing in the U.S. Economy," Washington International Trade Association, Washington, May 23, 2017.

11. US Department of the Treasury, "Household Income Mobility during the 1980s: A Statistical Assessment Based on Tax Return Data," Office of Tax Analysis, June 1, 1992. Also see R. G. Hubbard, J. Nunns, and W. Randolph, "Household Income Changes over Time: Some Basic Questions and Facts," Tax Notes, August 24, 1992.

12. Hubbard, Nunns, and Randolph, "Household Income Changes over Time," p. 12.

13. Hubbard, Nunns, and Randolph, "Household Income Changes over Time," p. 12.

14. Hubbard, Nunns, and Randolph, "Household Income Changes over Time," p. 14.

15. Daniel P. McMurrer and Isabel V. Sawhill, "Economic Mobility in the United States," Urban Institute, Washington, October 1, 1996, p. 2.

16. The mobility rates for those in the highest quintiles were 48 and 50 percent in the respective 10-year periods. McMurrer and Sawhill, "Economic Mobility in the United States," p. 2.

17. McMurrer and Sawhill, "Economic Mobility in the United States," p. 3.

18. McMurrer and Sawhill, "Economic Mobility in the United States," p. 3. Another study by the same two authors states, "The evidence on this point is clear: Mobility has not changed significantly over the last 25 years." See Daniel P. McMurrer and Isabel V. Sawhill, "How Much Do Americans Move Up and Down the Economic Ladder?," Urban Institute, *Opportunity in America*, no. 3, November 1996, p. 2.

19. Katherine L. Bradbury and Jane Katz, "Are Lifetime Incomes Growing More Unequal? Looking at New Evidence on Family Income Mobility," Regional Review, Federal Reserve Bank of Boston, Q4, September 2002, p. 4.

20. Bradbury and Katz, "Are Lifetime Incomes Growing More Unequal?," p. 4.

21. Bradbury and Katz, "Are Lifetime Incomes Growing More Unequal?," p. 5.

22. Robert Carroll, David Joulfaian, and Mark Rider, "Income Mobility: The Recent American Experience," Georgia State University, Andrew Young School of Policy Studies, Research Paper Series no. 07-18, March 2007, p. 7.

23. Carroll, Joulfaian, and Rider, "Income Mobility," p. 7.

24. Carroll, Joulfaian, and Rider, "Income Mobility," p. 7.

25. Studies also show similar findings for wealth mobility. In other words, the wealthiest individuals in a given year typically do not remain at the top of the wealth distribution every year. Over longer periods, neither those individuals nor their descendants remain at the top of the list. Chris Edwards and Ryan Bourne, "Exploring Wealth Inequality," Cato Institute Policy Analysis no. 881, November 5, 2019, pp. 8–11.

26. Gerald E. Auten and Geoffrey Gee, "Income Mobility in the U.S.: Evidence from Income Tax Returns for 1987 and 1996," US Department of the Treasury, Office of Tax Analysis Paper no. 99, May 2007; Gerald Auten and Geoffrey Gee, "Income Mobility in the United States: New Evidence from Income Tax Data," *National Tax Journal* 62, no. 2 (2009): 301–28.

27. Auten and Gee, "Income Mobility in the U.S.: Evidence," p. 8.

28. Auten and Gee, "Income Mobility in the U.S.: Evidence," p. 7.

29. Auten and Gee, "Income Mobility in the U.S.: Evidence," p. 7.

30. The authors adjust for inflation using the CPI. Auten and Gee, "Income Mobility in the U.S.: Evidence," p. 9.

31. Auten and Gee, "Income Mobility in the U.S.: Evidence," pp. 9–10.

32. This Treasury report also excludes taxpayers younger than 25 in the panel's initial year. The report does not name an author. See Department of the Treasury, *Income Mobility in the U.S. from 1996 to 2005: Report of the Department of the Treasury* (Washington: Department of the Treasury, 2007). For an updated study with similar results, see Gerald Auten and David Splinter, "Income Inequality in the United States: Using Tax Data to Measure Long-Term Trends," *Journal of Political Economy* 132, no. 7 (July 2024).

33. Department of the Treasury, *Income Mobility in the U.S.*, pp. 2–4.

34. Department of the Treasury, *Income Mobility in the U.S.*, p. 2.

35. Department of the Treasury, *Income Mobility in the U.S.*, pp. 9–10.

36. Jeff Larrimore, Jacob Mortenson, and David Splinter, "Income and Earnings Mobility in U.S. Tax Data," working paper, Washington Center for Equitable Growth, Washington, April 2016, p. 5.

37. Larrimore, Mortenson, and Splinter, "Income and Earnings Mobility in U.S. Tax Data," p. 12.

38. Mark Rank and Thomas Hirschl, "The Likelihood of Experiencing Relative Poverty over the Life Course," *PLOS One* 10, no. 7 (2015): 4–5.

39. Rank and Hirschl, "The Likelihood of Experiencing Relative Poverty," p. 6. Across the board, these percentages are lower for those in the bottom 10 percent.

40. Rank and Hirschl, "The Likelihood of Experiencing Relative Poverty," p. 6.

41. Rank and Hirschl, "The Likelihood of Experiencing Relative Poverty," p. 6.

42. Thomas Hirschl and Mark Rank, "The Life Course Dynamics of Affluence," *PLOS One* 10, no. 1 (2015): 5.

43. Hirschl and Rank, "The Life Course Dynamics of Affluence," p. 5.

44. Hirschl and Rank, "The Life Course Dynamics of Affluence," p. 6.

45. Hirschl and Rank, "The Life Course Dynamics of Affluence," p. 6.

Note: Information in figures and tables is indicated by *f* and *t*; n designates a numbered note.

NORBERT J. MICHEL is vice president and director of the Cato Institute's Center for Monetary and Financial Alternatives, where he specializes in issues pertaining to financial markets and monetary policy. Michel was most recently the director for data analysis at the Heritage Foundation, where he edited and contributed chapters to two books: *The Case against Dodd–Frank: How the "Consumer Protection" Law Endangers Americans* and *Prosperity Unleashed: Smarter Financial Regulation.* He is the author of *Why Shadow Banking Didn't Cause the Financial Crisis—and Why Regulating Contagion Won't Help* (2022) and coauthor of *Financing Opportunity* (2024).

Michel was previously a tenured professor at Nicholls State University's College of Business, teaching finance, economics, and statistics. Before that, he worked at Heritage as a tax policy analyst in the think tank's Center for Data Analysis from 2002 to 2005. He previously was with the global energy company Entergy, where he worked on models to help predict bankruptcies of commercial clients.

Michel holds a doctoral degree in financial economics from the University of New Orleans. He received his bachelor of business administration degree in finance and economics from Loyola University. He currently resides in Virginia.

Founded in 1977, the Cato Institute is a public policy research foundation dedicated to broadening the parameters of policy debate to allow consideration of more options that are consistent with the traditional American principles of limited government, individual liberty, and peace. To that end, the Institute strives to achieve greater involvement of the intelligent, concerned lay public in questions of policy and the proper role of government.

The Institute is named for *Cato's Letters*, libertarian pamphlets that were widely read in the American Colonies in the early 18th century and that played a major role in laying the philosophical foundation for the American Revolution.

Despite the achievement of the nation's Founders, today virtually no aspect of life is free from government encroachment. A pervasive intolerance for individual rights is shown by government's arbitrary intrusions into private economic transactions and its disregard for civil liberties.

To counter that trend, the Cato Institute undertakes an extensive publications program that addresses the complete spectrum of policy issues. Books, monographs, and shorter studies are commissioned to examine the federal budget, Social Security, regulation, military spending, international trade, and myriad other issues.

In order to maintain its independence, the Cato Institute accepts no government funding. Contributions are received from foundations, corporations, and individuals, and other revenue is generated from the sale of publications. The Institute is a nonprofit, tax-exempt, educational foundation under Section 501(c)3 of the Internal Revenue Code.

CATO INSTITUTE
1000 Massachusetts Ave. NW
Washington, D.C. 20001
www.cato.org